The Everyday State and
Society in Modern India

The Everyday State and Society in Modern India

Edited by
C.J. FULLER
and
VÉRONIQUE BÉNÉÏ

HURST & COMPANY, LONDON

First published in the United Kingdom in 2001
by C. Hurst & Co. (Publishers) Ltd.,
38 King Street, London WC2E 8JZ
by arrangement with
Social Science Press, New Delhi
© C.J. Fuller & Véronique Bénéï, 2001
ISBNs
1-85065-470-0 (hardback)
1-85065-471-9 (paperback)
www.hurstpub.co.uk

Set in Dante MT
Typeset by Eleven Art, Delhi-110035
Printed by Sanjiv Palliwal (6966093 , 6532878)
at Usha Offset , New Delhi-20

Contents

List of Contributors

1. Chris Fuller is Professor of Anthropology at the London School of Economics and Political Science
2. Véronique Bénéï is Research Fellow in Anthropology at the London School of Economics and Political Science; she is also a researcher at the Centre National de la Recherche Scientifique and a member of the Maison Française d'Oxford
3. John Harriss is Reader in Development Studies at the London School of Economics and Political Science
4. Thomas Blom Hansen is Associate Professor in International Development Studies at Roskilde University
5. Emma Tarlo is Lecturer in Anthropology at Goldsmiths College, London
6. Craig Jeffrey is Lecturer in Geography at the University of Edinburgh
7. Jens Lerche is Lecturer in Development Studies at the School of Oriental and African Studies, London
8. Arild Engelsen Ruud is Senior Researcher at the Centre for Development and the Environment, Oslo
9. Filippo Osella is Lecturer in Social Anthropology at the University of Sussex
10. Caroline Osella is Lecturer in Anthropology at the School of Oriental and African Studies, London
11. David Mosse is Lecturer in Anthropology at the School of Oriental and African Studies, London

Acknowledgements

The essays in this book are revised versions of papers presented at two workshops organized by John Harriss, Emma Tarlo and us on 'The anthropology of the Indian state', which were held in the Department of Anthropology at the London School of Economics and Political Science on 9 May 1998 and 15 May 1999. In addition to the authors represented in this volume, Mukulika Banerjee, Barbara Harriss-White and Johnny Parry also presented papers at the workshop. Our budget was limited and therefore we were unfortunately unable to invite scholars from India, the United States or other countries outside northern Europe. Nevertheless, the workshops were successful and for making them so, we thank all those who presented papers, Sunil Khilnani for his concluding commentary, Stuart Corbridge, Patricia Jeffery, Sudipta Kaviraj, Mattison Mines, K. Sivaramakrishnan and David Washbrook for acting as discussants, and everyone else who came and took part in two days of lively discussion.

In planning this book, John Harriss's contribution was invaluable and we are especially grateful to him. We also wish to thank our fellow authors for their exemplary efficiency and tolerance during the editing process and Esha Béteille for her advice and encouragement.

C.J. Fuller and Véronique Bénéï
London, December 1999

For an anthropology of the modern Indian state

C.J. Fuller and John Harriss

Over half a century ago, Radcliffe-Brown argued, in his preface to *African political systems* (1940), that the idea of the state should be eliminated from social analysis. He believed—as Philip Abrams (1988: 75) notes—that it had only created mystification, and argued that concepts of government and politics were all that are needed for an adequate grasp of the 'political'. It seems that his view has been influential amongst anthropologists. Certainly Joan Vincent's exhaustive review in *Anthropology and politics* (1990) suggests that anthropologists have not, generally, taken the state as an object of study. When they have, though Vincent neglects this in her discussion, it has often been the 'traditional' kingly state with which they have been concerned and the modern state has not usually been an object of study for anthropologists.

For Weber and most subsequent sociologists, the modern state is characterized by a system of administrative and legal order, which 'claims binding authority, not only over the members of the state, the citizens ... but also to a very large extent, over all action taking place in the area of its jurisdiction'. Thus the state is 'a compulsory association with a territorial basis'(Weber 1964: 156). The modern rational-legal state—partly because of its size—is not directly amenable to study by the ethnographic methods favoured by anthropologists (cf. Gupta 1995: 375), but given the difficulty of conceptualizing the state, to which Radcliffe-Brown referred, perhaps anthropologists have been well-advised in

Although this introductory essay is jointly authored, its first part is a revised version of Harriss's paper at the workshop and its second part was originally written by Fuller. We thank Véronique Bénéï, Thomas Blom Hansen and Johnny Parry for their incisive comments on earlier drafts.

steering clear of it. Yet this seems unlikely and Jonathan Spencer (1997), for example, is rightly critical of modern anthropology's neglect of politics and the post-colonial state. That neglect has contributed to the tendency in scholarship on the state to reproduce the Weberian argument that formal legal rationality eclipses substantive cultural factors, so that all modern states are fundamentally the same (Steinmetz 1999). As this volume's essays plainly show, the modern Indian state plays an important part in popular consciousness and understanding, as well in people's daily lives, and it does have some distinctively Indian characteristics. Anthropology, as a field of enquiry concerned with ordinary people's beliefs and practices, is therefore the weaker for its neglect of the state (in India or elsewhere); on the other hand, because of its special concerns, the discipline can also contribute much to analysis of the state within the social sciences.

The difficulty of studying the state[1]

Among political philosophers, scientists, sociologists and historians, the state and theories about it have perennially occupied the centre stage. Anthropologists will of course point out that 'the state', like 'the economy', is not a universal category. Nonetheless, in order to situate an anthropological approach to the Indian state in a wider context, we begin at a very general level with some remarks about theories of the state.

As Timothy Mitchell (1991) shows, American political scientists in the era of Easton and Almond in the 1950s and 1960s were actually with Radcliffe-Brown in rejecting the concept of 'the state', in their case in favour of 'the political system'. The concept of the state was, they felt, too vague, and it threatened to exclude important aspects of political processes from their studies. In practice, this 'political-system' approach did not solve, but rather tended to complicate, the problem of distinguishing the 'political' from the wider social environment. Thus it was that a later generation of political scientists sought to 'bring the state back in'—to cite the title of an influential book edited by Evans, Rueschemeyer and Skocpol (1985)—and they advocated adoption of a Weberian concept of the state as an 'actual organization' (Mitchell 1991': 86), which is clearly distinct from society and not identical to 'the political system'. According to Skocpol, 'the state properly conceived' consists of 'a set of administrative, policing, and military organizations headed, and more or less well coordinated by, an executive authority' (1979: 29). These organizations form only a part of any political system, which will also include non-state actors. But in Skocpol's own analysis of France, Russia and China (1979), it rapidly becomes apparent that 'the provincial and local power of the state is inseparable from the political power of the landed classes' (Mitchell 1991: 87). Thus the state is nothing like as discrete as the idea of its 'actual organization' would suggest, for 'the edges of the state are uncertain; societal elements seem to penetrate it on all sides, and the resulting boundary between state and society is difficult to determine' (Ibid.: 88).

Recognition of these difficulties in defining or conceptualizing the state has subsequently given rise to a narrower concept of it as a policy-making actor, frequently identified in the literature with 'the public interest'. This is indeed a very powerful view of the state in much discourse about 'development', which appeals to a notion of a benevolent Leviathan chartered to bring about growth or to eliminate poverty. But this concept is of course highly problematic. Quite apart from the implicit assumption in much of this literature that the state is a neutral arbiter of public interest, it also seems to presuppose a unified intentionality and internal consistency, whereas in practice state functionaries often, or even normally, pursue competing agendas at cross-purposes with each other.

Another tradition of thinking about 'the state' is in the Marxist vein, exemplified in the conflicting theories about the capitalist state propounded in books by Ralph Miliband (1969) and Nicos Poulantzas (1973). This debate has often been characterized as one between an instrumentalist view (associated with Miliband), in which an attempt is made to demonstrate empirically how the state apparatus furthers the interests of capital, and a so-called structuralist view (associated with Poulantzas). In practice, Poulantzas' analysis may be more aptly described as functionalist, because he argues, finally, that the state is the cohesive factor within the social formation. In Philip Abrams's view, however, both Miliband and Poulantzas—just like mainstream political sociologists and political scientists—remained trapped by reification of 'the state', for these Marxist authors 'have both perceived the non-entity of the state and failed to cling to the logic of that perception' (1988: 69). Hence although Miliband's work demonstrates extremely well how it is possible to study the cluster of institutions of political and executive control and their key personnel, as well as to trace their effects, it does not explain how the state is constructed as an 'illusory general interest'.

The notion of 'the state', as opposed to the cluster of 'concrete' institutions and personnel, seems to refer to some kind of structure or agency which lies hidden behind the concrete. Abrams suggests that sociologists, like most citizens, have often experienced this hidden entity on a common-sense level, and that the very difficulty of studying the state points to 'a backstage institutionalisation of political power behind the on-stage agencies of government' (Ibid.: 63). It was the structure hidden behind the concrete which Poulantzas sought to uncover, but failed to do so. Clearly, 'there is a political function of cohesion effected repressively, economically and ideologically in class societies', but 'to identify it as "the global role of the state" seems to me, by introducing a misplaced concreteness, to both over-simplify and over-mystify its nature' (Ibid.: 73). According to Abrams, the state is not an institution, let alone a thing, but 'an ideological project' (Ibid.: 75), so that the key to the problem is to acknowledge, as Poulantzas almost does, the 'cogency of the *idea* of the state as an ideological power and treat that as a compelling object of analysis' (Ibid.: 79). Hence in addition to 'a state-system in Miliband's sense', there is also 'a state-idea, projected, purveyed and variously believed in in different societies at different times'. It is important to study the relationship among the state-system and state-idea, and other forms of power, but a mistake to suppose 'that we have also to study the state—an entity, agent, function or relation over and above the state-system and the state-idea' (Ibid.: 82).

Mitchell's much-cited review of the mainstream political science literature leads him to a rather similar conclusion. He points out that a crucial weakness in the concept of 'the state', for the political-system theorists, is in fact what is significant about it. For Easton, the state seemed 'less an analytic tool than a symbol for unity, ... a myth', whereas for Mitchell the state is important because 'of its political strength as a mythic or ideological construct' (1991: 81). Mitchell's 'alternative approach' crucially depends on the argument that although there is no clear boundary separating the state from society, an apparent boundary between them is produced by the modern nation-state, so that 'the distinction between state and society ... [is] the defining characteristic of the modern political order' (Ibid.: 95). For Mitchell, who specifically distinguishes himself from Poulantzas, the state is not to be analysed as a structure, but 'as a structural effect', that is, as the effect of practices that make state structures appear to exist. Significant among these practices are Foucauldian 'disciplines' helping to produce the armies, schools, bureaucracies and other distinctive institutions of the modern state, and one of its particularly important characteristics, of course, is the territorial boundary policed by passports, immigration laws and the rest (Ibid.: 94). Because we all have to produce our passports whenever we cross into another country, we are all persuaded to take for granted the reality and legitimacy of the state. Thus passports, together with so many other institutions, arrangements and processes, create the structural effect of the modern nation-state as an almost transcendental entity set apart from the society from which it cannot in reality be clearly separated.

In a recent essay which slightly modifies parts of his earlier one, Mitchell cites Abrams, but argues that we should not 'separate the material forms of the state from the ideological, or the real from the illusory. The state-idea and the state-system are better seen as two aspects of the same process' (1999: 77). The process in question is the creation of the structural effect just mentioned. How Mitchell's more circuitous discussion of the 'appearance of structure' escapes the criticism aimed at Abrams's plainer focus on the state-idea is unclear. Yet it is surely right to insist that the idea of the state is itself a form of symbolic capital that enters into the material power of the state-system and is reciprocally upheld by it. Furthermore, to argue for the importance of the idea of the state and for the state as a structural effect in the modern world is not to deny the reality of bureaucracy or policing, or the state-system more generally, as the reference to disciplinary institutions should make clear. Mitchell's claim that the state-society distinction, rather than other possible criteria, is definitive of political modernity can obviously be challenged as well. Nevertheless, the question of the boundary between the state and society, both theoretically and empirically, is a recurrent theme in writing on the modern Indian state, including the essays in this volume. Partly for that reason, we have found Mitchell's theoretical concern with this boundary helpful and we shall briefly return to him in conclusion. At this point, however, we turn to a short review of the ways in which the modern Indian state, mainly in political science, has been analysed in some influential, recent literature.

The Indian state, the dominant classes and the 'passive revolution'

It is widely considered that 'a crucial feature of traditional Indian society was its ability to marginalise the political order ... the logic of political change remained isolated from the logic of social order' (Kaviraj 1984: 232). The further idea that the state was also conceptualized as distanced from and inessential to the moral core of society was most influentially developed in Dumont's *Homo Hierarchicus* (1970), which argues that secular power in traditional Hindu society was clearly 'encompassed by' and subordinate to religious values. Dumont's argument has been vigorously challenged by 'neo-Hocartians' such as Dirks (1987), and more generally by a host of scholars critical of his analysis of kingship. Sudipta Kaviraj and other political theorists who dwell on the 'marginality' of politics and the state in 'traditional' India are vulnerable to criticisms similar to those raised against Dumont. Here, though, we do not wish to cover this familiar ground again. What matters for our discussion is that India's post-independence leaders succeeded, as Sunil Khilnani argues, in establishing the modern state—in total contrast with the pre-colonial state of affairs—'at the core of India's society', so that it 'etched itself into the imagination of Indians in a way that no previous political agency had ever done' (1998: 41). The conception of the state enshrined in the Constitution of India is that of an entity which is subject to the 'sovereignty of the people'. The preamble to the Constitution begins: 'WE, THE PEOPLE OF INDIA, having solemnly resolved to constitute India into a SOVEREIGN, DEMOCRATIC REPUBLIC and to secure to all its citizens JUSTICE ..., LIBERTY ..., EQUALITY ..., and to promote among them all FRATERNITY ....' Some academic discussion has started with the same conception, naively or optimistically assuming (as Ashis Nandy points out) that India participates in a universal sociology of politics, so that—in time and as local distortions are gradually ironed out—the state will truly represent the interests of the majority of Indians as citizens. Many academic analysts, like independent India's first political leaders, also assumed that as the process of modernization proceeded, 'a more coherent form of Indianness would emerge and the diversity of the country would diminish to make India more governable' (Nandy 1989: 4).

Often, therefore, 'the state' in India has been conceived of on Weberian lines as an organization. Achin Vanaik argues explicitly that 'the state has to be seen ... in "organizational" and "realist" terms, as an actual organization with certain interests distinct from those of the dominant classes, controlling real peoples and territories' (1990: 15). Hence the politics and political economy of India have to be interpreted in terms of the relations between the 'state-as-actual-organization' and the dominant-class 'ruling coalition', which for Vanaik (as for many others) is primarily constituted by the agrarian bourgeoisie—or rich capitalist farmer class—and the industrial bourgeoisie led by big capital. The state's capacity to realize the democratic principles and aspirations of the Constitution is, in this widely-held view, chronically impaired by the power of the dominant classes. This also means, at least by implication, that the boundary between state and society is permeable or indistinct, or that the state is 'porous' because it can be permeated by the dominant classes and their interests.

The Rudolphs also argue (1987) that the state is 'a self-determining third actor' and hence an organization or distinct entity. The modern

Indian state is, they suggest, a 'weak/strong state'—also a formulation which corresponds well with widely-held ideas—because it is imbued with a considerable degree of autonomy (therefore 'strong') by virtue of the compromise of power between dominant classes, whilst at the same time and by the same token being very tightly constrained in what it is capable of doing (therefore 'weak'). The most influential development of this idea of the compromise of power has been in the work of Pranab Bardhan (1984), which is broadly endorsed by Vanaik and can fairly be claimed to represent the prevailing consensus. Bardhan describes the state in terms of conflicts and complementarities between three 'dominant proprietary classes': not only industrial capitalists and rich farmers, but also a class of bureaucrats and professionals, whose property is in their office. None of the three classes, however, is able to establish hegemony over the others and, in particular, the compromise of power between industrial capitalists and rich farmers leaves a space for the independent exercise of power by state office-holders, who derive an income from 'rents', for example from their authority over the allocation of permits and licences. In the work of Bardhan and other scholars of the Indian political economy, however, the state itself remains rather shadowy. Much of value is in fact said about the 'state-system', but the latter is still treated as a kind of residual category and the 'state-idea' features hardly at all. If the state is an 'actual organization', therefore, it is nonetheless one that is virtually subsumed by the relationships of power among the dominant classes.

A distinctive line of thought appears in the work of Partha Chatterjee and Sudipta Kaviraj, who despite their differences both draw on the Gramscian idea of 'passive revolution'. They largely accept the conclusions about the dominant classes just outlined, but their diagnosis of the Indian state's weakness is significantly different. Following Gramsci, Chatterjee argues that in the formation of capitalist nation-states,

> where an emergent bourgeoisie lacks the social conditions for establishing complete hegemony over the new nation, it resorts to a 'passive revolution', by attempting a 'molecular transformation' of the old dominant classes into partners in a new historical bloc and only a partial appropriation of the popular masses. (Chatterjee 1986: 30)

Chatterjee's 'bourgeoisie' denotes a progressive, modernizing class—rather than a broader class of capitalists both rural and urban—and in India, for example, there was an alliance, albeit uneasy, between this bourgeoisie and the rising rich peasantry, especially after zamindari abolition during the first phase of land reform shortly after Independence. As is well-known, the Nehruvian state was vitally committed to 'development' through planning, 'a utopian practice that would make India a modern nation' (Inden 1995: 248). Planned development did indeed become an absolutely central feature of the newly independent nation-state, whose new temples, in Nehru's famous phrase, were its dams and steel plants. In discussing 'Nehru and the passive revolution', Chatterjee (1986: ch. 5; cf. 1997: 287–90) bitingly dissects the illusions of the era. Planned development became the new, supremely statist utopia: 'Place all your prayers at the feet of the *sarkar*, the omnipotent and supremely enlightened state, and they will be duly passed on to the body of experts who are planning for the overall progress of the country' (Chatterjee 1986: 160). State planning was generally given strong support by the capitalist bourgeoisie, but in India, as the historical analyses of Hanson (1966) and Frankel (1978) document so clearly, the 'relative autonomy' of the state's planning elite—'the body of experts'— from a range of special interests in society was very rapidly eroded. The Indian elite's capacity to pursue the developmental project was therefore continually undercut, in contrast with their equivalents in more successful 'development states', like Taiwan or South Korea (cf. Wade 1990). As Kaviraj explains, in order to survive, 'the state elite began to seek alliances with pre-capitalist forces on a larger scale', so that it could no longer 'dictate to them' and instead began to reflect their interests (1984: 233).

Kaviraj further argues that a 'passive revolution' occurred because, in particular, the Indian modernizing bourgeoisie was relatively weak within society and politically isolated. Partly because of its linguistic isolation, it was also unable to exercise cultural leadership through society, so that it came to rely heavily on 'state-bureaucratic agency' (Ibid.: 225) for bringing about social transformation. Yet this agency was still based on the institutional structures of colonial rule, which 'had feet of vernacular clay. At the most general level, they lacked a precondition of institutions: ... to be part of an unforced common-sense' (Ibid.: 227). The Indian nationalist leadership and then the Nehruvian state failed to create the common-sense legitimacy which the colonial order had necessarily lacked. As Kaviraj puts it elsewhere, the 'elite around Nehru' 'neglected the creation of a common thicker we-ness (something that was a deeper sense of community than merely the common opposition to the British) and the creation of a single political language for the entire polity' (1991: 90). As the state expanded, a profound gap developed, too, between the bureaucratic elite, at home with a 'modernist discourse' which often corresponded fairly well with Weberian rationality, and the personnel at lower levels, whose 'vernacular everyday discourses' were not structured around principles of formal rationality at all. An important reason for the modern Indian state's failure to implement its policies successfully is therefore the fact that it is 'overstretched', and because policies are finally implemented 'very low down in the bureaucracy, they are reinterpreted beyond recognition' (Ibid.: 91).

Somewhat comparable arguments have been developed further by Chatterjee, who concludes that Indian nationalism created an 'inner domain of culture [which] is declared the sovereign territory of the nation, where the colonial state is not allowed entry', even though the 'outer domain' of state institutions remained under colonial control (1993: 237). After Independence, however, the post-colonial nation-state, 'embedded as it is within the universal narrative of capital', refuses to recognize 'any form of community' except the nation itself (Ibid: 238). Culturally distinctive expressions of community identity are therefore antithetical to the modern Indian state, which generally seeks to subjugate them (cf. Chatterjee 1998). Although expressed differently, T. N. Madan's diagnosis of 'the crisis of Indian secularism' proceeds along similar lines. The state's constitutional secularism lacks a popular ideological base—'it is not rooted in social thought' (1997: 38)—so that the programme and discourse of the secularizing elite make no sense to the mass of ordinary Indians. The religious nationalism and fundamentalism threatening Indian society and the state are primarily an outcome of the 'ambition and hubris' of the modern state's elite (Ibid.: 263), whose modernist values, Madan plainly implies, are incompatible with the religious beliefs and practices of almost all the Indian people.

It follows from such arguments that the institutions, disciplines, arrangements and practices associated with the post-colonial state have not been supported by a modernist ideology that has found popular acceptance, in the way presupposed by the modernizing aspirations of the political leadership and the state elite. The state-idea, in other words, is not part of ordinary Indians' understanding. What Satish Saberwal (1996: 39) describes as the segmentary 'cellularity' of traditional Indian society persists, and state institutions such as the courts and bureaucracies have not had the 'normative support necessary for their reliable, effective functioning' because their western logic 'does not command much of either understanding or respect on the ground' (Ibid.: 150).

We do not suggest that the authors just discussed—Chatterjee, Kaviraj, Madan and Saberwal—are all of one mind. Thus, for example, Chatterjee and Kaviraj emphasize the gap between the elite and the subaltern populace, whereas Madan and Saberwal are more concerned with the distinction between the modern and traditional in culture and society. Although modern values are in general attributed to the elite *anarcho-communitarians.*

and traditional ones to the masses, there are still differences in analytical approach among these various writers. Moreover, even though Chatterjee and Madan are sometimes linked (mainly by their critics) with Nandy, neither they nor Kaviraj and Saberwal espouse the radical anti-modernism found in Nandy's writings.

Yet it is not inaccurate to suggest that all these scholars, in spite of their differences, are essaying a distinctive culturalist critique which has in turn attracted criticism, for example from Bardhan (1998), who labels Chatterjee and Nandy in particular as 'anarcho-communitarians'. To imply that all culturalist critics are entirely misguided and reactionary, as Bose and Jalal (1998: 4) do, is too sweeping, but they are right to claim that at issue is a 'critique of modernity' identifying the crisis of the modern Indian nation-state 'in the very condition of modernity as transposed and superimposed by colonialism on the subcontinent' (Ibid.: 2). All the scholarship discussed in this section—from realist political economy to culturalist critique—concurs with the conclusion that the state-system in India is profoundly penetrated or influenced by social forces. Empirically, therefore, the boundary between the state and society is in reality unclear, blurred, porous or mobile, and ordinary people widely recognize that this is so.[2] The material in this volume's essays further confirm that conclusion, but on the whole they do not support the culturalist critique and to this particularly important point we return below.

Political theory and political science can take us only so far in studying the Indian state. As Sunil Khilnani explained in his concluding commentary on the workshop, calling for more work on the theory of the state may risk turning the state (misconceived as a unitary actor) into a master concept which purportedly explains more than it possibly can. And no such master concept can explain what Indians actually think and do; rather, the concept itself first needs to be explained by exploring what the state variously means and does—what in short the state is for people in India today—and for that exploratory task, the first requirement is plainly ethnographic evidence.

Anthropological and ethnographic perspectives on the Indian state

From the 1950s to the early 1970s, anthropologists wrote quite extensively on politics in India. One major contributor was F. G. Bailey, who also happens to be the only anthropologist of India to figure significantly in Vincent's account of the development of political anthropology. Bailey's analysis (1963) of the role of village faction leaders as brokers between local and state levels in Orissa made a seminal contribution to Indian political studies in the 1960s—for example, through its use by Hanson (1966)—and it influenced the later conceptualization of the state as crucially subject to rich-peasant as well as bourgeois power. In the same period, there were numerous anthropological articles on similar themes and a few books, notably Anthony Carter's study of politics in Maharashtra (1974). A lot of research focused on factionalism, but a lot was also about caste in politics, a topic most influentially raised by M. N. Srinivas in 1957 in *Caste in modern India* (1962: ch. 1). Caste and factionalism were both themes to the fore in Rajni Kothari's influential collection (1970), to which social and political scientists alike contributed. It is perhaps surprising that there has not been more empirical research in the same vein since the early 1970s. There are exceptions of course, such as Marguerite Robinson's *Local politics: the law of the fishes* (1988), an ethnographic analysis of the changes which have taken place, over a twenty-five year period in one district of Andhra Pradesh, in the political processes analysed by Bailey. In her apparently little-noticed book, Robinson provides a local study of a major shift in Indian politics, associated by political scientists with the deinstitutionalization of party politics brought about by Indira Gandhi in the 1970s. She also examines the significant change represented by widespread challenges to local authority and dominance in the countryside, which is commented on comparatively by Mendelsohn (1993) in anthropology, and by Frankel (in Frankel and Rao 1989; 1990) and Kohli (1990) in political science, although Lerche (1995) conversely shows how rich Jat landowners in Uttar Pradesh can still use the state-system to their advantage, so that generalizations about the decline of traditional authority are questionable.

Yet it can well be argued that Bailey and most other anthropologists mainly illuminate our understanding of local political action, but do not tell us much about the Indian state itself. In some very recent research focusing on religious nationalism, there is more explicit concern with the question of the state—partly because the protagonists themselves have forced it to the top of the agenda.[3] Nevertheless, we need more ethnographic research on the state, especially on lower-level officials as well as politicians, so as 'to illuminate the quotidian practices of bureaucrats that tell us about the effects of the state on the everyday lives of rural people' (Gupta 1995: 376).[4]

One study which looks at bureaucrats' practice is James Manor's investigation (1993) into a tragedy in Bangalore in 1981, when over 300 poor slum-dwellers died after consuming poisonous illicit liquor. Manor shows how bureaucratic incompetence and inflexibility combined with government policies, corruption among politicians and police, and the hooch producers' appalling recklessness to produce a disaster in which the government hospital's medical staff were virtually the only state personnel who ever tried to help the victims. Such tragedies, especially among the 'undeserving' poor, as the middle classes are wont to label them, are depressingly frequent illustrations of the modern Indian state's inadequacies.

Another important monograph, which also explores the state's failures and deals with the everyday actions of state functionaries, specifically the police, is Paul Brass's political ethnography of rural Uttar Pradesh, *Theft of an idol* (1997). In his synoptic account of modern politics, Brass (1994) is emphatic that India is mired in multiple crises, one of which pertains to the police and the breakdown of law and order. Violence perpetrated by numerous parties 'has contributed to an increasingly pervasive Hobbesian state of disorder' and 'in many parts of urban and rural India, the police are not in fact maintaining order, but are themselves among the most dangerous and disorderly forces in the country' (Ibid.: 60). This general observation is substantiated in his monograph by ethnographic evidence about a series of crimes and atrocities, which explains how increased violence in Uttar Pradesh— especially between Hindus and Muslims and between castes—is bound up with the development of close links among politicians, the police and criminals. Today, Brass argues: 'Villagers in north India do not discern a society based on abstract law and prevailing order' (1997: 273). Yet this does not mean that there is mere lawlessness. Rather, there is 'a network of power relations among police, criminals, and politicians' in which force and violence are commonly used. The police are neither just state agents upholding law and order, nor simply miscreants; 'They are doing what they normally do, entering into one side or another of a local conflict' (Ibid.: 275). That is the normality, at least in rural north India, and it can be summed up as 'a set of formal rules and practices obeyed by a few, a set of informal rules and practices followed by most, and a lack of legitimacy attached to both' (Ibid.: 279). Hence there is a real crisis of the state and significant numbers of Indians have lost all confidence in it, at least in any idea or system resembling the modern state enshrined in the Constitution of India .

Akhil Gupta's article (1995), which focuses on corruption and is also based on fieldwork in Uttar Pradesh, does not entirely support Brass's rather apocalyptic conclusions, although the latter are obviously influenced by the focus on violence. On the other hand, Gupta's argument that at the local level the boundary between the state and society is a blurred one does accord with Brass's account, as well as all the essays in this volume. Thus local state officials collapse the distinction between their roles and styles of operation as 'public servants' as opposed to 'private citizens' (Ibid.: 384) concerned with their position in their own social world. This point is of course a familiar one, especially in discussions about corruption, but it does need to be emphasized. It is made particularly forcefully by Barbara Harriss-White, in work based on her study over twenty years in the small town of Arni in northern Tamil Nadu. She notes that the growth of the informal economy here has been related to patterns of 'state failure', and that the inability of the local state to secure revenues for its developmental functions has created spaces for private security services or benefit providers. The result is a blurring of the boundary between state and society. India's intermediate classes— rich peasants and the 'lower middle class'—seek to further their interests by colonizing the state with their kin, and by expanding the scope of what can be described as a 'shadow state', existing alongside and in some ways interlocking with the 'formal' state (Harriss-White n.d.: 13).[5]

Nonetheless, even though Harriss-White's material demonstrates how blurred the boundary between 'state' and 'society' is, the idea of such a boundary is strategically significant for people in Arni, as elsewhere, and this relates to Gupta's main point that 'the discourse of corruption ... enabl[es] people to construct the state symbolically and to define themselves as citizens' (1995: 389). Newspaper accounts of official corruption portray 'the people' as powerless and exploited, but in democratic India it is in fact widely recognized that state employees are accountable to them. 'The discourse of corruption, by marking those actions that constitute an infringement of such rights, thus acts to represent the rights of citizens to themselves' (Ibid.: 389). Discourse about corruption implies or helps to produce the boundary between the state and society—perhaps even 'civil society'—and it also suggests that Kaviraj, for example, overstates the distinction between elite and popular understandings of the state.

Gupta's analysis is weakened by a typical use of the term 'discourse' to cover practice and action indiscriminately. It is also plain that most practice of corruption simply deprives citizens of their rights, rather than 'defines' them, and in some cases it helps to kill them, as in Bangalore in 1981. Yet he is probably right to claim that people's talk about corruption (and reports of it) can be important in how they see citizenship, the state and the distinction between state and society. Pavan Varma rightly argues that the 'folklore of corruption' (as he more plainly describes it) has helped to ensure that the existence of corruption even at the highest levels is now taken for granted as normal, but he is surely wrong that 'the perception that it was pervasive legitimized its existence' (1999: 87). However widespread corruption is assumed to be, it is nevertheless generally regarded as illegitimate and a violation of people's rights and entitlements.

In Jonathan Parry's ethnography of corruption (2000), based on research in and around the Bhilai Steel Plant, a very similar conclusion is forcibly advanced. Parry—who is discussing relatively small-scale 'retail corruption' among ordinary functionaries, not large-scale corruption by top politicians—insists that the Hindi words for 'corruption' and 'bribe' (*bhrashtachar* and *ghus*) are not 'morally neutral', and such payments are not normally regarded by contemporary Indians 'as legitimate perquisites of office ... especially when the office is somebody else's and it is they who are providing the perks. And what most fundamentally underlies their condemnation, I believe, is that [people] have to some extent internalised the universalistic and impersonal values associated with modern bureaucracy' (Ibid.: 29). In conclusion, Parry argues that the popular opinion in contemporary India that corruption has swollen over time—a 'fact' which cannot really be demonstrated—is a reflection of 'the widening *experience* of corruption [which] is an almost inevitable corollary of the expanded reach of the state' (Ibid.: 52). Moreover: 'Corruption has seemed to get worse and worse not (only) because it has, but also because it subverts a set of values to which people are increasingly committed' (Ibid.: 53).

This conclusion must remain debatable, mainly because sound evidence is so hard to collect. Using ethnographic data from a south Indian irrigation department, Robert Wade (1985) argues that corruption gets worse because, for example, it is encouraged by (and encourages) an increasingly systematic 'market for public office'. Parry's argument implies that Wade may have exaggerated because he might have believed too much of what he was told, but it is virtually impossible to be sure. Moreover, the reality of latter-day corruption, and talk about it, take many different forms, as several essays in this volume demonstrate, although corruption is only one of their themes and not necessarily the most important. Nonetheless, Parry's bold claim that the impersonal norms and values of the modern state have been widely internalized by ordinary Indians—lower-level bureaucrats, local politicians and ordinary citizens alike— is one that the material in this volume largely supports.

The contributions of this book

Each of the seven essays which follow provides further convincing ethnographic evidence that the state is not a discrete, monolithic entity 'acting' impersonally above or outside society. Rather, the *sarkar*—indifferently 'state' and 'government' in the commonest Indian vernacular term for them—appears on many levels and in many centres, and its lower echelons at least are always staffed by people with whom some kind of social relationship can or could exist; the 'faceless bureaucrats' actually do have faces. The boundary between the state and society, therefore, is not only unclear; it is also fluid and negotiable according to social context and position. Incidentally but not trivially, the ethnography also complicates, even if it does not necessarily undermine, the identification of a dominant class of state office-holders, because there appears to be little or no evidence that bureaucrats have any perceived common interests as a class. Yet none of this is likely to surprise anyone, except perhaps an unrealistically abstract political theorist, so let us now highlight some of this volume's positive contributions to our knowledge of the mostly everyday action and beliefs of ordinary people, officials and politicians in relation to the Indian state.

Despite this quotidian emphasis, the first essay in this volume is Thomas Blom Hansen's, which is explicitly concerned with how the modern Indian state seeks to sustain the 'myth of the state' as sublimely sovereign and how it thereby legitimates itself as the guarantor of order, security and justice for its citizens. In some places and for some groups, this myth was destroyed a long time ago, but in Mumbai it was particularly badly damaged during the bloody riots which followed the demolition of the Ayodhya mosque on 6 December 1992. Muslims in the city felt betrayed, especially by the collusion between Hindu rioters and the city's mainly Hindu police force, and for them the state, which had been progressively captured by the Shiv Sena and militant Hindu nationalists, completely failed in its duty to protect all its citizens. For many Hindus, especially supporters of Hindu nationalism, the myth was also shattered as they celebrated their 'victory' over a religious minority too long protected by the 'pseudo-secular' state. After the riots, the Maharashtra state government set up a commission of inquiry headed by Justice Srikrishna, whose lengthy public proceedings exposed the partiality of the police and the Shiv Sena's involvement in organized violence. After the Shiv Sena and Bharatiya Janata Party came to power in Maharashtra in 1995, the Commission was also asked to investigate the deadly bomb blasts executed by mainly Muslim gangsters in March 1993; those charged with the blasts were also prosecuted in a special terrorist court. Hansen argues that the Commission and the court 'should be seen as state spectacles, public displays of the state as a producer of impartial and universal justice', but both revealed as well the 'profane sides of state power' in the form of brutality and misconduct by politicians, officials and the police.

Hansen's interpretation of the Commission and the court derives much of its strength from his ethnographic knowledge of ordinary Hindus and Muslims in Mumbai, and some of his data on Muslims are reported in his essay. Since Independence, Mumbai's Muslims have become socially and economically more isolated, and the police force more dominated by Hindu nationalist sympathizers, so that police attitudes have hardened towards lower-class Muslims seen as 'irrational' slum-dwellers. Since 1992–3, however, neighbourhood committees have been established in riot-affected areas as part of police efforts to improve relations with Muslims, although the most striking development reported by Hansen is reconciliatory gesturing towards the police by Muslims. Senior police officers have distributed flowers outside mosques and they have been invited as guests of honour at Islamic religious events in place of the government ministers who used to come. In Muslim eyes, politicians from the Shiv Sena and the discredited Congress party are no longer acceptable representatives of the state, so that it is now police officers who officially confirm the Muslim minority's integral place in Indian society.

In conclusion, Hansen admits that we cannot tell how far the Srikrishna Commission actually succeeded in restoring the myth of the state in Mumbai. Maybe it did not, but it remains notable, argues Hansen, that the main perpetrators of violence in the city—the Shiv Sena, the police and the underworld—continue to depend on the state's resources and to define themselves, positively or negatively, in relation to its authority. The myth of the state's unity and coherence must still be kept alive, even as politics returns to 'business as usual' and effective governance progressively crumbles in the city.

In constitutional terms, the most dramatic crisis of the Indian state was the emergency between 1975 and 1977, but during the last two decades, as Emma Tarlo tells us, forgetting the emergency has been a 'national duty'. Especially important to forget are the campaigns of forced sterilization and slum clearance, whose vast numbers of victims included the mostly poor residents of an East Delhi housing colony studied by Tarlo. Her essay, part of a larger work which will contribute significantly to the neglected story of the emergency, explores the 'profane', mundane and banal bureaucratic workings of the state at the local level. One of her principal findings is that during the emergency, despite official denials, rights to housing—for the victims of slum clearance and others—were widely secured by undergoing sterilization or by 'motivating' someone else to do so. Furthermore, contrary to the popular belief that records about such matters were not kept during the emergency, they actually were as part of normal bureaucratic procedure.

Tarlo carried out her research in a municipal office, whose records—like so many bureaucratic files everywhere—'not only revealed official truths; they also concealed unofficial truths'. In uncovering the latter, Tarlo learnt much from the clerks who kept and still keep the records, and her essay is an exemplary demonstration of how the 'paper truths', which can become so vital in so many ordinary people's lives, do not record simple facts, but must be read as evidence about the often complex relationship of both bureaucrats and ordinary people to the state's administrative structures. As in all bureaucracies (however well or badly run), the clerks were knowledgeable about the system, so that they could explain their formally rational procedures in relation to the written contents of the files, as well as how to subvert those procedures. Tarlo, however, also shows how the ordinary residents in East Delhi did and do handle the bureaucratic procedures more or less competently, and during the emergency some people could actually take advantage of the rules about sterilization to obtain housing which they would otherwise not have got.

Moreover and more generally, even though their subjects' lives rarely correspond to what is written in their files, so that the files cannot represent reality, they are often taken to do so and thereby become a basis for action. Sometimes that action is denial, for example when officials tried to cancel housing rights made on the basis of sterilization in 1979, as part of a national move to forget the emergency. Actually, cancellation was not pushed through; instead the relevant files were buried among 'pending cases', where they still remain, leaving people to exist in a condition of bureaucratic limbo that may (or may not) catch up with them in the future. Thus do the urban poor of East Delhi and the lowly bureaucrats processing their files live their lives and do their work just a few miles away from New Delhi's seats of power.

Whereas the first two essays focus on people who have mainly suffered at the hands of the state, Craig Jeffrey and Jens Lerche discuss cases from rural Uttar Pradesh in which people benefit by exploiting it. Thus, for example, the rich Jat landowners studied by Jeffrey owe much of their economic success to their ability to secure a great deal more than their fair share of the state's resources, especially in the form of public-sector employment. In this part of India, as elsewhere, there is a 'market' in government jobs in which the amounts payable in bribes are fairly well-known, but in addition to money, information and contacts are also needed to secure the posts. Jats in the know, for example, have contacts with lower-level clerks, who act as intermediaries between candidates for jobs and recruitment officers. In general, however, only rich Jats can afford the bribes and they are also disproportionately able to cream off state resources through local *panchayats;* they can also obtain speedy police or legal action in defending their access to land, partly because they can rely on politicians to intercede for them. Jeffrey and Lerche's key argument here is that the reproduction of the class of rich Jat landowners significantly depends upon control of the economic and other resources located in the state, which has effectively been 'privatized' or captured by one stratum of society.

The essay looks at comparative examples studied by Lerche as well, and concludes with a discussion of the Scheduled Castes, who have found a new measure of confidence in themselves during the 1990s following the rise of the Bahujan Samaj Party. In some areas, they have improved their access to state resources in various ways, but scarcely by relying on constitutional rights granted to them by an impartial, protective state. Rather, the Scheduled Castes too try to secure state resources; they 'are eager to "misuse" the government administration as much as possible' and some low-caste people 'openly boasted about gaining more than their fair share of government programmes and of exaggerating Thakur violence against them in complaints to the police'. For the poor low castes, though still much less than for the rich high castes, as well as for officials and politicians, the state in rural Uttar Pradesh is primarily looked upon as a pool of resources to be exploited as effectively as possible.

It is of course because the state has been 'captured' by rich Jat landowners and similar groups in rural areas that the Indian state is often characterized as 'soft' or 'weak'. Moreover, the more completely the state penetrates the whole of the countryside, the more completely it can be exploited and the more normal such exploitation becomes. 'Business as usual' in a block office, for instance, is typically about diverting or pocketing public resources, and although misuse is still widely recognized as misuse, it is equally widely perceived as defining the quotidian reality of many people's relationship with the state.

While state resources can be exploited by a range of local magnates and leaders in Uttar Pradesh and many other regions, in rural West Bengal they are much more firmly controlled by the Communist Party of India (Marxist), the dominant party in the ruling Left Front government. Arild Engelsen Ruud's essay, which looks at the role of local politicians and leaders as intermediaries between the state and village society, is especially concerned with the moral ambivalence surrounding this role. Politics, it is generally assumed, is corrupting, so that even good people will become corrupt after entering politics. The ordinary villagers Ruud studied therefore distanced themselves from politics and politicians, but many of them were actually involved in it and to cope with their embarrassment, they sought to portray their own involvement as strategic.

To explore these issues, Ruud describes a village meeting called by CPM activists to elect a village committee. As everyone knew, no power was vested in the meeting except that granted to it by the CPM, which controls all important elections, financial allocations, patronage flows and the like within the area. Why then did anyone turn up to an apparently pointless meeting that was not very entertaining? Ruud argues that people came as loyal clients and supporters of local leaders because attendance at such meetings directly reflects on these leaders, who need to stay in the good books of the party, although ordinary people wanted to make it clear as well that they were not just clients. Yet people also recognize that leadership is based on power, which tends to generate more power, and leaders are men who can make things work. Because they require things to be done, ordinary villagers cannot avoid dealing with political leaders and getting entangled in politics, but they need to express their ambivalence about it, to themselves and each other. So they turned up at the meeting, but chattered and laughed during the speeches, and went home early in a 'reciprocal act of absolution'.

Ruud interprets the equivocal attitude towards politics in the light of the moral ambivalence attached to power and wealth (*artha*) in classical Hinduism, although it may have as much to do with the peculiar situation produced by the CPM's longstanding dominance, which has made the party virtually identical to the state. In a one-party state, the state itself is likely to be tainted by the corruption that elsewhere sticks more to political parties; perhaps for that reason, most ordinary people may be particularly keen to keep their distance from the state in West Bengal. The axiom that politics and politicians are (almost) always corrupt is of course ubiquitous in India, but the ambivalence reported from West Bengal is less apparent in our other studies from Kerala and Tamil Nadu.

In Kerala, argue Filippo and Caroline Osella, the annual Onam festival, which is the biggest of the year, is an occasion on which 'state' and 'people' construct 'intimate' patron-client relations with each other. Onam celebrates the annual return of the mythical demon-king Mahabali, who was destroyed by Vishnu; for most people in Kerala, Mahabali's kingdom epitomizes a lost golden age of tolerance and equality, which are seen as distinctively Malayali virtues. In that golden age, there was also no 'cheating', whereas today it is everywhere, especially in corrupt politics. The Osellas explain, however, that different kinds of illicit payments are evaluated differently, and ordinary people recognize that in order to support their families, state officials have to earn money where they can, just like everyone else. The tolerance of cheating as a venial part of daily life is definitively suspended at Onam, however, when Malayali social morality is collectively reconstituted. Then a failure to deal with cheating—for example, during a festival boat race—can cause politicians, state officials and other leaders to damage their reputation and power as patrons. At this time, powerful figures must strive to uphold king Mahabali's virtues and ordinary people—in a form of 'coercive subordination'—thereby acquire the ability 'to express their will and agency as clients'. The state, after all, is composed of people, and at Onam relationships between the state and its citizens are most dramatically made and expressed in an idiom of mutual closeness.

In both the cases described by Ruud and the Osellas, though in somewhat different ways, we see that ordinary people expect the business of politics and government to be thoroughly infected by corruption and cheating, but they also pragmatically recognize that they have to deal with politicians and officials. They try to keep their distance from the pollution, but in Kerala (as elsewhere in India) they also recognize that not all corruption is equally bad. In contrast to the West Bengal village meeting, which made visible people's normal distancing behaviour, the events at Onam are a kind of ritual of reversal in which people strive to bind themselves to their leaders in a morally perfect state imagined as Mahabali's kingdom. The Onam festival shows its citizens how the state could be, as opposed to how it profanely is, in a 'traditionally' Malayali 'state spectacle' that has more than a little in common with the Srikrishna Commission's public hearings in Mumbai.

The continued importance of kingship in Malayali notions of the ideal state has clear parallels in Tamil Nadu, as David Mosse shows in his essay on the former kingdoms and zamindari estates of Ramnad and Sivaganga. There are also obvious parallels between Mosse's and Jeffrey and Lerche's material on how the resources of the state are exploited by powerful groups and individuals in the countryside. Mosse's historical and ethnographic study focuses on irrigation systems, which well illuminate 'the shifting boundary between state bureaucracy and community institutions, and the intermingling of state power and local authority at different historical moments'. During the colonial period, the British sought to make improving landlords out of the erstwhile 'little kings' of Ramnad and Sivaganga, but the latter continued to use productive resources as political assets for ruling in the old way.

Government efforts to force the zamindars to invest in irrigation and to collect land revenue systematically mostly failed, and 'land and water continued to be ruled rather than managed'.

After independence, zamindars were soon abolished and the new, independent Indian 'development state' increasingly involved itself in managing irrigation systems. As the idea of the state became stronger, however, it correspondingly evoked stronger ideas of the 'community', and the state-community dichotomy has partly obscured the survival of old ideas about rule which are still important. Thus for example, village headmen have privileged access to major public works contracts for irrigation improvement, although they also have to share out their gains with government officials and politicians; in these respects, 'business as usual' works much as it does in the region discussed by Jeffrey and Lerche and all over rural India. Mosse, however, also emphasizes that private gains have to be redistributed locally—especially through religious donations—so that headmen and other local magnates can legitimate their claim on state resources and 'transform state public works into personal patronage'. Much of the old kingly order survives and is often reproduced through local leaders' control of the endlessly multiplying local 'community' associations, which the government, as well as non-governmental organizations, encourage as channels for their development expenditure. For understanding the state's role in this region of Tamil Nadu, therefore, one of Mosse's most significant findings is that the local 'community' is dialectically generated by the modern state within a framework that is also markedly shaped by a notion of rulership, which is distinctively pre-modern and in some respects characteristically Tamil.

Véronique Bénéï's essay is also about the importance of a regionally distinctive, pre-modern idiom, in this case in Maharashtra. Bénéï explores the ways in which the idea of the Indian nation is inculcated in schools, which are of course one of the modern state's principal disciplinary institutions, and more explicitly than our other authors, she focuses on the state as the nation-state. In all Maharashtra's primary schools, there is (or should be) a daily session of 'value education' at which children and their teachers together sing the national anthem, recite the pledge of India and complete a 'nationalist liturgy' in which the idea of India is ingrained by a combination of repetitive bodily techniques, and rote-memorization and recitation. In the children's separate classrooms, this collective daily session may be followed by a simple act of Hindu worship and further recitation of memorized lists, closing with one for Indian currency, in an enactment of 'banal nationalism' tinged with Hinduism.

A central thesis in Bénéï's essay is that the idea of the Indian nation is actually mediated through the region, here Maharashtra. Historians of India have already shown how regional 'old patriotisms' were instrumental in the growth of all-Indian nationalism, but Bénéï argues that they are still important, even within the post-colonial Indian nation-state, so that loyalty to and love for the nation are in fact developed from a Marathi patriotism anchored in the *desh*. The term *desh*, significantly, is used indifferently for either Maharashtra or India, whereas the term *rashtra*, usually translated as 'nation', is rarely employed. (On the evidence available, the 'segmentary' meaning of *desh* and the relatively rare use of *rashtra* are features found throughout India, not just Maharashtra.) In some respects, Maharashtra is an unusual case, because its distinctive regionalism is so strongly focused on glorification of the seventeenth-century hero Shivaji and his Maratha empire. Conquest and statecraft are thus central in Maharashtrian regional patriotism, whereas in Bengal or Tamil Nadu, for example, great traditions of language and culture are more heavily emphasized. On the other hand, the anachronistic conversion of Shivaji into a founder of modern India is, of course, typical of nationalist history-making. In their essay, the Osellas show that the Malayalis' position within the nation and their version of the national rhetoric of the 'development state' are constructed at Onam by invoking Mahabali's rule; Mahabali is not (yet) a maker of modern India, but the evidence from Kerala further supports Bénéï's general argument that among ordinary people—and for schoolchildren—Indian nationalism comes in a patriotic idiom perceived as dependent on regional traditions. Thus in a daily routine, the idea of the glorious nation-state is re-enacted in Maharashtra's schools by drawing on a pre-modern regional patriotism; this patriotism is in turn reinforced by a modern nationalism which, at least in this part of India, is now being 'saffronized' by the educational policies of the Hindu parties.

Conclusion

We need not belabour the point that our seven essays, and the other anthropological and ethnographic studies referred to earlier, do not amount to a representative survey, let alone a comprehensive one, so that it would be foolhardy to advance grand generalizations. On the other hand, the evidence in this book clearly does confirm previous findings that the modern Indian state (no doubt like all other states) is not a discrete, unitary 'actor', because it does not consist of an 'actual organization' separated from society. Moreover, its multiple agencies are staffed by personnel who rarely act in full coordination with each other and are often in dispute or competition. For these reasons among others, bureaucrats—unlike industrial capitalists or rich farmers —never even begin to form themselves into an organized dominant class.

The state, however, is also an idea as well as a system, as we have already seen. In making sense of the modern nation-state in India, it is vital to recognize that it is precisely that—modern, national and a state. Thus for instance, to follow Mitchell (1991: 94) again, the Indian state possesses the characteristic institutions of an army, a school system and a bureaucracy; it also has a territorial boundary which it polices and has more than once defended to the inch across uninhabitable glaciers. Through all these characteristics and in all these respects, the state can and often does appear to people in India as a sovereign entity set apart from society by an *internal* boundary that seems to be as real as its external boundary. A local administrative office, a government school, a police station: to enter any of these is to cross the internal boundary into the domain of the state, whose conceptual separation from society is perhaps most ubiquitously symbolized by all its special-purpose buildings with their painted notice-boards outside.

In support of his point about blurred boundaries between the state and society, Gupta comments on the local village officials who are more likely to be found 'at the roadside tea stalls and in their homes than in their offices' (1995: 384). His point is a fair one, but it needs qualification in relation to discourse about the state. Even if many petty officials do not spend much time in their offices, many others do, and nobody imagines that the endless cups of tea and coffee drunk in India's government buildings turn them into tea shops or homes. Furthermore, people in India also know that modern impersonal norms of secularized government and formally rational bureaucracy do or should apply in government offices and other locales of the state. Of course, deferential feet-touching is quite common in government offices, but that does not mean that ordinary Indian citizens do not grasp the logic of impersonal norms. On the contrary, we would argue that many or most of them do, so that touching the feet of a superior administrative officer, for example, is an action which undermines the impersonal, bureaucratic norms that certainly the officer, and probably the supplicant as well, both know should prevail in such a context. It is true that many of the same norms apply (or should do) in all modern, secular institutions—factories, offices, schools, hospitals and so on—even if they are private ones in which people lack some of the rights and responsibilities they have (or should have) in state institutions. At issue here, though, is Gupta's point about blurred boundaries between the state and society, between the domain of public servants and the world of private citizens. The ethnographic evidence, we believe, shows that although these boundaries may be blurred or porous or contextually shifting, they nonetheless are perceived as boundaries, so that the threshold of a government office symbolizes an internal boundary—a 'wall of separation' to adapt a famous American phrase—by which the state is ideologically parted from the society that it governs.

Our assertion that many or most Indians understand bureaucratic norms does of course contradict Saberwal's contention (1996: 150), which we cited above, that the opposite is true. More generally, it runs counter to the arguments of culturalist critics who contend that the modern state is in some sense incompatible with the structure of Indian society and its indigenous demotic values, and that the latter-day 'crisis of the state' in India is fundamentally a result of that incompatibility. The evidence in this volume scarcely supports this thesis, because it consistently shows an everyday understanding of the workings of the state and its administrative procedures among ordinary people which could hardly exist if there were such a profound incompatibility. Certainly, police officers may be invited as guests of honour to Islamic festivals in Mumbai or rural magnates in Tamil Nadu may redistribute state resources through religious gifting, but such actions do not imply any misunderstanding about the role of the police or the rules applicable to public funds. Rather, they mainly demonstrate how 'the "modern" sector as the leading element within the nation' is legitimated in 'pre-modern' terms, to cite Chatterjee (1997: 295) from an article which (*pace* some of his other writings) undermines the culturalist critique. To put it in Weberian terms, these cases exemplify a distinctive combination of state-based legal authority and traditional authority.

This takes us to a crucial point about the domination and extensiveness of the modern Indian nation-state. Khilnani eloquently explains that 'towering over [Indian] society today is the state. This state is far from supremely effective. ... Yet it is today at the very centre of the Indian political imagination' (1998: 59). For all sorts of reasons which Khilnani considers—some of them discussed in this volume, like the capture of state resources by local elites—the modern Indian state's deficiencies have arguably put it in crisis. And the continued salience of regional distinctiveness, also prominent in this volume, certainly confirms that the state does not represent a unifying idea and concept, the basis for 'a single shared sense of India' (Ibid.: 2). In his discussion, Khilnani places great weight on the role of democracy in generating the rapid transformation that now means that 'everyone can imagine exercising some influence' upon the ever-expanding state and its resources (Ibid.: 60). As Bardhan (1998: 192) observes, this has led to a 'demand overload' partly caused by the energetic and assertive way in which 'the masses' have taken to 'the democratic project initiated by the modernizing elite'. Furthermore, electoral democracy in India, as is widely recognized, has increasingly become majoritarian populism in pursuit of ballot-box victory, at the expense of much respect for checks and balances or for the rights of minorities. Thus it has been plausibly proposed by Hansen that the rise of assertive Hindu nationalism as a political force is one outcome of 'the less than orderly democratization of Indian democracy' (1999: 58).

Pursuing a similar line of argument, Kaviraj emphasizes the changes since the early years of Independence; then the state was 'spectacular, mysterious and distant', but now it 'has become something vast, overextended, extremely familiar at least in its sordid everyday structures—the *panchayat*, the revenue department ... and above all the elections'. Today, the state's domination of Indian society, in one form or another, is 'historically irreversible' (1997: 243–4). Thus the democratization of democracy has been accompanied by what we might call the routinization of state authority, whose modern rational-legal form (perhaps paradoxically) once seems to have possessed its own charisma. True, there is a danger here of exaggerating the majesty of Nehru's India. Nonetheless, in all those 'everyday structures', bureaucratic procedures have now become extremely familiar, so that demotic discourse about government is at least as much modernist as traditionalist.

Partly as a result of their familiarity (and the contempt that it may have bred), bureaucratic procedures can also be readily distorted and subverted by groups which demand their 'democratic' share of public resources (or more than it), and by individuals—mostly politicians and officials—who know how to work things to their personal advantage. The outcome is normally unfair, but it is also notable that even the poor, low-status and weak can sometimes benefit from their own adequately competent manipulation of political and administrative systems. Thus we find victims of the emergency in East Delhi, Scheduled Caste members in rural Uttar Pradesh or ordinary villagers in West Bengal pragmatically trying to deal with political and bureaucratic agencies, rather than striving to resist them. Clearly, the evidence in our seven essays is not decisive, but given the obsession with 'resistance' in so much current scholarship, it is striking that the ordinary people described in this volume are mostly not resisting the state, but using the 'system' as best they can.

Before closing, let us briefly refer to Spencer's persuasive criticism of political anthropology for its lack of interest in key concepts like the 'state' and 'democracy', and his call for a study of politics 'that would endeavour to gaze wide-eyed' at the 'political' however it might be culturally defined (1997: 15). Spencer recalls Geertz's influential article of 1963 on 'primordial sentiments and civil politics', which compared seven different 'new nations', including India. Set within the modernization paradigm of its time, the article now sounds almost weirdly dated in its discussion of the 'thrusting of a modern political consciousness upon the mass of a still largely unmodernized population' (1993: 269). Yet Geertz's article was a rare example of serious anthropological writing at that time on post-colonial nation-states, although it actually says very little about the civil and modern, as opposed to the primordial and traditional (Spencer 1997: 6–7). Moreover, across the world in the last two decades, religious nationalism in particular has forcibly shown us that 'primordial sentiments' (often more new than old) can actually flourish all too well within modern states. Geertz does recognize that 'primordial and civil sentiments are not ranged in direct and implicitly evolutionary opposition to one another' (1993: 308). In that respect, therefore, unlike much crude but influential modernization theory, Geertz also allowed for the possibility that an 'unmodernized' population in India (or elsewhere) might actually become thoroughly at home as well with electoral democracy and governmental bureaucracy—in short, with the modern nation-state.

And so it has turned out. Anthropologists are well-equipped to study the 'everyday state', and although we naturally hope and believe that none of the essays below reproduces the dullness of a dusty office file, our collective gaze shows how banal, mundane and routinized—how unexotic—so much of the state now is in contemporary India. The idea of the state and the myth of its sublime qualities are still extant, as we have seen, but the everyday structures and institutions of the nation-state, in most political and administrative contexts, are now very prosaically at the centre of modern India's imagination.

Notes

1. This title is taken from that of the paper by Philip Abrams, written in 1977 and published (posthumously) in 1988, which is referred to in the text.
2. It plainly follows from all this that the idea of a distinct 'civil society'—as a sphere of freely associating individual citizens —which is presupposed by the logic of the modern democratic state, is highly problematic in the Indian context (though it is scarcely simple anywhere) and certainly cannot be adequately analysed by dwelling, out of disenchantment with the state, on

the significance of non-governmental organizations or 'traditional' community groups. For a short but trenchant discussion, see Béteille (1999); he comments that in the debate on civil society in contemporary India, 'the arguments are so often either inconsistent or vacuous' (Ibid.: 2591).

3. An example of such research, partly based on ethnography, includes Hansen's on Hindutva in Maharashtra (1996; 1998; 1999), although a range of other authors could be listed. Also worth noting here owing to its direct focus on politics and the state is Burghart's research on Nepal, which was always situated in a wider South Asian context (1996: chs. 8, 9, 11).

4. Some of the work which does illuminate the quotidian practices of bureaucrats is now quite old: Dube's account (1958) of the activities of Village Level Workers in the 1950s, or, from within political science rather than anthropology, Heginbotham's (1975) and Mook's (1982) studies of local administration in Tamil Nadu, based on fieldwork carried out in the late 1960s and early 1970s. More recent ethnographic accounts of the quotidian practices of state functionaries include Breman on labour inspectors (1985), Jeffery, Jeffery and Lyon on local health workers (1989), and Wade on irrigation department officials (1982; 1985).

5. Harriss-White goes on this paper, and in more detail in her forthcoming book *Working India, India working* (based on the Smuts Lectures delivered in the University of Cambridge in November 1999), to develop the most coherent alternative to the political-economy approach to Indian state, exemplified by Bardhan (1984), which we have described as 'the prevailing consensus'. As against the notion of the 'dominant proprietary classes' set out by Bardhan, Harriss-White draws on Kalecki's idea of 'the intermediate regime' to argue that an intermediate class made up of traders and small businessmen, petty officials and the richer peasants (frequently connected by caste and kinship relations) is dominant. This approach shows how the neat structures of the 'dominant proprietary classes' model disappear when we view the state at the local level in terms of actual and multiplex social relationships.

References

Abrams, P. 1988. Some notes on the difficulty of studying the state. *Journal of Historical Sociology* 1, 1: 58–89.

Bailey, F. G. 1963. *Politics and social change: Orissa in 1959*. Berkeley: University of California Press.

Bardhan, P. 1984. *The political economy of development in India*. Oxford: Blackwell.

———. 1998. The state against society: the great divide in Indian social science discourse. *In* S. Bose and A. Jalal, eds, *Nationalism, democracy and development: state and politics in India*, pp. 184–95. Delhi: Oxford University Press.

Béteille, A. 1999. Citizenship, state and civil society. *Economic and Political Weekly* 34: 2588–91.

Bose, S., and A. Jalal. 1998. Nationalism, democracy and development. *In* Bose and Jalal, eds, *Nationalism, democracy and development: state and politics in India*, pp. 1–9. Delhi: Oxford University Press.

Brass, P. 1994 [1990]. *The politics of India since Independence.* Cambridge: Cambridge University Press

———. 1997. *Theft of an idol: text and context in the representation of collective violence.* Princeton: Princeton University Press

Breman, J. 1985. 'I am the government labour officer. ...': state protection for rural proletariat of south Gujarat. *Economic and Political Weekly* 20:1043–55.

Burghart, R. 1996. *The conditions of listening: essays on religion, history and politics in South Asia* (C. J. Fuller and J. Spencer, eds). Delhi: Oxford University Press.

Carter, A. 1974. *Elite politics in rural India: political stratification and alliances in western Maharashtra.* Cambridge: Cambridge University Press.

Chatterjee, P. 1986. *Nationalist thought and the colonial world: a derivative discourse?* London: Zed Books.

———. 1993. *The nation and its fragments: colonial and postcolonial histories.* Princeton: Princeton University Press.

———. 1997. Development planning and the Indian state. *In* Chatterjee, ed., *State and politics in India*, pp. 271–97. Delhi: Oxford University Press.

———. 1998. Community in the east. *Economic and Political Weekly* 33: 277–82.

Dirks, N. B. 1987. *The hollow crown: ethnohistory of an Indian kingdom.* Cambridge: Cambridge University Press.

Dube, S. C. 1958. *India's changing villages: human factors in community development.* London: Routledge and Kegan Paul.

Dumont, L. 1970. *Homo Hierarchicus: the caste system and its implications.* London: Weidenfeld and Nicholson.

Evans, P., D. Rueschemeyer, and T. Skocpol, eds. 1985. *Bringing the state back in.* Cambridge: Cambridge University Press.

Frankel, F. 1978. *India's political economy 1947–1978.* Princeton: Princeton University Press.

———, and M. S. A. Rao, eds. 1989. *Dominance and state power in India: decline of a social order,* vol. 1. Delhi: Oxford University Press.

———. 1990. *Dominance and state power in India: decline of a social order,* vol. 2. Delhi: Oxford University Press.

Geertz, C. 1993 [1963]. The integrative revolution: primordial sentiments and civil politics in the new states. *In* Geertz, *The interpretation of cultures*, pp. 255–310. London: Fontana.

Gupta, A. 1995. Blurred boundaries: the discourse of corruption, the culture of politics and the imagined state. *American Ethnologist* 22: 375–402.

Hansen, T. B. 1996. The vernacularisation of Hindutva: BJP and Shiv Sena in rural Maharashtra. *Contributions to Indian Sociology* 30: 177–214.

———. 1998. BJP and the politics of Hindutva in Maharashtra. *In* T. B. Hansen and C. Jaffrelot, eds, *The BJP and the compulsions of politics in India*, pp. 121–62. Delhi: Oxford University Press.

———. 1999. *The saffron wave: democracy and Hindu nationalism in modern India.* Princeton: Princeton University Press.

Hanson, A. H. 1966. *The process of planning: a study of India's five-year plans, 1950–1964.* London: Oxford University Press.

Harriss-White, B. n.d. The state and informal economic order in South Asia. Unpublished working paper, Queen Elizabeth House, University of Oxford.

Heginbotham, S. 1975. *Cultures in conflict: the four faces of Indian bureaucracy.* New York: Columbia University Press.

Inden, R. 1995. Embodying God: from imperial progress to national progress in India. *Economy and Society* 24: 245–78.

Jeffery, P., R. Jeffery, and A. Lyon. 1989. *Labour pains and labour power: women and childbearing in India.* London: Zed Books.

Kaviraj, S. 1984. On the crisis of political institutions in India. *Contributions to Indian Sociology* 18: 223–43.

———. 1991. On state, society and discourse in India. *In* J. Manor, ed., *Rethinking third world politics,* pp. 72–99. London: Longman.

———. 1997. The modern state in India. *In* M. Doornbos and S. Kaviraj, eds, *Dynamics of state formation: Europe and India compared,* pp. 225–50. New Delhi: Sage.

Khilnani, S. 1998. *The idea of India.* Harmondsworth: Penguin.

Kohli, A. 1990. *Democracy and discontent: India's growing crisis of governability.* Cambridge: Cambridge University Press.

Kothari, R., ed. 1970. *Caste in Indian politics.* New Delhi: Orient Longman.

Lerche, J. 1995. Is bonded labour a bound category? Reconceptualising agrarian conflict in India. *Journal of Peasant Studies* 22: 484–515.

Madan, T. N. 1997. *Modern myths, locked minds: secularism and fundamentalism in India.* Delhi: Oxford University Press.

Manor, J. 1993. *Power, poverty and poison: disaster and response in an Indian city.* New Delhi: Sage.

Mendelsohn, O. 1993. The transformation of authority in rural India. *Modern Asian Studies* 27: 805–42.

Miliband, R. 1969. *The state in capitalist society.* London: Weidenfeld and Nicolson.

Mitchell, T. 1991. The limits of the state: beyond statist approaches and their critics. *American Political Science Review* 85: 77–96.

———. 1999. Society, economy, and the state effect. *In* G. Steinmetz, ed., *State/culture: state-formation after the cultural turn,* pp. 76–97. Ithaca: Cornell University Press.

Mook, B. 1982. Value and action in Indian bureaucracy. Discussion paper 65, Institute of Development Studies, University of Sussex.

Nandy, A. 1989. The political culture of the Indian state. *Daedalus* 118: 1–26.

Parry, J. P. 2000. 'The crisis of corruption' and 'the idea of India': a worm's eye view. *In* I. Pardo, ed., *The morals of legitimacy,* pp. 27–55. Oxford: Berghahn.

Poulantzas, N. 1973. *Political power and social classes.* London: New Left Books.

Radcliffe-Brown, A. R. 1940. Preface. *In* M. Fortes and E. E. Evans-Pritchard, eds, *African political systems*. London: Oxford University Press.

Robinson, M. 1988. *Local politics: the law of the fishes—development through political change in Medak district, Andhra Pradesh (south India)*. Delhi: Oxford University Press.

Rudolph, S. H., and L. I. Rudolph. 1987. *In pursuit of Lakshmi*. Chicago: University of Chicago Press.

Saberwal, S. 1996. *The roots of crisis: interpreting contemporary Indian society*. New Delhi: Sage.

Skocpol, T. 1979. *States and social revolutions: a comparative analysis of France, Russia and China*. Cambridge: Cambridge University Press.

Spencer, J. 1997. Post-colonialism and the political imagination. *Journal of the Royal Anthropological Institute* 3: 1–19.

Srinivas, M. N. 1962. *Caste in modern India and other essays*. Bombay: Asia.

Steinmetz, G. 1999. Introduction: culture and the state. *In* Steinmetz, ed., *State/culture: state-formation after the cultural turn*, pp. 1–49. Ithaca: Cornell University Press.

Vanaik, A. 1990. *The painful transition: bourgeois democracy in India*. London: Verso.

Varma, P. K. 1999. *The great Indian middle class*. New Delhi: Penguin.

Vincent, J. 1990. *Anthropology and politics: visions, traditions and trends*. Tucson: University of Arizona Press.

Wade, R. 1982. The system of administrative and political corruption: canal irrigation in south India. *Journal of Development Studies* 18: 287–328.

———. 1985. The market for public office: why the Indian state is not better at development. *World Development* 13: 467–97.

———. 1990. *Governing the market: economic theory and the role of government in east Asian industrialization*. Princeton: Princeton University Press.

Weber, M. 1964. *The theory of economic and social organization*. New York: Free Press.

Governance and myths of state in Mumbai

Thomas Blom Hansen

> In all those tasks that need no particular and exceptional
> efforts, no special courage or endurance, we find no magic
> and no mythology. But a highly developed magic and
> connected with it a mythology always occurs if a pursuit
> is dangerous and its issues uncertain.
>
> (Ernst Cassirer, *The Myth of the State*, 1946, p. 350).

Shattered myths

A passage in *The moor's last sigh* by Salman Rushdie (1995: 123–6) captures
the gap between the dominant self-images of the nationalist elite and
the cultural practices of the popular worlds in Mumbai: every year during
the Ganpati celebrations, when the elephant-headed god Ganesh is
celebrated in huge public processions, the modernist painter Aurora
Zogoiby dances in her white dress on top of her house at Malabar Hill,
displaying her rebellious sophistication towards tradition, as well as her
contempt for what she regards as a primitive Hindu mass-festival
unfolding on the popular beach far below her. This constitutive split in
the life and imaginings of the city was once again highlighted by two
rounds of bloody riots between Hindus and Muslims in Mumbai in
December 1992 and January 1993, which left more than 1,000 persons
dead, many more wounded and more than 150,000 people displaced.

I am indebted to Véronique Bénéï, Chris Fuller, Jonathan Parry, Jonathan Spencer,
Finn Stepputat, Oskar Verkaaik, Akhil Gupta, Daniel Herwitz, Vivek Narayanan for
helpful comments and suggestions that enabled me to improve and sharpen my
argument.

The riots dealt a major blow to the image, favoured by the middle class, of Mumbai as the epitome of Indian modernity and the site of a pragmatic, enterprizing capitalist ethos. The ferocity, scale and political character of the riots made it clear that sectarian violence emanates not just from residues of irrational belief among the ordinary masses, as conventional wisdom has it, but also remains central to India's experience of modernity and capitalism. One of the central themes in Rushdie's novel is exactly that Mumbai's official face and the life of its affluent elite depend on extensive involvement in the city's murkiest sides: massive corruption, organized crime and communal politics. During the riots and their aftermath, these forces and dynamics—immensely powerful but denied—acquired an unprecedented visibility, which was deplored by prominent citizens, who bemoaned the demise of public order, tolerance and cosmopolitanism in Mumbai (e.g. Padgaonkar 1993). Scholars and activists saw the proliferation of crime and sectarian politics as an effect of the 'lumpenization' of the city as its industrial economy and its large working class have given way to real estate speculation and small service industries (e.g. Lele 1995).

My basic proposition in this essay is that these concerns were symptoms of a wider anxiety. Centrally at stake was the 'myth of the state', the imagination of the state as a distant but persistent guarantor of a certain social order and a measure of justice and protection from violence. The shattering of this myth appeared in different guises to different groups and communities. To the Muslims in Mumbai (approximately 17 per cent of the city's population), who bore the brunt of police brutality and the ethnic rage of militant Hindus in both rounds of violence, the riots marked the culmination of a long process of political marginalization and everyday harrassment by the city police and Hindu extremist political forces. For more than a decade, Muslims had been the targets of relentless stigmatization by militant Hindu nationalist organizations such as the Shiv Sena. Aided by the police, the mainstream press in Mumbai had consolidated older images of the city's Muslim areas as dens of drug-peddling, smuggling and violence, and peopled by clannish, fanatic and hostile Muslims, paying allegiance to dreaded 'mafia' dons like the Dubai-based gangster-king, Dawood Ibrahim.

The anti-Muslim bias of the city police force became more obvious than ever during the riots when police officers issued 'shoot to kill' orders for Muslim demonstrators, while generally milder forms of riot control were administered on Hindu crowds. During one week of riots, killings and arson in the city—organized and encouraged by the Shiv Sena—the police actively assisted Hindus, protected them from Muslim counter-attacks or simply turned a blind eye to the atrocities and plunder by Hindu militants.[1] The presence of leading Congress ministers in Mumbai during the riots, and their deployment of the newly-formed 'Rapid Action Force', did not curb the sustained attacks on Muslims.

These circumstances gave rise to a range of rumours and conspiracy theories. To most of my informants in the Muslim neighbourhoods in central Mumbai, older imaginings of the upper echelons of the state and the Congress party as sites of justice and protection gave way to a radical sense of isolation and betrayal. In March 1993, a group of people, mainly Muslims affiliated with gangster organizations in Mumbai, executed a series of bomb blasts killing hundreds of civilians on a single day, and wrecking bus terminals as well as the city's stock exchange. A few weeks later, consignments of arms and explosives were recovered at several places along the Maharashtrian coast. Allegations that the secret and independent Pakistani intelligence unit, ISI, was assisting local underworld networks in Mumbai were immediately raised by the police, as well as by Hindu nationalist and more moderate public figures.[2]

Regardless of the factual complexities surrounding the bomb blasts, it soon became a well-established popular truth that the blasts constituted a Muslim answer to militant Hindus, a message of 'don't mess with us', sent by the legendary Dawood Ibrahim – now elevated to the status of a stern godfather—on behalf of some sections of the Muslim community. A Muslim female teacher from Nagpada echoed what I found to be a widespread sentiment when she told me in 1993:

We all felt horrible during those four months [December 1992 to March 1993]; all over you would hear these derogatory remarks about Muslims, you felt the hostility all over, in the trains, in shops, in my school. I recall riding on a train when a group of Hindu women spotted me and started talking quietly. One said 'We Hindu women should also do something. Look at that Muslim woman there—one should throw her off the train ...'. All this stopped after the bomb blasts—not because they accepted us, but because they feared us.

Among substantial sections of the Hindu middle classes and the slum-dwellers who supported militant Hindu nationalism, the shattering of the myth of the state appeared in an altogether different form. Here it was a triumphant sense of 'teaching the Muslims a lesson', of overruling and defying the state, of celebrating an ethnic-majoritarian justice in the face of what Hindu nationalist leaders had decried as the state's 'pampering' and protection of minorities. During these heated months in Mumbai, it was as if the earlier practice of more restrained and guarded modes of naming and talking about Muslims had disappeared, and given way to the most radical xenophobic fears and fantasies, which circulated widely from rickshaw drivers to respectable family doctors.

The supreme dictatorial leader of the Shiv Sena, Bal Thackeray, has made a name for himself through colourful and provocative rhetoric, his radical abuse of Muslims and political opponents, his outspoken contempt for the judiciary and his populist attacks on everything associated with *sarkar* (the state/government) (see Hansen 1996). Since the riots, the Shiv Sena has consolidated its position year by year. In the 1995 elections which brought the Shiv Sena to power in the state of Maharashtra, the party completely swept the polls in the metropolis. In spite of massive evidence of increasing corruption at the highest level, open contempt for legal processes and democratic procedures, and Thackeray's celebration of his own 'remote control' of the government, the party's popularity was not affected for several years, so that it once again swept the polls at the municipal elections in 1997 in Mumbai and several other cities in the state (Hansen 1998). Did this signify a mandate to ethnicize the state with a demise of older notions of the secular state as a neutral adjudicator of conflicts? Before answering these questions, let me briefly consider how we can think of 'the state'.

Governance and the imagined state

In popular political imaginaries and in the eyes of political strategists, the state is often reduced to a pliable apparatus in the hands of political forces. At the same time, it is also clear to most people that the state is something more permanent, more omnipresent and more central to their lives, something larger and more durable than the prevailing regime in power at any one time. The state is a name given to various practices and institutions of government, not only as an analytical concept but also as a locus of authority invoked and reproduced by an endless range of interventions—from validating documents and checking motor vehicles, to prohibiting substances or encouraging forms of behaviour that promote public health, and so on. The state, in other words, is an organizing concept through which people in Mumbai, as well as in other modern societies, imagine the cohesion of their own society, its order, its sovereignty—but also its hidden secrets, sources of violence and evil.

In the history of the west, the idea of the state emerged as a site of sovereignty, a symbolic centre of political will and power above partial interests. According to this tradition, a state needs to govern but must also reproduce something more, an imaginary dimension that separates its own actions from those of any other agency. The generation of legitimacy takes more than hegemonic imposition of categories and epistemic regimes. It requires the enactment of the state as a symbolic centre of society, an arbiter of conflicts and the site of authorization, which can delegate power as well as rightfully 'write society' through law, the constitution, rules and certificates.

Ernst Kantorowicz (1957) has shown with great subtlety how a legal-political theory of the 'King's two bodies' developed in medieval Britain. The political authority was constructed as a dual structure: the notion of a sublime, infallible and eternal body of the King (the Law), and the profane, human and fallible body of the king (the giver of laws). Kantorowicz quotes Blackstone writing on the sublime dimension of royal authority: 'the king "is not only incapable of *doing* wrong, but even of *thinking* wrong: he can never mean to do an improper thing: in him is no folly or weakness"' (qu. in Kantorowicz 1957: 4). As Lefort points out, the efficiency of this construction flows precisely from the separation and unity of these two bodies, from the combination of the profane and the sublime in the eyes of the subjects:

It is the image of the natural body, the image of a God made flesh, the image of his marriage, his paternity, his liaisons, his festivals, his amusements and his feasts, but also the images of his weaknesses or even his cruelties, in short, all the images of his humanity, that people their imaginary, that assure them that the people and the king are conjoined (Lefort 1988: 245).

This union of the two bodies was later reconfigured as the nation, the people or the leader, which took the place of the sublime-abstract body and made governance of the empirical and profane people possible in the name of that higher principle (Ibid.: 254). Lefort argues that with the advent of democracy this mythical and 'original' source of power becomes radically empty as it can only be temporarily occupied by representatives of the people or nation (Ibid.: 17). These representatives represent the people by occupying exactly that which is more permanent and enduring: the central institutions of the state.[3]

I suggest that the imagination of the state is marked by a deep and constitutive split between its 'sublime' and 'profane' dimensions. The latter encompass the incoherence, brutality, partiality and banality of the technical sides of governance, and the rough and tumble of negotiation, compromise and naked self-interest displayed in local politics. These features stand opposed to 'sublime' qualities imputed to a more distant state: that is, to the opaque secrets and knowledge of the state's higher echelons, to its hidden resources, designs and immense power, and to the higher forms of rationality or even justice believed to prevail there.

One of the effects of this split, as I will indicate below, is that the sublime qualities imputed to the state make it possible to transform otherwise dispersed, and maybe utterly senseless, procedures of bureaucracy, into meaningful signs of something larger, as minor bits in a more complex design or plan.

We need to recognize and understand this crucial duality in the cultural construction of the state if we are to fully understand why the state's political forces and agencies felt the need to launch various initiatives in Mumbai in order to create mechanisms for reconciliation, or at least cohabitation, between Muslims and Hindus after the riots, and how Muslims especially have reacted to these initiatives. I will argue that these initiatives have been launched to reassert the state's authority partly by reorganizing techniques of governance, but also by reconfiguring its legitimacy with the aim of retrieving a myth of the state without which no democratic state can govern—even a state headed by a government which nurtures a most anti-democratic form of majoritarianism, as is the case with the Shiv Sena.

Before proceeding to the complexities of contemporary Mumbai, let me briefly consider whether such a line of reasoning derived from medieval western political thought can be made relevant to contemporary India. Are there any 'sublime' dimensions of the state and political authority in modern India at all? Should one instead adopt a longue durée perspective and inquire into how older registers of kingship and the Brahman-Kshatriya relations are played out today? There is no doubt that notions of honour, patronage and the appropriate behaviour of the landowning aristocracy and dominant castes in various parts of India have shaped the construction of politics there in profound ways. These cultural repertoires seem, however, insufficient to capture the meanings evoked by the term *sarkar* in contemporary India.

In spite of deeply segmented and competing notions of power, leadership and legitimacy in post-colonial India, its public culture has produced a large reservoir of shared symbols, languages and references—from war heroes, politicians and film heroes to sports teams, cultural events, brand names and styles of consumption shared across the length and breadth of India, sometimes across caste and class as well. This national, or at least nation-wide, culture has been systematically promoted by the state whose crucial role in producing a national imaginary can hardly be overestimated, as Khilnani (1997: 19) has pointed out. Admittedly, the political field abounds with religious imagery, and politicians invoke pre-colonial aristocratic splendour in dress and speech, and refer to the wisdom of religious texts, when they attempt to represent the authority of the nation-state. However, education, command of English and competence in the world of science and administration constitute equally, if not more, powerful registers of authority and sublime qualities. The bureaucrat, the planner and the scientist, the member of the Indian Administrative Service—the heavily mythologized 'steel-frame' of the state—occupy crucial positions in contemporary political imaginaries, not least for the large middle class. The bureaucrat was for decades the hero of modern India and, until the 1970s, was depicted in Hindi films as a man of character and insight.

Until quite recently, this 'modern nationalist aristocracy' of high-ranking bureaucrats, scientists and politicians was referred to with awe and respect. The mark of these ideal national citizens manning the bureaucracy was exactly their combination of moral integrity, commitment to the notion of a larger abstract nation and deep technical insights. The authority of education, especially English-medium education, also remains crucial among ordinary people, for whom it often generates more respect than wealth. According to my own experience, many ordinary people in India attribute considerable authority and sublime qualities to institutions such as courts, as well as to judges or senior bureaucrats. This testifies to how effectively the modern nationalist elite in India throughout this century has made education, science, the rule of law and the role of the public sector the core signifiers of the modern nation. Complementing older registers of public conduct, the nationalist register has also evolved a complex web of public languages and political imaginaries that shape discourses on the state and boost rumours and stories about rule-breaking, corruption and abuse of governmental authority. It is the sense of violation of the idealized sublime qualities imputed to the state that makes such stories worth telling at all. It may well be that ordinary Indians are less in awe of the state than a few decades ago, but it is still regarded as indispensable for public order and for recognizing communities, leaders or claims as legitimate. Bureaucrats, judges and officers are called upon every day to authenticate, inaugurate and authorize—in brief, to act as transient incarnations of authority and symbols of the state. These manifestations of the state's authority may well be a structural effect of governance, as Mitchell (1999: 9) contends, but they are also important public performances which need to be studied in their own right.

I will illustrate the split representation of the Indian state as both sublime and profane by, firstly, analysing judicial initiatives, especially the work of the Srikrishna Commission inquiring into the riots and bomb blasts of December 1992–January 1993, and March 1993 respectively, and the proceedings of the special Terrorist and Disruptive Activities

(TADA) court investigating only the bomb blasts in March 1993. Secondly, I will discuss how the government maintains public order in central Mumbai and how the so-called 'mohalla committees' were set up by the police and non-governmental organizations (NGOs) in these neighbourhoods in 1994. I look at the trajectory of these initiatives and how they impacted on local perceptions of state and authority in the context of the strained everyday encounters between police and Muslims in the city.

The Srikrishna Commission: catharsis and the politicization of truth

A few weeks after the riots in January 1993, the Government of Maharashtra decided to set up an inquiry commission headed by the High Court judge, Justice Srikrishna. The massive evidence of open involvement by the Shiv Sena and other parties in organizing the violence, and of police mistreatment of Muslims, made it clear that in order to re-establish its authority in the eyes of the minorities and human rights organizations, the government had to demonstrate its commitment to justice. The commission began its work in June 1993, with a mandate to establish 'the circumstances, events and immediate causes of the incidents which occurred in the Bombay Police Commissionerate area in December 1992 on or after the 6th December 1992, and again in January 1993, on or after the 6th January 1993.' The commission was further mandated to identify 'individuals, or groups of individuals or any other organisation' responsible for the riots, as well as to assess the effectiveness of the Bombay Police in handling the situation (Srikrishna 1998: 1).[4]

The commission was supposed to work like a public hearing and initially called 'all persons having knowledge about facts touching upon the Terms of Reference to come forward and file affidavits before the commission' (Ibid.: 2); it also called upon the police and the government to submit their versions of the events in the city. Altogether, 2,126 affidavits were filed, two from the government, 549 by the police and 1,575 by various individuals and organizations. The political mandate made it clear that it was the prerogative of the state government of Maharashtra to decide whether, when, and in what form, the Srikrishna report (submitted in March 1998) would eventually be made public. The cabinet of the Shiv Sena-Bharatiya Janata Party (BJP) government delayed the report's release for five months and it appeared in August 1998, five and a half years after the riots took place. It was left to the state government to decide whether the massive evidence gathered by the commission would be made available to the Advocate-General to allow the state to institute criminal prosecutions.

Public inquiries into serious conflagrations, major policy failures or disasters, such as famines or revolts, have been carried out in India since the 1870s. The inquests of the colonial state were normally carried out by civil servants interviewing police officers, victims, witnesses, and others in order to establish the factual circumstances and to apportion responsibility. In the independent post-colonial state, these techniques of governmental self-diagnosis continued but acquired new moral and political dimensions, because they became intensely preoccupied with rooting out harmful practices and with reforming society through reform of the state (Visvanathan 1998a: 15). When the Shah Commission in 1977 probed into the excesses of the 'emergency' imposed by Indira Gandhi, a new and more openly 'cathartic' mode of enquiry was created. The Shah Commission was more like a hearing, with submissions from victims of excessive use of state power, as well as from responsible bureaucrats and politicians, and it sought to make its style and proceedings as close as possible to those of a courtroom.

The Srikrishna Commission emerged more like a public tribunal; it was decided to make the proceedings public, and to call upon interested organizations and parties to be represented through legal counsel along with the commission's own official advocate. Between 1993 and 1997, a number of organizations and parties were represented before the commission: the Shiv Sena and the BJP (which were ruling the state during most of the tenure of the commission), the All-India Milli Council (a coordination group for a number of Muslim organizations), the Jamiyat-E-Ulema (Council of Islamic Scholars), the Communist Party of India (until 1995) and a variety of human rights associations, such as the Lawyers' Collective and the Committee for the Protection of Human Rights. The commission could call upon any public servant and ask him or her to testify under oath before it, whereas ordinary citizens only appeared according to their own wish. The same voluntary principle applied to elected officials, but given the public nature of the hearings there was pressure on public figures to appear in person and let themselves be cross-examined. The hearings began as systematic inquiries into the events unfolding during the critical period in the twenty-six affected police districts in the city. Based on independent investigation / and affidavits from citizens and police officers, the commission and legal counsel summoned and cross-examined witnesses and officials. After each cross-examination, Justice Srikrishna drew his conclusions about causes and effects, and his brief summaries and the mass of written material was summarized in the final report.

The material the commission dealt with was intensely political, just as the form and public nature of the hearings—closely covered by the press—often made them rhetorical platforms for the counsel of different parties. In so far as it was the political parties that were represented, the rhetorical battles at the hearings very often came back to the question of whether one or another 'community', party or organization was responsible for a certain act, and how that act could be justified as retaliation for previous atrocities by 'the other community', and so on.[5]

Reconstructing 'truth' after the fact

Before looking at the intricate relationship between the state government, the commission and the ruling parties, let me offer a few glimpses into how various materials were presented before the commission.[6]

When the decision to set up a commission of inquiry was taken by the state government in February 1993, Mumbai's Commissioner of Police during the riots, Shreekant Bapat, was transferred and A.S. Samra, a highly respected officer was brought in to reform the city's police force. Samra had been very successful in preventing the massive riots in Mumbai from spreading to Thane north of the city, an industrial district that had seen the worst rioting in the country in the 1980s, and as a Sikh he was widely assumed to be neutral in the Hindu-Muslim conflict. Samra's arrival and the wording of the commission's mandate made it clear to many police officers that the state government was ready to put most of the responsibility on the police force. Hundreds of officers who had been in command at police stations and in the field became busy writing lengthy affidavits explaining their actions and perceptions during the riots. More than five hundred of those were submitted to the commission.

The two handfuls of affidavits I managed to get access to all ran along similar lines. They began with a long, often rosy account of the career of the said officer and his specific qualities, often pointing to his long experience in handling 'mobs' or crowds. One officer referred to his long experience at police stations in Mumbai's mill district where on many occasions he had dealt with demonstrators and 'violent mobs'. Another used almost ten pages listing all the demanding postings he had been in—ranging from Dharavi, the biggest slum in Asia, to Agripada, one of the most 'notorious trouble spots in Bombay'—and he provided a virtual catalogue of situations he had dealt with: mass meetings, Hindu-Muslim violence after cricket matches between India and Pakistan, religious processions turning into 'rampaging mobs', and so on and so forth.

Armed with these credentials the officers then turned to describe the areas they were posted in during the riots. One officer described the Muslim-dominated Dongri area in central Mumbai as a dangerous and unpredictable place:

This locality has a long history of communal riots [that have] been occurring here at frequent intervals since 1893. ... Though by and large the residents are peace loving citizens, incidents of anti-national character committed by a few mischief mongers tend to cause sudden escalation of tension. The area has earned such a notorious reputation that the police machinery has to be alert round the year. However, it is not always possible to predict how and to what extent a situation can deteriorate.

The officers' accounts then gave vivid and detailed descriptions of the events and their actions, the orders issued, the number of rounds fired, etc., during both series of riots in their respective areas. From these accounts what emerges is a picture of chaos, drama and confusion; of a city exploding in what the officers describe as random and unintelligible violence, looting and arson. Violence, said officers, often broke out behind the police even as they dealt with one situation, and while fresh reports of police vehicles being stoned and attacked by rioters in new areas were pouring in. These were stories of a force not properly prepared for such situations, of confusion and of a fear of mobs which—in accounts from the Muslim parts of the city—seemed intensely hostile to the police.

In cross-examination, most officers defended their actions and asserted the need for public order. One maintained that the so-called *ghanta naad* promoted by the Shiv Sena, when Hindus rang the temple bells on 6 December 1992 to celebrate the demolition of the mosque in Ayodhya, 'was treated as religious activity exempted under the ban order of the Bombay Police Act'. A senior inspector from the Nagpada Police Station admitted that although he was aware that Shiv Sainiks (Shiv Sena activists) made highly provocative speeches in connection with the bell-ringing, 'it did not then occur to me to take any action'. An inspector was asked by counsel for the Milli Council to justify calling Muslims 'aggressors'. He replied: 'Muslims were aggressors because they came out in large numbers (and) they did resort to violence. The police had to take effective action and the Muslims who were on the streets had to bear the brunt of the police action'. According to this officer, the question of why the events took place, who was shot, and so on, was not relevant to policing. Their job was to restore public order and those who got in the way could get shot.

The issue of whether the police used excessive force against Muslim rioters in particular was discussed at length in the commission proceedings. A police officer defended the immediate use of 'extreme force', which is to shoot directly at rioters in order to kill. He said: 'I do not think that it is always necessary to use graded force when dealing with a situation of violence. If extreme force is resorted to, at the very first stage, in order to put down the riots firmly, I would consider it justified'. Affidavits from ordinary constables tell a less orderly story, full of horror of advancing mobs: 'the mob did not respond to our teargas ... on the contrary, they indulged in heavy stone throwing ... then someone fired a gun at us'. An elderly constable related how he was attacked with a sword and how his colleagues withdrew into the police post: 'I was then left alone in the hands of the mob, I was terribly frightened ... someone attacked my face and neck with a sword'.

Most of the accounts by constables seem to reflect both fear and incomprehension, as if rioters were a sort of natural calamity, displaying an aggression that the policemen did not seem to connect to their own status as police. Instead, many of them depicted themselves as the victims of the riots. Judging from my conversations with policemen, this was not an attempt to exonerate themselves or their actions. None of the policemen I talked to denied that they had shot people dead or wounded them. To them it was self-defence, the only way to respond to the mobs they dreaded so much. The sense of being unjustly targeted while doing your job, of being hated by the local people, of detesting the same local people, and being stabbed in the back by political leaders, was a common experience. In some ways it appeared to me to be the strongest bonding among them, a sort of negative *esprit de corps*.[7]

The bulk of the evidence presented to the commission was, however, affidavits submitted by victims and bereaved families, mostly Muslim, as well as social workers, local organizations, journalists and many others who did not share the police's perspective. There were harrowing accounts of the brutality and rage of mobs or groups of men attacking Muslims in streets and homes, attacks often led and organized by local Shiv Sainiks, and there were frightening accounts of the anti-Muslim bias of the police in their 'clean-up' operations. A young man who worked in a Muslim-owned bakery gave this account to the commission:

Commandos in light uniforms and bulletproof vests entered the building. I peeped out from my hiding and saw Samshad standing, two commandos pointing their guns at him. He folded his hands and sat down near the commandos and pleaded that he was a Bhaiya (from U.P.). One of the commandos kept saying that Sanshad was a Pakistani, the other said that he was Kashmiri. ... I concealed myself again, then I heard firing and it became quiet. I saw Samshad writhing in pain, blood flowing out. He said his prayers for a minute or two, and then he was quiet.

It was, however, testimonies from leading police officers which elicited most interest from journalists and others interested in the proceedings.[8] V. Deshmukh, former leader of the Special Branch (SB) in Mumbai, was the first high-ranking police officer to appear before the commission. Deshmukh, a well-spoken man with intellectual inclinations, appeared very humble that day in mid-February 1997 as he stood in his uniform in the dock in a large spacious room in the Bombay High Court, a fine example of colonial architecture on the Maidan in Mumbai. Deshmukh was more frank in admitting the SB's failures than anyone had anticipated. In his deposition, Deshmukh explained the lack of intelligence work by the fact that he, as well as many others, 'was led to believe that the government would protect the mosque (in Ayodhya)'. He said that he was well aware of the Shiv Sena's capacity for violence, that the party 'had incited hatred against the minority community', and that '*maha artis* were started by the Shiv Sena in late December 1992 with the purpose of forcing the minority community to give up their *namaz* on the streets'.[9] He also stated that the SB knew all the key personnel in communal organizations in the city, but chose to do nothing because he and other police officers were reassured that nothing would happen in Ayodhya.

In his cross-examination of Deshmukh, the Shiv Sena's counsel, Balakrishna Joshi (a Shiv Sena MLA), followed a course he had pursued throughout the hearings. Instead of challenging the evidence of Shiv Sena involvement (which would have been a futile exercise), Joshi focused almost exclusively on alleged aggression and attacks on the police and Hindus by Muslims. During the riots, rumours were rife that Muslims collected arms in mosques and that their loudspeakers were used to incite attacks on Hindus. But Deshmukh stated that the SB did not recover any weapons from mosques. Questioned by Srikrishna about why the SB had failed to monitor the activities of the Shiv Sena more closely, Deshmukh answered: 'The SB received reports on December 10 that masjids maybe were used to instigate violence, but issued no instructions in this regard ... nor did it act against two Muslims who gave provocative speeches in November 1992'. Deshmukh's reaction revealed that he subscribed to the widespread notion of communal violence as an enactment of retributive justice, where killings on each side cancel each other out and make the two sides even. Similarly, the grave failure of the SB to monitor the Shiv Sena can be counterbalanced by its equally culpable leniency towards Muslim communal organizations. One inaction makes another inaction acceptable.

The perception that Muslim anger or 'aggression' justified police brutality and later Hindu 'retaliation' also informed the testimony from Shreekant Bapat, the former Commissioner of Police in Mumbai. Bapat was widely believed to be sympathetic to the Shiv Sena and BJP and he had submitted a 175-page affidavit. For over a week, he was cross-examined by five counsel, including Mr Hudlikar, who represented the police force. According to the clerks outside the courtroom, Hudlikar only appeared when high-ranking officers were giving testimony. Hudlikar was generous in his questioning and gave Bapat ample time to expand on what he had stated in writing. Bapat was particularly adamant in rejecting the charge of anti-Muslim bias: 'According to me the larger number of minority community casualties during December 1992 can be explained on the basis of the much greater aggression of the minority community mobs'. Shortly after Mr Muchalla, the soft-spoken counsel for the Milli Council probed further into this, Bapat said angrily: 'It is not true that action against the minority community in December 1992 was wholly unjustified'. Muchalla then confronted Bapat with the police's own statistics, which showed that in January 1993, when Hindus led by Shiv Sainiks were also the undisputed aggressors, most of the victims of police firings were Muslims. Bapat replied: 'I cannot comment on that'. Then the commission's own counsel took over and when he asked why his affidavit never mentioned even once the role played in the riots by the Shiv Sena, by then well-established, Bapat replied: 'If there is reference to Shiv Sena it should be there. If there is no reference, there is none'. He continued: 'The police is concerned with offence, not with political affiliation'.

At this point, Justice Srikrishna lost patience, and asked Bapat why the issue of organizational involvement in the riots was omitted. Visibly disturbed, Bapat assured him that the police before the riots 'had taken action against organizations known to be violent'.

Srikrishna	:	If this was done, why is there no reference to organizations in your affidavit?
Bapat	:	We had no material at hand at this point in time, indicating that any organization was involved in the riots.
Srikrishna	:	Were you not aware that Shiv Sena leaders claimed that their volunteers had demolished the Babri Masjid? [This news item was splashed across front pages of newspapers in most of the country a few days after the demolition.]
Bapat	:	No, I was not aware of such statements being made.

Here the judge sighed, leaned back and said 'Thank you, sir'.

The politics of balancing guilt

The interpretation of communal riots in terms of apportioning and 'balancing' collective guilt and responsibility among faceless and abstract communities, which emerged from the commission hearings, clearly reflected a dominant and widespread politico-moral discourse. But it did not produce material suitable for prosecuting individuals for specific crimes committed. As the Commissioner of Police, A.S. Samra, stated emphatically a few days before he was appointed:

Our penal code and our idea of justice revolves around the idea that individuals commit crime and are punished, whereas political parties as a whole do politics. There might be individuals within these parties who commit crimes, even leaders, but they must be punished as individuals ... what can we do to an organization? Ban it? That is difficult to do more permanently in a democracy.[10]

When appearing before the commission in April 1997, Samra reiterated this point of view, and declined to name particular organizations responsible for violence. When Justice Srikrishna pointed out that a range of organizations, such as the Shiv Sena, Vishwa Hindu Parishad and various Muslim organizations, were listed in the government of Maharashtra's 'Guidelines to handle communal riots' issued in 1986, Samra said: 'It is true that they were active in social activities, but it did not come to my notice that they as organizations indulged in illegal acts. Some of their members have done so' (*Mid-Day*, 12 April 1997). Like other high-ranking officers, Samra appeared to be mainly concerned with protecting the police force. In his deposition, Samra depicted the police as the protectors of society by conveniently blaming the riots on Dawood Ibrahim and other criminal networks and 'landgrabbers'. These criminals felt threatened after the crackdown on illegal constructions by the Municipality and the police force in the preceding year and, Samra stated, 'they hit back by exploiting the feelings of the people after the demolition of the Babri Masjid' (*Mid-Day*, 16 April 1997).

Yet the public nature of the Srikrishna Commission's proceedings turned it into a running tribunal that inadvertently exposed the complex links among political parties, the state and the legal system. This became particularly evident when the main perpetrator of violence, the Shiv Sena, assumed office in the state government in 1995. The principal area of contention between the government and the commission concerned the release of documents and files related to the inquiry. The commission had to seek permission from the Advocate-General for the release or declassification of documents. In some cases, this was refused on the basis of 'interest of the state' or other compelling reasons, but generally (according to the Public Inquiry Act) the state could not in principle claim privilege and refuse to hand over the required documents. After the Hindu nationalist coalition government came to power in Maharashtra in March 1995, twelve of more than twenty pending cases against Thackeray for incitement to violence were withdrawn or 'classified', by being made into security questions which could not be the object of public prosecution or scrutiny by the commission. After a protracted legal tussle, the state government agreed to hand over the files of four of these cases to Srikrishna.[11] The commission could now show that no government agency had dared to take action for years and that Shiv Sena leaders had almost openly tried to threaten previous Congress governments into withdrawing the cases. Police Commissioner Tyagi stated that if the government decided to withdraw the cases 'in the interest of communal peace and social justice' it would be understandable and the police force would have no objections (*Times of India*, 4 April 1997). It should be added that Tyagi, after his retirement from the police force in 1997, was nominated as a Shiv Sena candidate in the 1998 general elections but failed to win a seat.

When the Shiv Sena and BJP came to power in Maharashtra in 1995, the new government began a process of obstructing the course of the investigation. Papers and documents were not released or were delayed. As mounting evidence pointed to the Shiv Sena's crucial role in both rounds of violence, as well as to the many links between the party and the police force, it was decided on 23 January 1996 to dissolve the Srikrishna Commission. While the state in a strict sense had the legitimate power to dissolve the commission, and the Shiv Sena had sworn to do so during the election campaign in 1995, there were very few precedents for dissolution, none of which involved such blatant and transparent *mala fides* as in this case.

It was nonetheless clear that the issue of legitimate authority was at stake. Could the state actually sustain a credible myth of impartiality when, in such an unmitigated manner, it was exercising a clear ethnic-majoritarian form of justice? In the ensuing debate, activists, intellectuals and political figures argued that the commission should be reinstated to consolidate communal peace and harmony, whereas questions of justice and prosecution of the perpetrators of violence played a very minor role. After pressure from the short-lived BJP government in Delhi in May 1996, it was decided to restore the commission but with an expanded mandate. It was now decided that the commission should include the bomb blasts in March 1993 'to give a clearer and more comprehensive picture of the patterns of violence and civil disturbances in the city', as argued by the Advocate-General (*Indian Express*, 29 May 1996).[12] Including the bomb blasts was a rather transparent attempt to deflect the course of the investigation, but it nonetheless enjoyed considerable support in the public debates following the move. This reflected the widespread currency gained by the dominant, and official, interpretation of the riots as irrational excesses spontaneously committed equally by faceless Hindu and Muslim communities (but not organizations or individuals) in extraordinary situations. The government's decision actually authorized the formula of 'balanced and equally apportioned guilt': that every murder by Hindus could be ethically neutralized by demonstrating a corresponding atrocity committed by Muslims. The logic of 'retributive justice', which the Shiv Sena's counsel and the Shiv Sena-led government had been at pains to establish in order to exonerate itself, was slowly imposing itself on the commission's work.

There was a glaring contrast between the slow, contested and in many ways academic character of the work of the Srikrishna Commission, and the simultaneous prosecution of those accused of responsibility for the bomb blasts in March 1993. In the weeks following the bomb blasts, more than 200 people, mainly Muslims, were rounded up and detained under the stringent Terrorist and Disruptive Activities Act (TADA), an anti-terrorist law passed in the 1980s and designed to combat Sikh militants in Punjab. As many as 189 persons were accused of complicity in the conspiracy. Most of these detainees were subjected to the most humiliating and brutal forms of interrogation, and only few of them were granted bail. Even those who were accused of playing minor roles in connection with the arms consignments landed on the coast of Maharashtra in February 1993 were kept imprisoned for more than two years, before they were released because of lack of evidence. A brand-new, high-security TADA court was erected in Mumbai, and the police displayed unusual diligence in producing and gathering a massive amount of evidence in the cases. Before the Central Bureau of Investigation in Delhi took over the case, the Mumbai Police had charged all the accused with one of the most serious offences in the Indian Penal Code, 'the waging of war against the state'. These charges were withdrawn only after a much delayed intervention by the Attorney-General (Visvanathan 1998b: 127–8). Most of the evidence gathered by the Mumbai Police to indict this large number of innocent people on such flimsy grounds was either irrelevant or of low quality. By contrast, corrupt officials in police and customs departments, who had made the entire import of advanced explosives into Mumbai possible, had not even been questioned.[13]

The proceedings of the TADA court went on at a brisk pace and they were closed to the public because of the allegedly sensitive character of the evidence presented there.[14] Individuals were targeted for prosecution and the Shiv Sena government had on several occasions stated explicitly that it wanted to speed up the process against what it called 'Muslim gangsters' responsible for the blasts. Some of the accused were sentenced to ten or twenty years of imprisonment. A number of the key accused, connected in one way or another with Dawood Ibrahim, are still on the run. Although the case was not fully concluded at the time of writing, it appears unlikely—given the strong political pressure on the TADA court—that those sentenced could expect a new trial or that the government would be willing to concede that many people have been convicted on questionable grounds.

Diagnostics, prescriptions and state spectacles: the report of the Srikrishna Commission

The status and authority of a report of a commission of inquiry are always precarious. Such a report is not just an expert's opinion or a piece of research commissioned by the government. Whether the government agrees with the conclusions or not, the report is inevitably an authoritative statement on the matter under scrutiny. However, the government is not compelled by law to implement or even accept the commission's findings and recommendations. The complicated and contested trajectory of the Srikrishna Commission—more clearly than for any other commission I know about in India—had sometimes turned this inquiry into a spectacular clash of radically different notions of the state. On one side was the decent High Court judge, supported by human rights activists and large sections of the press, defending the idea of the state as impartial, above society, and committed to a universal form of justice. On the other side were the administrative machinery, the police employing its own armoury of techniques to delay, obstruct or influence the inquiry to protect its own 'secrets' and cover up its failings, and the political forces governing the state, committed to a majoritarian notion of 'retributive justice', and bending and threatening the administration to serve its ends. Although public in its form, this debate on state power remained internal to the state, both in terms of its mandate, resources and method, and of its authoritativeness. It was not a citizens' tribunal or an independent investigation.[15]

I would argue that both the Srikrishna Commission and the TADA court should be seen as state spectacles, public displays of the state as a producer of impartial and universal justice. At the same time, the very simultaneity of the two proceedings—one indicting Hindus and the police, the other 'Muslim goondas'—was also a spectacle representing the discourse of 'retributive justice'. Both proceedings were marked by the crucial duality inherent in the representation of the state. The Srikrishna Commission revealed numerous examples of the profane sides of state power: the deplorable quality of policing and police intelligence, the partial, biased and brutal conduct of the police force, and a series of blatant attempts on the part of the government to obstruct the proceedings and to prevent powerful political figures such as Bal Thackeray from being prosecuted. At the same time, the very existence of the commission, the tenacity and integrity of Justice Srikrishna, and the public exposure of misconduct, corruption and liaisons between politicians and the police force, have also provided a site for a certain process of public catharsis.

In this capacity, to Muslims as well as to concerned citizens, the commission has become a symbol of the resilience of a higher and more benevolent form of justice, and thus a sign of the permanence of the sublime dimension of the state. In a sense, this duality was also represented in the very choreography of the proceedings: before the bench were a string of counsel seeking to extract their particular, interested and intensely politicized claims from the stream of witnesses passing through, while the judge, positioned three feet above them, concluded each cross-examination with a summing-up supposed to extract the reasonable and the factually plausible—the negotiated truth—from the maze of interpretations before him.

The commission's final report adopts a medical language; like a doctor, Justice Srikrishna diagnoses and prescribes a possible cure for what he terms the 'communal malady': 'Communal riots, the bane of this country, are like incurable epileptic seizures, whose symptoms, though dormant over a period of time, manifest themselves again and again. Measures of various kinds suggested from time to time dealt with symptoms and acted as palliatives without effecting a permanent cure of the malaise.' The judge argues further that until there is a complete change in social outlook and the level of education, 'communal riots must be treated, perhaps, as an incurable disease whose prognosis calls for suitable measures to contain its evil effects' (Srikrishna 1998: 4). In keeping with this diagnosis, the judge is brief in his examination of the causes behind the riots, admitting that they grow out of complex dynamics of demography, class and the political discourse of organizations. Mumbai had an unfortunate combination of an increasingly impoverished and isolated Muslim community and a set of very aggressive Hindu organizations (Ibid.: 25–9). Srikrishna is emphatic in his statement that no 'known Muslim individuals or organizations were responsible for the riots', and equally emphatic in pointing to the responsibility of Shiv Sena, not as an organization *per se*, but because 'the attitudes of Shiv Sena leaders (as reflected in) its doctrine of "retaliation", were responsible for the vigilantism of Shiv Sainiks' (Ibid.: 30).

Srikrishna regards communal riots as incurable, and he notes in a more poetic vein that because 'the beast in man keeps straining at the leash to jump out' (Ibid.: 63), effective measures are of paramount importance. The most interesting part of the report is the judge's diagnosis of the structure and shortcomings of the police force in Mumbai, and the string of recommendations he makes to remedy these (Ibid.: 31–62). Srikrishna paints a gloomy picture of a complacent, biased, disorganized force where even everyday routines like filing of cases, physical training and discipline are incoherent if not absent. Returning to the diagnostic mode he sums up: 'Despite knowledge of the fact that the force had been infected by communal virus, no effective curative steps were taken over a large period of time as a result of which, communal violence became chronic and its virulent symptoms showed up during the two riot periods' (Ibid.: 35). The entire report maintains this measured distance from the interested parties and it gives critical and considered summaries of the events unfolding around each police station. The judge examines the depositions by leading police officers and political leaders, former chief ministers and the former Minister of Defence, Sharad Pawar. Reading through these pages one gets an ever clearer picture of the theory of the state to which Srikrishna subscribes. The tone is not legalistic but moral. He is highly critical of non-adherence to rules and regulations in the police force, but even more critical of the ostensible lack of commitment and moral outlook that he detects in leading police officers and many political figures. Srikrishna's view is clearly that a sense of duty towards the nation and an ethical view of life must be the basis for the representatives of the state. Srikrishna's formula seems to be 'the higher the rank, the deeper the commitment'—a formula that resonates with the dominant discourse of the post-colonial nation state in India. The idea of the state as a moral entity, once again enunciated in an official report, remains exactly its most unattainable and, therefore, most precious and sublime dimension.

In the case of the TADA court, the representation of the state was slightly different. Here, the rhetoric of secrecy and the practice of classifying even the most banal piece of evidence to protect the supposed interest of the state contributed to create a sense of urgency, that something larger threatening the nation was at stake. The Mumbai police eagerly projected the enormous amount of material it had gathered to generate the same illusion of effectiveness and ubiquity in the state's knowledge and capacity for taking on public enemies. The profane dimensions were equally obvious in the brutality and partiality of the police investigations and in the harshness of its treatment of the detainees. However, the serious character of the crimes, the alleged connections of the 'Muslim gangsters' to Pakistan, and the secrecy surrounding the case meant that these obvious abuses and human rights violations never generated the kind of public concern and debate which have surrounded the Srikrishna proceedings, not least in the English-language press catering for an educated middle-class audience. In a conversation in 1997, a liberal Hindu businessman expressed quite succinctly how the scale of knowledge and violence at the disposal of the state acquire sublime dimensions: 'See, many of the accused in this case are well-known criminals. They have committed a terrible crime—even Muslims admit that. We should not be soft on them .... Besides, there are so many things we are never told. The government has a lot of information it cannot disclose'.

The deep divide between the social worlds of Hindus and Muslims today traversing the city seems not only to have affected the sense of public justice, but also the public interest in these two sets of proceedings. Many educated people from all communities have taken a keen interest in the Srikrishna Commission. A series of independent reports documenting suffering and abuse have emerged from NGOs and civil rights activists. Many ordinary Hindus, nonetheless, according to my impressions from discussions and interviews over the last four years, seem to approve of the formula of balanced apportioning of guilt and responsibility for the riots. This is a convenient non-legalistic framework that enables the ordinary citizen to bracket these events as ones without actors, which were an unfortunate aberration from the normal order of things. To most ordinary people I met, the Srikrishna Commission appeared as a somewhat inconsequential sign of 'the state', a manifestation of authority that was simply expected to restore the public order upset by the riots. But the rhetoric of the state as a moral entity, as well as the legal intricacies of the proceedings, were mainly directed at the educated, literate middle class, which always has been the primary constituency and concern of the post-colonial state.

Among ordinary Muslims in central Mumbai whom I got to know, the commission figured less prominently, although Srikrishna was praised as a 'secular person', in the sense of being highly educated, impartial and critical of the Shiv Sena. The Muslim social world in Mumbai is not only spatially separated from that of the Hindus, but is also demarcated by the existence of a local Urdu public sphere with its own newspapers, journals and cable television. To the ordinary Hindu conversant with Marathi and Hindi, this world appears closed and even threatening, and the Urdu press is routinely accused of spreading anti-Hindu propaganda. Such accusations were also presented to the Srikrishna Commission, but they were never substantiated. Rather than being a vehicle of sectarian ideology, however, the Urdu press seems to be strongly introverted and preoccupied by issues internal to the Muslim community. It was unsurprising, therefore, that the TADA case was attributed more importance and concern than the proceedings of the Srikrishna Commission. Muslim organizations documented the harsh treatment of the predominantly Muslim detainees under TADA, which became a symbol of the inherently anti-Muslim bias of the state. Calls to stop the case, and to dismantle the TADA laws altogether, have for some years been high on the agenda of local organizations and several Urdu newspapers, and the issue is often raised in campaigns by local Muslim politicians. As we shall see, the TADA proceedings resonate with a long tradition of enmity between Muslims and the police in lower-class neighbourhoods in central Mumbai.

Governing the Muslim *badmash*

Colonial rule in India organized its object of governance, the natives, into two categories. On the one hand was the huge mass of ordinary people, peasants, artisans—in brief, subaltern groups—regarded as irrational, passionate and traditional and, therefore, in need of firm governance as subjects of the colonial state. On the other hand, there were the educated middle classes, literate elites in provincial towns, zamindari landlords, and 'natural' leaders of sects, castes, petty kingdoms and religious communities, who were considered amenable to reasoned persuasion and negotiation. These latter groups were the pillars of colonial rule, entrusted with the local administration below the district level, revenue collection, the management of affairs 'internal' to communities and so on. It was also these groups which, from the late nineteenth century onwards, were accorded certain rights to political representation and a public space wherein a rich and diverse range of cultural and civil associations arose within vernacular public spheres.

The uncontrollable, deeply-rooted religious sentiments that made the Orient oriental, however, existed more among the 'masses' than the reasonable 'educated sections'. During the Hindu-Muslim riots in

Bombay in August 1893, the *Times of India* observed 'a disturbing and most dangerous element in the riots—that the mill-hands responded in large and apparently well organised gangs' (14 August 1893). However, the *Bombay Gazette* reported on the same day that 'one gratifying circumstance in this outbreak of lawlessness is that amongst the hundreds that have been arrested, there is not a single respectable Hindu or Mahommedan'. Press, police and officials agreed that the cause of the riots was incitement of the 'lower classes' and instigation by criminal *badmash* residing in the slums (Krishnaswamy 1966:39). The Police Commissioner decided to call a meeting of 'representatives and respectable members of the communities' to discuss how normality could be restored and how the corrupting influence of the *badmash* on the lower classes could be curbed (Ibid.: 29).

As industrial capitalism developed in the Bombay region in the first decades of the twentieth century, the mill districts and adjoining popular neighbourhoods developed quickly afterwards.[16] The Bombay Police had for several decades tried to decipher the dynamics of the working-class neighbourhoods they tried to police, but with little success. The theory of 'hooliganism' relied on by the police was that 'it is not generally speaking, the ordinary resident with a home and an occupation who keep the police and the military busy. It is the riff-raff, the scum of the city that gives the trouble'.[17] During the prolonged disturbances in 1929, which took the form of a 'low-intensity riot' marked by scattered and recurrent episodes of killings throughout the central parts of the city, 'the hooligan became the universal embodiment of "the other"' (Chandavarkar 1998:174). These events further entrenched anxieties about the 'roughs' from the working-class neighbourhoods and paved the way for the emergence of the Muslim *badmash* as the most dreaded figure in the city.

The 1930s and 1940s saw an incipient isolation of the Muslim working class in the economy as well as spatially in the city, and the process became even more pronounced after Independence. The big naval strike launched against the British in Bombay quickly spilled over into a full-scale Hindu-Muslim riot in February 1946, which left 250 people dead and more than 1,000 wounded. Concerns were expressed regarding the 'alarming degree of instigation by *goondas* (criminals)' which, according to the editorial in the *Bombay Chronicle* (28 February 1946), meant 'widespread involvement of domestics and paupers in looting and arson'. Newspaper editors were, however, critical of the brutal conduct of the police and troops in quelling the riot, and activists of the Indian National Congress launched the so-called 'Peoples' Peace

Brigades'. Brigade volunteers, who dressed in shorts, white blouses and caps, patrolled the streets in open lorries and sought to intervene to stop violence. Police officers did, however, express concern over the large number of casualties among these volunteers (*Bombay Sentinel*, 25 February 1946).

After the riots, the Congress set up an inquiry committee and urged the police to cooperate. Police Commissioner Butler was unwilling to do so and felt threatened by the political interest in the work of the police. Testifying before the Municipal Corporation, Butler issued this unveiled threat: 'You must trust your police. If you push me down, if you don't stand by me, so help you God'. The tough line of the police against 'goondas and troublemakers' from the lower classes was, however, supported by most members of the Municipal Corporation. One of them, Mr Sabawala, stated: 'No [*sic*] government that does not fire and resolutely restore order, ceases to be called a government' (*Bombay Chronicle*, 8 March 1946).

As already mentioned, the position of the Muslim community in Mumbai since Independence has been marked by an increasing level of socio-economic isolation (Hansen 1996). This has been combined with an intensified level of policing in the Muslim areas, which have more police stations and 'chowkeys' than non-Muslim areas in the city. ('Chowkeys' are police posts on strategic street corners, which are built in stone; as in the colonial period, they are equipped to be barricaded and turned into bunker-like structures.) As we saw in the depositions from police officers at the Srikrishna Commission, in Muslim areas the 'police machinery must be alert around the year'. In spite of all the assurances about a change in the police attitude after the 1992–3 riots, the policing infrastructure in these areas was expanded considerably in the next four to five years. The practice of making 'preventive arrests' of what the police term 'notorious characters' or just 'rowdy young men' prior to festivals, elections and so on, is widespread and widely accepted as legitimate.[18] It is no exaggeration to say that for young Muslims in these areas, the police force is the ever-present, dreaded representation of the state.

The police force in Mumbai is overwhelmingly Hindu and is recruited from the social groups and caste communities from which the Shiv Sena's masculine Hindu chauvinism has also emerged. In the predominantly Muslim areas in Mumbai where I worked, I frequently went to two police stations and met officers and constables there, as well as in their chowkeys. Inside each of the compounds of what is supposed to be the strong arm of the secular state, I found two or three small temples

devoted to Ganesh or Hanuman (the monkey-god associated with cour-
age and fighting spirit). These had been financed by donations from officers and constables and constructed within the past decade. 'Some of
us have questioned whether it is appropriate', an officer from a Christian background told me, 'but my superior simply replied that if there
were more Christian officers and constables, he wouldn't object to us
having an image of Virgin Mary in one corner of the compound'. I must
have appeared unconvinced by the officer's demonstration of secularism because a few days later, another policeman offered to take me to
the police station in nearby Dongri, another 'notorious trouble spot', as
he said. There a Muslim *dargah* (shrine) had been built inside the police
compound back in 1923, and later a small Shiva temple had been placed
next to it. After the riots in 1993, a senior police inspector initiated renovation of the *dargah* and invited both Hindus and Muslims to cultural
programmes involving devotional *qawwalis* and *bhajans*. 'This initiative
has really improved the relations between the police and the general
public here', a police officer explained to me. Talking to policemen, I
got a clear sense that the earlier 'vulgar sociology' of the 'hooligan',
which had earlier informed police work in Mumbai's Muslim neighbourhoods, had evolved into a certain simplified 'sociology of Muslims', based
on a mixture of stereotypes, rumours and stories, many of them modified versions of those actually circulating in the neighbourhoods. Consider the following example, based on the stereotype that Muslims di-
vorce their wives and abandon their children all the time. An officer
explained: 'One reason for the high level of crime is that all these young
boys grow up without a proper father—this is because there are so many
divorces and the men just leave their families behind'. The following
'off-the-record' statement by a young and inexperienced officer testifies
to the enormous gap between the social worlds of the predominantly
Hindu police and the Muslims:

In the beginning when I came here, I was nervous when we went on patrol,
especially at night. This hostility was something I never experienced before ...
but then after some time I started to look them right in the eyes and pretend
that I was indifferent to them. I also learned more of the dirty language they use
around here ... that helped a lot. Now I get answers to my questions and I feel
more respected.

Generally, postings in the Muslim areas are considered strenuous, full
of hard work and dangerous, but there are also considerable rewards
and bribes from the brisk flesh trade and drug economy in parts of central Mumbai. As a rule, officers are rarely posted for more than twelve

to eighteen months in one police station, while constables typically serve two to three years. The police force, therefore, vitally depends on its neighbourhood network of informers, which is created and maintained though flows of *hafta* (bribes and pay-offs) and other economic transactions.

It is noteworthy that all of this resonates remarkably well with methods of colonial policing. The low quality of policemen recruited into the force in the city was a constant source of worry to colonial officers. Bombay was a difficult place to police, densely populated, full of hooligans, prostitutes and other temptations for the constable. The authorities were constantly worried by the low quality of information being received and they obviously had an uncanny sense that they did not know what was happening in their areas (Chandavarkar 1998: 187–219).

In his deposition before the Srikrishna Commission, the Special Branch chief in Mumbai revealed that there had been a so-called 'Communal riots prevention scheme' in existence for the last thirty years. Under this scheme, police stations in sensitive areas are supposed to keep track of communal organizations with a capacity for violence, as well as of their leaders, and are required to arrest these individuals whenever the situation so demands. It was, however, indicative of the distance between the police leadership and the lower ranks that virtually none of the sub-inspectors and responsible officers at the police stations scrutinized by the commission were able to define the precise criteria for identifying persons labelled as 'communal *goondas*'. Leading police officers had also shown very little interest in implementing the prevention scheme. Instead, the provisions for carrying out 'preventive arrests' were often employed according to the will and whims of commanding officers, or at the behest of local political forces.[19]

The depositions before the commission also revealed some of the many ties between the police force and local political organizations, particularly the Shiv Sena. It is important for the police not to destroy the intricate web of *hafta* and the tacit understandings between local operators and *dadas* (strongmen-cum-politicians), upon which daily police work depends. These multidimensional webs were very fluid; they cut across lines of caste and religion, and operated on the basis of rumour and gossip. Thus the identity of an 'informer' was never based on solid facts, and claims by policemen that someone 'works with us' were often made strategically and themselves became rumours floating around in the clan-like *biraderi* networks.[20] I only got to meet the 'public' friends of the police, men who trade openly with policemen, drink with them, 'fix' various things for the officers and walk in and out of the police station. Many of these helpers were men at the margins of the powerful networks, often small traders from low-status families, some of them with criminal records.[21]

One of the more arresting paradoxes of the relationship between a brutal, incompetent and biased police force and the Muslim communities in central Mumbai was the reconciliatory gestures and signs of respect displayed by Muslims towards police officers. During the Id festival in early 1994, senior police officers, determined to renew their relations with the Muslim community, waited outside several of the large mosques in central Mumbai, and distributed flowers and greeted hundreds of men and boys as the congregations left after prayer. Rumours of this gesture spread like wildfire and the officers were soon surrounded by massive crowds, initially hesitant but increasingly enthusiastic. I heard dozens of accounts of this incident, which in spite of its obvious banality, 'had a soothing effect. It made possible the process of reconciliation that followed. What impressed people was that these were not local officers from our police station, but the top-brass people who stood there', as a local *imam* of Madanpura explained to me. In the following years, new connections developed between leading police officers and Muslims. The relationships of patronage and recognition between the Congress government and the Muslim community were ritually confirmed each time Congress leaders and ministers came as honoured guests at cultural events and religious festivals in central Mumbai. After the riots of 1992–3, there was a strong sense of betrayal by the Congress and no dignitaries were invited during 1993–4. When the Shiv Sena and BJP came to power in 1995, the sense of alienation from ruling political parties became even more pronounced. 'We don't regard these people [Shiv Sena] as worthy representatives of the Indian state. They may be ministers of my state, but they are not my ministers. Why should we honour them by inviting them here?', asked Maulana Kashmiri, a well-known conservative figure among the Bohra Muslims, when I interviewed him in 1996. Instead of ministers, senior police officers were invited to honour religious events, not because the police as such was trusted, but because these officers, owing to their seniority and rank, represented 'the state' rather than the government. Thus the police could perform the function of officially confirming that the Muslim community was integral to the larger Indian society—a function which, needless to say, was crucial at this juncture.

Another dimension of this paradoxical relationship between Muslims and the police is the way in which local politicians and businessmen in central Mumbai strive to establish good relations with the police force, not tacitly as a decade ago, but as publicly as possible. One finds, for instance, well-constructed chowkeys carrying a plate saying 'donated by the honourable Shri—, Member of Legislative Assembly', as well as small structures at street corners providing shade for police constables, which carry conspicuous advertisements for the local shops, restaurants and firms that have sponsored them. Why has this happened? Basheer Patel, one of the influential politicians known for such donations to the police said rather bluntly:

In 1993, we paid the price for our bad relations with the police. We Muslims have always blamed the police for everything, we never tried to understand their point of view. Now, I realize that working with the police is the way to prevent another riot here. I represent this area—it is my responsibility to protect my people ... before I was treated with suspicion when I took a complaint to the police. Now all that is much easier.[22]

I can only make guesses about the complex alliances and strategies developed by a skilful, shrewd operator like Basheer Patel. Today, Patel has emerged as one of the most powerful operators in central Mumbai, because he has forged all these links and appears to recognize that in his area the police are the foremost representatives of the state. Not that the police necessarily control the neighbourhood, because there are other contenders for dominance over these areas, such as criminal outfits as well as religious and ethnic organizations. Patel's point, however, seems to be that the strong presence of the police in the area means that it is much easier to work through them than outside them.

State spectacles and politics in the *mohalla*

In 1994, *mohalla* committees were set up throughout the areas affected during the riots. These were launched to create 'communal reconciliation' in the city, as well as to facilitate the future governance of the urban territories in central Mumbai. Peace committees are hardly a novelty in the city, as we saw above, but are as old as communal disturbances themselves. After the riots in Thane in 1984, which also affected large parts of Mumbai, peace committees were formed in a number of mixed neighbourhoods such as Mahim, Bandra and Byculla. Over the years, however, they evolved into platforms for local politicians, who saw the committees as an opportunity for forging ties with the police, as well as strengthening their position in the neighbourhood. None of these committees played any role in preventing violence in 1992–3, and they were dissolved quickly afterwards.

Police Commissioner Sahani, known for his inclinations towards what one officer disapprovingly described to me as 'intellectual policing', launched a new reconciliation scheme after a series of unprecedented initiatives. Thus, for example, police officers were told to cooperate closely with social activists, and to attend long sessions where riot victims gave detailed and moving accounts of their loss of children and spouses at the hands of the police; they were also made to sit through week-long courses on Islam and Muslim culture conducted by people such as Asghar Ali Engineer, a well-known activist and vocal critic of the police force. The action plan implemented in 1994 required the police to initiate the formation of *mohalla* committees at every police station in the so-called 'problem areas', almost all of which turned out to be areas with substantial Muslim populations. The initiatives had many parallels with similar techniques of governance employed over the past century: bodies of concerned and 'respectable' citizens from all communities in a neighbourhood were called upon to take responsibility, to calm down sentiments and to assist the police in taking preventive action. Just as importantly, the committees aimed at 'recreating confidence in our institutions and in our democracy among the Muslims in this city', as one of the driving forces behind the initiative expressed.[23] When the *mohalla* committees were set up in 1994, they mainly recruited members from the Muslim middle classes. Many committee members were known in their localities as respected figures, who were often involved in voluntary work and were in close contact with institutions of the state. A young progressive lawyer, known for her controversial support for divorced Muslim women and active in the committee in Nagpada, stated:

The fear of the intentions of the police was the biggest problem, and then the fear of attending meetings inside the police compound itself. Only educated people who knew they enjoyed some respect among constables and officers were willing to do that in 1994. You can imagine how the atmosphere was at that time.[24]

Among police officers it was broadly assumed that the Muslims, especially the poor and the uneducated *badmash*, constituted the main problem. In the police analysis, riots started when such people were in-cited and manipulated by local political leaders and their *imams*. The police saw the committees as a way to 'depoliticize' and contain com-munalism, by reducing it to occasional outbursts of irrational social be-haviour and by removing the element of 'political manipulation' which, according to standard common sense among police officers (and many social scientists) in India, is the main reason behind riots. Members of political parties and politicians elected in the area were not admitted into the committees. Based on their earlier experience, the police wanted to remain firmly in control of these committees, to keep politics away 'in order to curb the divisive effects of partisan interests', as a high-ranking officer put it. The objective this time was more ambitious, for, as he said, 'we want to create a new leadership among Muslims'. The police wanted to bypass and exclude the established 'brokers' and *dadas* in the *mohallas*, so that Muslims would instead be represented by 'civilised' citizens. These citizens, according to the standard assumption so central to governance in India for a century, would be Muslims who, by virtue of their education, had abandoned primitive beliefs and had become amenable to reason and persuasion. The entire community could then be addressed and governed through these representatives.

Mohalla committee members told me that initially the meetings were tense and serious. A retired judge who served on a *mohalla* committee related:

In the beginning, all the top officers from the station were present at the meetings. On Fridays when the streets were full of people assembling for the Friday *namaz*, we would all come out with the officers and stand around the crowd, very alert, watching passers-by and making sure that no one made any provoking moves. There were tense moments, but I think we were successful.

As political attention faded in 1995–6, the committees were subtly transformed. At the initiative of the new and flamboyant Police Commissioner Tyagi, the committees were enlarged from a maximum of fifty members per police station to as many as two hundred.[25] Many of these were the 'marginal men' used by the police to know the neighbourhoods. They desired some recognition and standing in the community, and the police rewarded their loyalty by conferring on them an official status as community representatives. The effect of this expansion and inclusion of larger groups of people in the committees have been several. First, the social prestige of sitting on the committees was immediately reduced. For example, the Nagpada *mohalla* committee included a rag merchant, who had become rich by buying from and exploiting the rag-pickers in the area. He was a big hefty man known for his violent temper and the long whip he carried when ordering his many workers around; he was feared but not respected. Another new face was that of a man known as a supplier of all kinds of goods to the police. He walked in and out of the station, was always excessively servile to commanding officers, and was constantly joking with the constables. He had a small office in the building opposite the police compound, with nothing but a table, a telephone and a chair. From there he could fix anything, he boasted: 'Just tell me, you are my friend, I will get it for you.'

When the campaign for the municipal corporation elections started in January 1997, many of those recruited by the police because they claimed to be non-political actually tried to convert their new-found visibility and public standing into a bid for a political career. As a result, a large number of committee members, strictly speaking, had to be excluded because of their 'pollution' by the political world. This was, however, of little consequence, because many political figures had already begun to attend the meetings after the committees were enlarged. On several occasions, prominent political figures not only attended meetings, but even began to preside over functions organized by the *mohalla* committees. Very few of those who were politically involved actually left the *mohalla* committees, whose increasingly infrequent meetings at police stations began to resemble public functions, often lavishly hosted by the 'helpers' and friends of the police.

Another consequence of the committees' expansion was that certain police stations began to assume new functions of brokerage and 'fixing' local problems, which ran parallel to the activities of the local politicians they had sought to marginalize and also resembled the tangible service provision which local Shiv Sena branches had made their trademark throughout the city. An officer at the Agripada police station told me enthusiastically about his new-found role as 'fixer':

Now many people come to us with their usual problems—sewage, water, telephone connections, school admissions, etc. For us it is very easy to solve—we just make a few phone calls. When I present myself to these lazy bureaucrats at the Municipal Corporation, things start to happen [nodding towards a line of people waiting in the compound]. ... So, as you can see with your own eyes, people have gained confidence in us. They can see that we actually solve their problems.

The *mohalla* committees, and the newly assertive friendliness of the police, have indeed reduced the level of tension in Muslim areas, but they have removed neither the mechanisms producing communal enmity nor the organizational structures that perpetrate violence. On the contrary, the committees have in many ways merely provided the police with a set of new techniques for keeping order in 'trouble-spots', using a network of underworld operators, liaisons with political figures, and direct intervention in the distribution of public services. The *mohalla* committees are, in many respects, just the most recent means of governing the *badmash*.

Whither the state?

The many continuities in how to govern the *badmash* in Mumbai show that the post-colonial state in India continues to represent itself as a locus of higher rationality, outside and above the complexities and irrationalities of the lives of the masses. Both the Srikrishna Commission and the *mohalla* committees were interventions and spectacles that supported this style of governance. In both cases the 'sublime' dimensions of the state—fairness, reasonableness, tolerance and justice—were being represented to its preferred audience, the educated middle class.

As relative peace began to prevail in central Mumbai in the later 1990s, middle-class society—the high-ranking officers, the educated and the activists—withdrew from the *mohalla* committees, so that more everyday, profane forms of governance and networking were reconstructed. The public spectacle of the Srikrishna Commission also came to an end, and the report can be found in libraries and in limited circulation among intellectuals and political activists. At the time of writing in 1999, it still remains the task of those most strongly indicted by the report, the Shiv Sena and the Mumbai police, to decide whether and in what form the commission's recommendations about reform of the police should be implemented. The political world in Mumbai appears, in other words, to be conducting 'business as usual'. This raises the question of whether the 'state spectacles' analysed above have actually been able to resuscitate the myth of the state.

The answer cannot be precise but let me by way of conclusion offer a few reflections. The Shiv Sena's hold on Mumbai points to a transformation in the aura of the state as a site of neutrality and a certain predictability, based on impersonal rules and laws and technical expertise, which both the colonial and post-colonial state painstakingly sought to construct and maintain. This transformation not only occurs in the practices of governance but also in popular political imaginaries. Listening to the maze of rumours and tales of conspiracy that constitute an important part of the popular debate on government and state, one gets a sense that politics is widely understood as a game, and that control of government institutions and their resources is the prize to be won by parties and the communities they are believed to represent. The prevalence of such political imaginaries has made the Shiv Sena's style of governance possible. On the one hand, the party celebrates its conquest of the state government on behalf of the majority of ordinary Hindus, and enacts this in grand populist spectacles and equally grand promises of employment or free housing to the slum-dwellers. On the other hand, from the top leadership to the local *shakha pramukhs* (local branch leaders), there has been an indulgence in corrupt practices, land speculation and overt criminal activity unprecedented even in a city like Mumbai. All these activities have enabled the party to extend its complex networks of patronage, dependence and alliance across all levels in the city and the state. Moreover, Bal Thackeray's continual assertions about his autonomy, as well as his contempt for the judiciary and the Srikrishna Commission, remain central to his popularity and to his attempt to construct himself and his movement as a site of authority that openly defies and challenges the state's authority. Whether this defiance militates against the desire for social respectability that is equally strong among Shiv Sena supporters, so that it will rebound on the party at future elections, remains to be seen. Nevertheless, the older myth of the state as the uncontested centre of society does indeed appear enfeebled in contemporary Mumbai.

It is significant that many Muslims do not look to the government, but to Dawood Ibrahim and the powerful, legendary big *dadas* for protection from the Shiv Sena. I suggested above that the attribution of sublime qualities to the state is linked to its capacity for violence. As older myths of the state and its monopoly of violence seem to crumble in Mumbai, competing myths of authority and tales of fear cluster around the real perpetrators of violence in the city—the Shiv Sena, the police and the underworld. The paradox of this process of segmentation of authority is, however, that each segment remains dependent on the continued existence of the state—as a pool of resources, as the source of legitimate violence, or as an order to be defied and opposed. Even while effective state governance crumbles and fragments, the myth of the unity and coherence of the state must still be kept alive

Notes

1. I happened to be present in the city during the riots and on several occasions observed policemen literally protecting arsonists, and turning their backs on rampaging mobs. Similar incidents all over the city were reported widely by journalists of the English-language press, especially the *Times of India*.

2. In the official report of the Srikrishna Commission inquiring into the riots as well as the bomb blast in the city, it is stated that 'a grand conspiracy was hatched at the instance of the notorious smuggler Dawood Ibrahim Kaskar, operating from Dubai, to recruit and train young Muslims to vent their anger and wreak revenge by exploding bombs near vital installations and also in Hindu dominated areas so as to engineer a fresh bout of communal riots' (Srikrishna 1998: 60). Justice Srikrishna further expresses his satisfaction with the effective police investigations revealing this conspiracy (Ibid.: 61) but fails to mention the vital role played by corrupt customs and police authorities in the entire operation. The complicity of high-ranking officials in an operation that was intended to cover most major cities in India, but

failed to do so because 'Tiger Memon', the main accused in the bomb blast trial, panicked, has recently been documented by Visvanathan (1998b: 118–28).

3. Just as the domain of the sacred is fraught with ambivalence, with bliss as well as horror, so the sublime dimension of the state is also dependent on its dark sides. The fascination with spies and secret services, from James Bond to *Nikita* to *Men in Black*, to mention some recent films, is premised on awe of the state and fear of its brutality and ruthlessness. The state appears sublime because of its inordinate power to condone, redeem and even purify violence, as René Girard (1977) has also pointed out in the context of violence and sacrifice in religious rituals.

4. The commission was also asked to recommend steps to be taken to improve the performance of the police force and to recommend administrative measures that could reduce the likelihood of such incidents repeating themselves. The task was in other words daunting and deeply controversial, as it was bound to collide with entrenched political and bureaucratic interests in the government and the police force.

5. It is indicative of the perception of the Congress, among its own leadership and in the press, that it saw itself as represented through the state. After the party was ousted from the state government in 1995, it did not seek representation. 'We are represented in the spirit and mandate of the commission which we created. The commission has its own able counsel. There is no need for us to be there', as a Congress MLA told me in 1996.

6. This draws on my own presence at hearings in November 1996 and February-March 1997, as well as on written affidavits from a range of police officers and civilians obtained from court officials .

7. Summing up on the low morale of the police, Justice Srikrishna writes: 'The police, by their own conduct, appeared to have lost moral authority over the citizens and appeared to evoke no fear. ... The criminal elements were emboldened to hurl a crude bomb at the Police Commissioner and hack constables to death without fear. The police developed a psychological fear about attacks on them' (1998: 34).

8. I was fortunate to be able to attend most of these hearings and the quotes and observations in the following are all from my personal notes and not the official transcript.

9. *Maha arti* is mass prayer on streets and footpaths around temples; it was invented and organized by the Shiv Sena and other radical Hindu organizations in this period in order to mobilize Hindus against Muslims.

10. Interview, 18 February 1993.

11. The legal intricacies of this unprecedented move are outlined by R. Padmanabhan in *Frontline*, 18 April 1997. An important part of this process was that the High Court in Mumbai actually rejected the government's request for withdrawal and furthermore sentenced Thackeray to a week of 'simple imprisonment' on the grounds of contempt of court. Thackeray was forced to appear in the magistrates' court in the Mumbai suburb of

Bandra on 17 February where he was released on bail. Meanwhile, the court was surrounded by thousands of angry Shiv Sainiks shouting slogans and demanding the immediate release of the *Senapati*, the commander of the army, as he is known among the rank and file (*Mid-Day*, 18 February 1997).

12. The terms of reference of the commission were expanded to include an investigation of 'the circumstances and the immediate cause of the incidents commonly known as the serial bomb-blasts of the 12th March 1993, which occurred in the Bombay Police Commissionerate area', and further whether these were linked by common causes or 'a common design' to the riots investigated by the commission (Srikrishna 1998: 58).

13. For an overview of the proceedings of the TADA court, see the article 'Justice for Whom' in *Humanscape*, December 1995.

14. The secrecy of the TADA proceedings has produced the interesting paradox that the Srikrishna Commission has encountered many difficulties in fulfilling its revised and expanded mandate because it has been impossible to get access to the many classified documents used in the TADA court.

15. An independent human rights group organized the 'Indian People's Human Rights Commission', which shortly after the riots set up an inquiry headed by two retired judges of the Bombay High Court. Their report, *The People's Verdict*, was published in August 1993 and concluded that the main responsibility for the riots should be laid on the Shiv Sena and a partial and incompetent police force.

16. For a richly textured analysis of these areas, see Chandavarkar (1994: 168–238).

17. Memo from the Commissioner of Police, Bombay, December 1926 (qu. in Chandavarkar 1998: 161).

18. See the excellent piece on police practices concerning arrests of young 'rowdies', their subsequent classification as 'rowdy-sheeters', etc., by Vivek Dhareshwar and R. Srivatsan (1996).

19. During the municipal elections in Mumbai in February 1997, the supposedly 'reformed' gangster Arun Gawli, who had been befriended by leading Shiv Sena men, created an independent political party, *Akhil Bharatiya Sena*, to contest the elections and threaten the Shiv Sena's position in the Agripada working-class area in central Mumbai. One week before the election, Gawli was picked up and detained under the prevention scheme and released the day after the elections were over.

20. In the predominantly Muslim neighbourhoods where I worked, most families come from north India. For them, *biraderi* networks in which there are durable relationships of trust among families mostly (but not always) of the same caste, are of paramount importance when it comes to mutual help, getting jobs, arranging marriages, recruiting new labour from the villages, lending money, etc. However, in the urban economy, other relationships and economic networks cut across the *biraderis*, which often seem to function as defences of last resort in times of crisis or serious decision-making.

21. A large number of the residents in these areas are Muslim weavers of north Indian descent, mostly from the Julaha community, a low-status, lower-caste community which higher-status Muslims did not recognize as proper Muslims. The Julahas began in this century to claim recognition by calling themselves Ansaris, the Arabic word for 'helper', referring to those who helped the Prophet flee from Mecca to Medina. The contempt for Julaha/Ansaris still prevails. A high-status Muslim in the neighbourhood said this about the police informers: 'Some of these people call themselves Ansaris. But who are they helping? The police! These men are Julahas, we know who they are'.

22. Basheer Patel, MLA, Samajwadi Party (interview, Umerkhadi, 10 December 1996)

23. Sushoba Bharve, activist and a self professed Gandhian social worker (interview, Worli, 19 February 1997).

24. S. Bharve (see n. 23) confirmed this view when she said, 'See, respectable people are not very interested in working with the police. The tout will always come forward, but we did not want that. So we worked really hard to find good people with constructive views. It was very difficult'.

25. Tyagi also started a range of slightly more creative initiatives, such as regular sports days where police teams would play cricket against the local Muslims, or where a team of Hindus would play against a Muslim team, as was done in Agripada, which has long seen almost ritualized clashes between Hindus and Muslims after cricket matches between India and Pakistan. In this neighbourhood, where the Hindu side is known as Jammu and the Muslim side as Kashmir, the concept worked quite well. 'Now they fight it out, but we are there watching them so it does not go out of hand', an enthusiastic police constable told me.

References

Cassirer, E. 1946. *The myth of the state.* New Haven: Yale University Press.

Chandavarkar, R. 1994.*The origins of industrial capitalism in India.* Cambridge: Cambridge University Press.

———. 1998. *Imperial power and popular politics.* Cambridge: Cambridge University Press.

Dhareshwar, V., and Srivatsan, R. 1996. 'Rowdy-sheeters': an essay on subalternity and politics. *In* S. Amin and D. Chakrabarty, eds, *Subaltern Studies IX.* Delhi: Oxford University Press.

Girard, R. 1977. *Violence and the sacred.* Baltimore: Johns Hopkins University Press.

Hansen, T. B. 1996. Recuperating masculinity: Hindu nationalism, violence and the exorcism of the Muslim 'Other'. *Critique of Anthropology* 16, 2:137–72.

———. 1998. BJP and the politics of Hindutva in Maharashtra. *In* T.B. Hansen and C. Jaffrelot, eds, *The BJP and compulsions of politics in India,* pp. 121–63. Delhi: Oxford University Press.

——. 1999. *The saffron wave: Hindu nationalism and democracy in modern India*. Princeton: Princeton University Press.

——. n.d. Segmented worlds: work, livelihood and identity in central Mumbai. Paper at *Workers in Mumbai* conference, 20–23 November 1997, Mumbai.

Kantorowicz, E. 1957. *The king's two bodies*. Princeton: Princeton University Press.

Khilnani, S. 1997. *The idea of India*. Harmondsworth: Penguin.

Krishnaswamy, J. 1966. *A riot in Bombay, Aug. 11, 1893: a study of Hindu-Muslim relations in western India in the nineteenth century*. Ph.D. dissertation, Department of History, University of Chicago.

Lele, J. 1995. Saffronization of Shiv Sena: the political economy of city, state and nation. *In* S. Patel and A. Thorner, eds, *Bombay: metaphor of modern India*, pp. 165–212. Bombay: Oxford University Press.

Lefort, C. 1988. *Democracy and political theory*. Cambridge: Polity Press.

Mitchell, T. 1999. Society, economy and the state effect. *In* G. Steinmetz, ed., *State/culture: state–formation after the cultural turn*, pp. 76–97. Ithaca: Cornell University Press.

Padgaonkar, D., ed., 1993. *When Bombay burned*. Delhi: UPSD Press.

Price, P. 1996. *Kingship and political practice in colonial India*. Cambridge: Cambridge University Press.

Rushdie, S. 1995. *The moor's last sigh*. London: Jonathan Cape.

Srikrishna, B.N. 1998. *Report of the Srikrishna Commission*, 2 vols. Mumbai: Punwani and Vrijendra.

Visvanathan, S. 1998a. The early years. *In* S. Visvanathan and H. Sethi, eds. *Foul play: chronicles of corruption 1947–97*, pp. 15–44. New Delhi: Banyan Books.

——. 1998b. Notes on the Bombay blast. *In* S. Visvanathan and H. Sethi, eds. *Foul play: chronicles of corruption 1947–97*, pp. 118–28. New Delhi: Banyan Books.

Paper truths: The emergency and slum clearance through forgotten files

Emma Tarlo

In 1995, I began working on a project about furniture and the uses of the body in an area locally known as Welcome—a poor resettlement colony in the densely crowded margins of East Delhi.[1] Like Delhi's forty-six other resettlement colonies, Welcome was home principally to evicted slum-dwellers who had been displaced from inner city locations during a series of demolition drives initiated by the Delhi Development Authority (DDA) and the Municipal Corporation of Delhi (MCD) between 1963 and 1977. Given that the colony was essentially a planned space, I thought it might be useful to scan the housing records of the slum department in order to get some background information about the history of the colony. However, what began as background soon became foreground and my work in the records room was to radically transform the nature of my project as a whole. Two particular issues arrested my attention: on the one hand the records revealed new and disturbing information about what had occurred in Delhi during the 'emergency' when Indira Gandhi temporarily suspended democratic rights for a period of nineteen months (June 1975 to January 1977). On the other hand, they raised a number of questions about the status of official documents as 'evidence',

I am grateful to the British Academy and the Economic and Social Research Council (ESRC) for supporting various phases of this research and to the London School of Economics and Jawaharlal Nehru University for their institutional backing. Earlier drafts of this paper were presented in seminars held at the Universities of Edinburgh and Cambridge and the LSE. This paper forms part of a much larger project about representations and experiences of the emergency in Delhi. I would like to thank my research assistant, Rajinder Singh Negi, for his invaluable help and companionship in the records room of the slum department in Welcome where this research began.

suggesting rather that their relationship to reality is open to manipulation and fraught with ambiguity. By the time my assistant and I had waded our way through some 3,500 files, I had decided to make the emergency the central focus of my study and to use the records as an avenue through which to begin to explore the relationship between the state and the urban poor during this critical moment of modern Indian history—a moment too recent to have attracted the attention of historians but too significant to be ignored by anthropologists.

To give some background: the early 1970s were a period of considerable political agitation in India. In June 1975, Indira Gandhi, the then Prime Minister, was found guilty of election malpractices and debarred from office for a period of six years. Instead of stepping down, she responded to the court judgment against her by declaring a state of internal emergency. This gave her special powers which she used to impose censorship, arrest political opponents and enforce the acceleration of a number of measures which had long been sitting on the back burner of Indian politics. Prominent amongst these were the two controversial policies of 'resettlement' (the other side of which was slum clearance) and 'family planning' (which became synonymous with sterilization). The scale of these projects was phenomenal. According to official statistics, between 1975 and 1977, in Delhi alone, some 700,000 people were expelled from the city centre (which was almost 15 per cent of the population) and over 161,000 were sterilized.

The inhabitants of Welcome were amongst the thousands of Delhi's poor targeted in the slum-clearance and sterilization drives. Indeed many found themselves trapped at the painful point of intersection where the two policies met. But although much of my work focuses on their personal narratives (Tarlo n.d.), I want, in this essay, to concentrate on the pile of dusty files that had led me to work on the emergency in the first place. My objectives are twofold. At one level, my aim is to use the information contained within the slum department files as a form of evidence which enables us to challenge the silence that surrounds the emergency. At another level my aim is to explore the grey zone of ambiguity that the files represent. By treating the slum department office as an ethnographic terrain, I also seek to highlight the role of local government officials as intermediaries, who negotiate between the state and the residents of the colony on the one hand, and between the anthropologist and the archive on the other. But before turning to the files and outlining their significance, I want to begin by introducing some of the problems inherent in trying to work on the emergency.

The emergency: an area of silence

Like all attempts to rewrite the past, writing a history of the emergency is fraught with difficulties: there is the problem of the nature of the material available; the veracity of the statistics; the difficulty of distinguishing reconstructions from realities in people's memories of the past. But although these problems are inherent in all historical ventures, they are, I think, particularly pertinent here owing to the fact that the emergency has largely been effaced from the country's own renderings of its past. Despite having once been recognized as a moment of crisis—perhaps *the* most critical moment of India's post-colonial development—the emergency has since been forgotten. Just as it was characterized by silence and censorship at the time, so it has, over the years, been built as an area of collective silence, a moment not to be remembered for reasons I shall come to shortly.

Such forgetting is not neutral. As the writer and political scientist, Ashish Nandy (1995), recently commented: 'Enormous political weight has gone into *wiping out* the emergency as a live memory'. Now this has obvious methodological implications. It means that any attempt to understand the period involves plunging into an area of silence and trying to uncover or activate memories which work against it. It also raises the fundamental question of whether it is in fact possible to write the history of a moment which has been so effectively effaced.

In asking this question, I am not alone. Similar questions have been raised by the historian, Shahid Amin (1995), in his attempt to stitch together an account of the violent events which took place at the hands of Indian nationalists in the small town of Chauri Chaura in Uttar Pradesh in 1922, an event which has been subject to what Amin calls the 'imperatives of historiographical amnesia'. Similarly, Gyan Pandey (n.d.) speaks of the difficulty of writing a history of the violence of partition in 1947–8, a difficulty compounded by the fact that the entire episode has been sidelined, underplayed, or passed off as a brief moment of madness, a terrible accident, an atypical example of history derailed.[2] Such unwritten moments of the Indian past share at least one common factor: they do not fit comfortably into the national picture of how things are meant to be. Like Chauri Chaura and partition, the emergency is a violent moment, difficult to digest. Not only does it threaten the precarious image of India as 'essentially non-violent'—an image increasingly difficult to sustain—but it also implicates the state as the key agent of violence. More threatening still, the emergency challenges the discourse of democracy which claims an unbroken hold over India's past from the present day right back to the attainment of Independence in 1947.

This is not to argue that the emergency has always been a forgotten moment. On the contrary, for the brief period of twenty-one months of Janata Party rule immediately after the emergency (1977–9), remembering the emergency, exposing its atrocities and judging its perpetrators attained the status of a national imperative, a personal and collective duty. Indira Gandhi's election defeat, which brought down her emergency government, was followed not only by the establishment of an official commission, compared in scale and scope to the famous Nuremberg trials, but it was also followed by a flurry of political exposés with dramatic titles like *Operation emergency, Experiment with untruth, An eye to India: the unmasking of tyranny,* in which the emergency was portrayed as a moment of severe and terrible oppression, a cacophony of torture, censorship and violent abuse. For a brief period the emergency was built as the ultimate lesson for the future, as the memory that would never fade, leading John Dayal and Ajoy Bose (1977), who wrote two books at the time, to argue with conviction: 'Nothing that happens in the future can undo this past'.

There is no space here for tracing the mixture of nationalist sentiment, party political interests, and chance events which served to nip this effervescent moment of memory in the bud. But a few points are worth mentioning. First, Indira Gandhi was voted back to power by democratic means in January 1980, which inevitably dealt a serious blow to all attempts to portray her as a monstrous tyrant, 'a second Hitler'; that it was in her interests to draw a veil over her brief moment of unpopularity and subsequent rejection goes without saying. The fact that her infamous son, Sanjay Gandhi, who had spearheaded the sterilization campaign, died in a plane crash in July 1980, also served conveniently to remove the most controversial of all emergency figures from the picture. Meanwhile, Indira Gandhi's assassination by Sikh extremists in 1984 served to extinguish further memories of her dubious past by elevating her to the noble category of martyr of the nation. All of this means that although allusions may be made to emergency atrocities and to the misdeeds of Indira Gandhi in the discourse of marginal political groups and left-wing academics, such opinions are little more than mere whimpers in the face of the dominant discourse, in which Indira Gandhi laid down her life for the nation and the emergency is quite simply absent, missing or little more than an empty label.

My reason for raising this issue of the status of the emergency as a forgotten moment is that it highlights the problems one inevitably encounters in trying to recapture something of that moment. Two problems converge here. One is the almost total absence of material about the emergency from the 1980s onwards, and the other is the nature of the material that does exist, mainly from the mid- to late 1970s. On the one hand, we have contemporary publications written *during* the emergency, but this was a time of censorship when most journalists, academics and politicians who wanted to avoid being jailed either wrote in support of the emergency or else kept silent. On the other hand, we have the outrage literature of the *post*-emergency period (buttressed also by some of the underground resistance literature of the emergency). Here the discourse of resentment, the sense of guilt, the backlash to censorship, the fervour of political will, the desire for sensationalism, and an inability to distinguish rumour from fact retrospectively, combine to ensure that this narrative (which like the emergency, lasted no more than twenty-one months) is as unsatisfactory as 'historical evidence' as the propaganda of the emergency itself.

Apart from these two narratives, there are the specialist discourses which box up emergency experiences to conform to academic disciplines or administrative categories. The 'slum clearance' issue is therefore discussed within the context of literature on housing and urban development, whereas the 'sterilization' issue is discussed within the context of population studies and family planning, which rapidly became redefined as 'family welfare' after the emergency in a vain attempt to escape the negative connotations.[3] But the drawing of boundaries between specialist areas of administrative concern has meant that although it is generally recognized that it was the poor in Delhi who bore the brunt of both the sterilization and slum-clearance drives, very little effort has been made to see how these two policies might have operated in relation to one another, and how the individuals and families targeted by one policy may actually have been the same people caught by the other. Interestingly, novelists have been willing to enter where social scientists fear to tread, but reading Rohinton Mistry's novel, *A fine balance*—set during the emergency—I cannot help but feel that he has absorbed uncritically the outrage literature of the post-emergency period, and has reproduced its very particular catastrophic and sensationalist reading of the past, without recognizing the extent to which that reading was a product of a very particular time (the post-traumatic recovery period). Hence his two Scheduled Caste tailors in (fictionalized) Bombay are not only displaced and sterilized, but one ends up with his legs amputated, and the other ends up castrated, in a novel which degrades into a cocktail of high melodrama and torture.

It is within the context of this apparent dearth of satisfactory forms of information about the emergency, that I would like to introduce the housing records of the slum wing of the Municipal Corporation of Delhi (MCD) east zone B, one of the seven regional offices of the slum department. There are various reasons why I decided to focus on the records. First, as I mentioned before, it was with the files that my research on the emergency began, for they alerted me to the significance of this forgotten moment of Indian history and gave me the background to enable me to pursue the topic with residents of the colony. However, the files are far more than simply a background record to the personal narratives of the residents of Welcome, for they constitute a very particular type of evidence, essential to the project as a whole. Unlike personal narratives, the files provide, not retrospective accounts of what went on in the colony twenty years ago, but contemporary ones. They represent, not history remembered and recomposed in the presence of an inquisitive anthropologist, but remnants of history in the process of being made. In other words, they tell us about the functioning of the bureaucracy in the present of the past. Of course this does not make them truer than personal narratives, for what they provide is, after all, only an official version. But it does give them an immediacy in temporal terms which retrospective memories of the emergency cannot have.

Finally, as an anthropologist working on the records of the immediate past, I had the advantage of being surrounded by present-day bureaucrats, who not only helped me interpret the files but also offered their own interpretations. For, although to all intents and purposes, the records room of the slum department looked like a dead archive—and was even replete with the carcasses of small hairy rodents which sometimes dropped out of the files—it was in fact a living archive, still in the process of being made. This meant that the record keepers of the slum department were not simply librarians or archivists, distanced from the contents of the files, but were the actual record makers themselves, some of whom had even been around during the emergency. Their commentaries on and interpretations of the official version of the past contained within the files formed an essential part of my research, turning my work in the records room into a form of fieldwork in itself.

Fields of files

Following ethnographic convention, I want to begin by asking my readers to imagine themselves in the field—in this case a field with neither grass nor trees—a dingy and discoloured concrete block in a dusty and neglected corner of the metropolis. It is hot, stiflingly hot. Every window of the building has been smashed. Dust storms rage outside, sugaring the burgeoning heaps of files within with layers of grey-brown sediment. Pigeons fly in and out of the empty window-frames, nesting on dysfunctional fans and depositing their droppings on the crumbling grey-brown files which line the walls on steel shelves in varying degrees of collapse. Electricity has not functioned here for several years. This is the records room of the slum wing in Welcome, a room which no doubt finds its equivalent in the townships of developing countries all over the world. In the corridor and the next door room, seven officials cluster in marginally better conditions, staving off a lethal combination of boredom and heat. There are seven such zonal offices of the slum wing in Delhi, which cater collectively to the forty-seven resettlement colonies of the capital. The colonies provide land on a leasehold basis to those whose homes have been demolished under the slum clearance scheme, which was first activated in 1960, greatly accelerated during the emergency, and still continues to function today at a much slower rate. Although my own work was restricted to the offices of Welcome, there is no reason to suppose that the other zonal offices would be any more luxurious or that the details found within their files would have been much different.

What these decaying but nonetheless active records contain is an official memory of the emergency embedded within the context of housing policies which have preceded and succeeded it. The emergency in historic and administrative perspective, the emergency as a humdrum fact of everyday existence rather than as a fleeting moment of high drama. Viewed from this angle, the distinguishing feature of the period is not so much the fact of slum clearance (for the colony had begun catering to displaced slum dwellers back in 1963), as the fact that many people had during the emergency secured their rights to housing through participation in 'family planning' (for which read sterilization). Case-by-case and file-by-file the records pertaining to Welcome bear witness to the granting of housing rights on the basis of sterilization, a fact previously suggested by a few outraged post-emergency authors, but vehemently denied by the ex-head of the Delhi Development Authority, Jagmohan, who had been in charge of the resettlement activities during the emergency. In his book, *Island of truth*, published in 1978, Jagmohan (who is still very much present in Delhi politics) presents himself as a lone voice of reason speaking out in a wilderness of hypocrisy, superficiality and sensationalism. 'Mine', he writes, 'is an island of truth—truth in its essence, truth in its basic framework. I intend to take you to this island ... I hope to show you a few spots from which the reality may emerge, and you may be able to see true reflections even in a cracked mirror'. In response to the British journalist David Selbourne's sensational accusation that 25,000 people whose homes had been bulldozed had been subject to compulsory sterilization as a prerequisite to resettlement, Jagmohan asserted plainly: 'Not in a single case, was compulsory sterilization made a pre-condition for allotment of land or plot to those who were affected by the clearance-cum-resettlement operations' (1977: 82). The records, then, are interesting in providing a new type of evidence from the slum wing (then under the DDA, now under the MCD), which directly contravenes the DDA's own official version of what happened during the emergency.

Why, one might ask, have such records never been studied before? Why has the issue not moved beyond the conflicting opinions of different authors? Why did the notion of displaced people being sterilized never attain more than the status of rumour? One reason is quite simply that, according to popular imagination, such records do not exist. It is part of the mythology of the emergency that controversial things such as details of the bureaucracy's role in enforcing sterilization were not recorded in anything other than general terms. This was the time of secrecy, when everything was done by word of mouth. And so the silence of the past serves to reproduce the forgetting of the emergency in the present, this time by denying the existence of 'the evidence'. This struck me particularly forcefully when I recently got into conversation about the records with a journalist, who had in fact been working for a national newspaper in Delhi during the emergency—presumably under the conditions of censorship which then prevailed. As soon as I mentioned that I was working on the DDA records pertaining to the slum wing's role in sterilization activities during the emergency, he immediately retorted: 'The DDA never had any role in sterilization activities. That is just a baseless rumour spread by sensation-hungry foreigners'—a category to which I was obviously assigned. Nonetheless, the records do exist and they provide some threads with which we can weave a new narrative of the emergency—that works against the prevailing trend of silence and denial. Lifting the veil of secrecy, which in this case has proved more fictitious than real, we are left with the documents, previously unexplored and unacknowledged.

To understand these documents, we need to see them within the context of the slum department records more generally. Needless to say, there is no convenient classification of records according to period, no pile neatly labelled 'emergency'. Rather, what we have are 3,459 'personal files', each file containing the documents pertaining to a single resettlement plot in Welcome. Collectively the files represent 80 per cent of the allotments made in the colony, the other 20 per cent being either destroyed or misplaced. The squalor and filth of the records room ensure that no-one who works there enters it unless strictly necessary. Generally it is only the low-level employees of the slum department who dirty themselves by rummaging though the dust, feathers and pigeon-shit in search of a file. This seems to be a relatively rare occurrence, which takes place perhaps once or twice a week. That my assistant and I spent every day in the records room for a period of approximately two months (give or take frequent national holidays) was a cause of disbelief, humour and disgust.

A slum department personal file comes into being when a plot of land or occasionally a built-up tenement is allocated to a family whose home has been demolished, usually as a result of slum clearance policy, occasionally as a result of flood or fire. In most cases, what is allocated is a small rectangular plot of 25 square yards, on which the allottee has the right to build some form of structure and for which he or she is expected to pay a very nominal licence fee. Since files correspond to allotments rather than demolitions, it is impossible to judge from them how many of the displaced failed to obtain a plot or tenement. What we have here are files which begin with the successful acquisition of a plot, but which often contain information relating to several different families as the plot changes hands over the years. Some files dated back to the early 1960s when the colony was founded and when almost two-thirds of it had been laid, whilst others dated back to the emergency years when an additional 1,483 plots had been created, making a grand total of 4,034 residential plots, 415 tenements (flats) and 198 shop plots. Some files were almost empty, containing only an allotment slip which gave the name, block and plot of the original allottee. But most files contained some form of demolition slip, an allotment order, a list of resettlement regulations, a photograph of the original allottee, an affidavit signed or thumb-printed by the allottee, and a few receipts for licence payments or the payments of damages. The precise wording of the documents varied from year to year, largely in accordance with changes in administration as the slum department got shunted back and forth between the MCD and the DDA.

Also included in some files were death certificates, applications for mutation, documents of purchase, eviction orders, papers relating to court cases, papers relating to sterilization, letters to and from residents of the colony and, from time to time, a survey form, dated 1989, which was aimed at establishing how many of the original allottees had left the colony. By tracing the paperwork relating to each plot, one could in theory establish the history of the plot and the fate of its inhabitants. In practice, however, things were not that simple owing to the slippage between official truths and realities. This slippage was not peculiar to the emergency as such, but was characteristic of the records more generally.

As mentioned earlier, unlike historians sifting through the records of the distant past, my assistant and I were in the fortunate position of having access to present-day housing officials who could and did assist us in decoding official realities. What soon became apparent was the discrepancy between the official reading of a particular document taken at face value and the numerous other possible readings that could be made of the same document. For documents not only revealed official truths; they also concealed unofficial truths and no one was more helpful in explaining this than the lower divisional clerk of the slum department. A couple of examples serve to illustrate the point.

According to the rules of resettlement, only the original allottee and or his or her blood relatives were entitled to live on a given plot and to pay the licence fee for it. It was, we were told, in order to distinguish between original allottees and illegal impostors (that is those who had rented, purchased or squatted on plots) that the MCD had introduced a system of taking photographs of allottees, in which the latter clutched a small black board on which their names, their fathers' names and the numbers of their plots were chalked. These photographs, reminiscent of penal records, were used for identification purposes at the time of payment. At least that was the official version. But in actual fact, as the lower divisional clerk explained with a twinkle in his eye, many of the people paying the fee were not the original allottees, since many had illegally purchased plots or were living there on rent. The slum department's usual response to this was not to evict the impostors, but rather to tell them that as long as they had possession of the documents belonging to the original allottee and as long as they continued to pay the license fee *in the name of* the original allottee, then the slum department would turn a blind eye to their irregular status. This meant that however regular documents in a given file might appear to be, it did not necessarily mean that they represented a regular situation, a possibility which became particularly relevant during the emergency.

A second example—also common—concerned the situation in which it came to the official notice (as opposed to the unofficial notice) of the slum department that the person residing on the plot was not the original allottee. In such cases the slum department issued a document entitled 'Show Cause' in which the residents had to establish their rights to the plot within seven days under threat of eviction. What residents usually did in such cases was to compile a whole dossier of documents including photographs, ration cards, and power-of-attorney documents recording the purchase of the plot, accompanied by a request for the property to be transferred to their names. Such requests were, it seems, systematically refused by the slum department for, as the lower divisional clerk insisted, it was strictly forbidden to buy or sell a resettlement plot, making transfer of ownership a total impossibility. The department's usual response, however, was not to evict the illegal purchaser but to charge him 'damages' calculated at Re 1 per square yard per month. (This worked out at Rs 25 a month as opposed to the licence fee which was fixed at Rs 8 per month.) Illegal purchasers who paid damages were given the recognized status of 'unauthorized occupant', a curious institutionalized form of unofficial status which revealed the ambiguity and malleability of the system as a whole.

These discrepancies are important, not only because they reveal the extent to which such records are misleading if read purely at face value, but also because they hint at the various levels of ambiguity in the status of many people living in such colonies. Further examination of the files reveals that the vast majority of so-called original allottees had not paid their licence fees for several years. When I examined more closely the terms and conditions of resettlement at various times, it did in fact become quite difficult to see how anyone could be living within the rules of resettlement at all, for the rules appeared to have been formulated with almost total disregard for the lifestyles and futures of the resettled. This was particularly striking in the case of people resettled in the early 1960s, all of whom had put their signatures or thumb-prints to documents in which they promised not to build any permanent structure on their plots, which were referred to as 'temporary camping sites' and could be reclaimed by the government at any time following two weeks' notice. Others had signed documents in which they swore not to keep animals and not to use their properties for anything other than domestic use. But since many of the resettled were craftspeople who had worked from home for generations, and some of them reared buffaloes, chickens and goats, the chances of their abiding by the rules seemed very remote. In fact, what came across very strongly from the records was the alienating nature both of resettlement rules and of the documents themselves. The thumb-print signatures of allottees seemed to indicate the layers of distance that separated them from the bureaucracy, a distance marked not only in the heavily-coded official jargon of the documents, but also in the choice of the English language, the medium of writing itself and the very fact that 'official truths' necessarily took on a paper form.

A fair amount of general information can be gleaned from these official papers despite the gap between paper truths and realities. From the names of the original allottees, it was usually easy to guess their religion, establishing that there were both Hindus and Muslims resettled in the colony. From the occupations listed in some files, one could also draw up some sort of occupational profile of the resettled, most of whom belonged not surprisingly to the lower end of the socio-economic scale, engaged as petty traders, craftspeople, rickshaw-drivers and low-level government employees such as sweepers, railway coolies, peons, gardeners and so forth. From demolition slips, it was also possible to learn where such people had been living in Delhi before being resettled and from power-of-attorney documents, one could trace how certain properties had changed hands. But conversations with officials of the slum department taught us to be wary of such papers by indicating what they might conceal. The greatest value of the files lay not so much in the accuracy of the statistics they generated, as in the insights they provided into the changing regulations, priorities and functioning of the slum department over time. It is through the paperwork in the files that we can trace the process by which the sterilization imperative was accommodated within the existing structure of the slum department during the monsoon season of 1976.

Sterilization plots

It is within this context that I would like to introduce a small and seemingly unpretentious document, entitled a DDA Family Planning (FP) Centre Allotment Order. Of the 3,459 personal files available in Welcome, 975 (28 per cent) contained this form, which reads as follows:

1. Name and Age
2. Father's name
3. Plot
4. No. of family members
5. Date of voluntary sterilization
6. Nature of assistance claimed
7. Order

Signature of applicant   Officer in Charge
Date

Here, the FP allotment order is just an empty form, devoid of details, but since each form must have been empty before being filled, it is worth pausing to contemplate it in its original empty state. Clearly the title alone gives official acknowledgement of the fact that the DDA was issuing plots on the basis of family planning. But what does it mean by 'family planning'? For this we have to go to point 5, which demands bluntly 'Date of voluntary sterilization'. So 'family planning' is defined as 'sterilization' and 'sterilization' is defined as 'voluntary' before the form is even filled. In these small slips of paper we find official family planning euphemisms in operation at a local level during the emergency.

On first encounter, the presence of these allotment orders would appear to confirm Selbourne's claim that those whose homes were demolished in the slum clearance scheme could only get resettlement plots by being sterilized at the hands of the DDA. But there are various facts which seem to suggest that the simple formula, demolition leads to sterilization, leads to plot, cannot fully explain the complexity of the situation. First, there is the fact that the FP allotment orders are not found in all the files pertaining to the new plots allocated during the emergency. Clearly a number of people were resettled during the period without getting sterilized. Secondly, well over half of the sterilization cases that were recorded referred to plots which dated back to the 1960s. In other words, these were old plots being secured through sterilization, not new allocations of land. And thirdly, there was the question of the identity of the person sterilized. For not only did the forms record the date and sterilization number of applicants, but they also recorded one of two phrases: either 'self sterilization', or 'motivated case.'

The term 'self sterilization' seemed clear enough, suggesting that in return for sterilization a person was able to obtain a plot. But the term 'motivated case' was by no means self-explanatory, and led me and my assistant to turn to the slum department officials for an explanation. It soon became apparent that the term referred to an unofficial financial transaction, a deal, between a person wanting a plot and a person willing to get sterilized for money. In effect the former could avoid getting sterilized for a plot by paying someone else to take his or her place on the operating table. In such cases the former became a 'motivator' in official family planning parlance, and the latter became the 'motivated case.' Of the sterilization cases for which details were given in Welcome, about half were classified as 'motivated'. I do not want to digress here into how this system of motivation functioned on the ground—something I was only able to establish through in-depth interviews with residents, and which I have discussed elsewhere at some length (Tarlo 1995). But suffice it to say that the image of the motivator thrown up by the explanations of slum department officials was very different from that thrown up by the family planning literature, in which the 'motivator' is generally a health worker who gains a petty financial bonus for fulfilling targets by persuading people to get sterilized.

These conundrums seemed to suggest something much more complicated than a straightforward insistence by the DDA that all displaced slum dwellers should be sterilized. So how did the system work? To establish this, we need to return to the files: which files contained family planning allotment orders, under what conditions did the document seem to become a requirement, and what were the benefits or rights that such a document promised to secure? This last question could be answered by reading the responses to point 6 on the form: 'nature of assistance claimed'. Here the two most common responses written in by housing officials were 'regularization of a residential plot' or 'allocation of a residential plot.' Occasionally the plot was a 'shop plot' and in all cases the concerned official had written the phrase 'allowed provisionally'. Examining these responses in relation to other information contained within the same files, it soon became clear that 'regularizations' occurred in those situations where the sterilized person or motivator was already residing on a plot but was not the original allottee; in other words, these were people living in that grey zone of recognized irregularity that we have already encountered. Such cases occurred mainly in the files pertaining to plots in the older section of the colony which had been developed back in the 1960s.

In the files pertaining to the newer section, it was more common to find the phrase 'allocation of a plot', but this did not mean that all the people applying for such plots were from outside the colony. On the contrary, the demolition slips of a number of them suggested that they were already living in the colony, not in authorized plots but in unauthorized *jhuggis* (shacks). Their affidavits contained, amongst other declarations, the phrase: 'I solemnly declare that I ... was residing in ... jhuggi for the last ... years and that I have voluntarily demolished my jhuggi and vacated Government land'. It should perhaps be noted here that resettlement colonies have, over the years, become popular places for new incoming migrants to squat, leading to the development of what Sabir Ali (1990) has termed 'slums within slums'. The difference between having your *jhuggi* demolished in a central Delhi location and having it demolished in the marginal space of a resettlement colony was that only in the latter case was sterilization likely to be a prerequisite to resettlement. At least this is what the records in Welcome suggest. Those whose *jhuggis* were demolished in central locations had been allocated plots without having to produce evidence of sterilization. Only those whose homes were demolished within the colony and the surrounding marginal area of East Delhi had been obliged to produce DDA Family Planning Centre Allotment Orders. This perhaps accounts in part for confusion about whether or not the DDA had demanded sterilization certificates from those whose homes had been newly demolished under the slum-clearance scheme. The answer is that they *did* do so, but only in certain circumstances, linked partly to the location and more importantly to the visibility of that location. Resettlement colonies are marginal spaces away from the public eye of journalists, dignitaries and so forth. The sterilization of the displaced in such areas was unlikely to cause public outrage.

The question remains, however, as to how the DDA managed to extract its sterilization cases and under what conditions. One way of approaching this issue is, of course to speak to residents of the colony and ask them directly, but even before I had got to this stage, there were slum department officers willing to explain—not openly exactly, but nonetheless willing. Significantly, our most interesting conversations about the records generally took place in the marginal space of the corridor at the liminal phase of the end of the day, when the head clerk had left and the need to present an official version seemed less imperative. It was in just such a situation that the upper-divisional clerk one day explained: 'Looking through the files, you will get the impression that people were voluntarily getting sterilized, but actually that is not the case. It was done by force'. Asked who was doing the forcing, he explained:

Government employees ... people from the slum department. They would go around door to door and ask to see people's allotment papers. They were under a lot of pressure. They had been told that they would lose their jobs if they didn't fill targets for sterilisation. They were under force. If the residents couldn't provide all the relevant documents, they were threatened with eviction then told they could save themselves by getting sterilized or giving a case [that is, by 'motivating' someone].

This, then, is what was meant by the phrase 'regularization of a residential plot'. Regularization took place under threat of eviction. The clerk went on:

Take the iron market. ... It was demolished. At the time of demolition the traders were told that they could not get new plots unless they were sterilized or gave cases.

In this second example, the clerk had decoded what was meant by the phrase 'voluntarily destruction of one's own jhuggi'. First the building was destroyed by the DDA, and then the inhabitants were made to sign papers to the effect that they had demolished the property themselves before they were allocated a plot, in this case a commercial plot. It is no doubt the formula used in these official papers that enabled Jagmohan to state that 'compulsory sterilization' was never a prerequisite for obtaining a plot. The sterilizations were, after all, like the demolitions, 'voluntary'.

Reassessed in the light of these clarifications, the files of Welcome record the process by which the DDA, caught within a wider national structure of sterilization targets, cast its bureaucratic net over the colony in search of victims for sterilization. It found them in that ambiguous space which had always existed and which, as we have seen, still continues to exist, between the official and the unofficial. Just as today the colony contains '*jhuggi* dwellers', 'unauthorized occupants' and illegal purchasers who pay the licence fee in the name of the 'original allottee,' so in the mid-1970s it was home to a number of people who were living in the loophole between official policies and officially recognized irregularities. During the emergency that loophole tightened. Instead of being a space for negotiation it became a noose which squeezed its victims into participation in family planning, by offering them a choice between getting sterilized, paying someone else to get sterilized, or losing their access to land altogether. The rules and regulations of the colony had suddenly lost their flexibility. They now functioned as official levers with which to scoop up sterilization cases from those residents who found themselves cornered by the finer print of the law.

At first sight, the system appears to be based on a straightforward totalitarian model of a pyramid of power, in which Indira Gandhi's son, Sanjay Gandhi, imposed targets on top bureaucrats like Jagmohan who, in turn, put pressure on lower-level government employees, in this case the housing officials of the DDA. The pressure continued to accumulate downwards until it reached the individuals and families whose security and reproductive capacities were placed under direct threat. But on further perusal, there are various things that do not fit the model: in particular, the 'motivation structure' which seemed to suggest that the poor were themselves looking sideways, making deals which enabled them to avoid the imperative of the state, although in avoiding it they were simultaneously perpetuating it by getting others sterilized. Such 'motivators' seemed to conform neither to the profile of a victim nor to the profile of the official agent of the state. There was also the wider question of whether the system had really lost its flexibility, or whether it was simply that the terms and conditions of negotiation within the pyramid of power had been redefined. After all, there were some cases in which residents appeared to be using the sterilization drive as a means of negotiating a better situation.

This was suggested by the so-called 'transfer cases', in which residents tried to shift from one colony to another for whatever reason, usually to be near relatives or their place of work. Judging by the records, transferring to and from Welcome had always been difficult and applications were often refused. During the emergency, however, getting a transfer seemed to become easier. All one had to do was get sterilized or pay someone else to get sterilized in your place and the transfer was granted. Then there were the cases, not many, but a few (eleven in total), in which people had motivated their own relatives. When I tried to ask the peon why this happened, he explained that the head of the household only had the right to have one plot registered in his name. There was no point in him registering for a plot through self-sterilization if he already had a plot. But suppose his son registered for a plot in his own name by giving the motivated case of his father. That way, the family would obtain an additional plot of land without going against DDA regulations; the son would retain his fertility and the ageing father who already had enough children would get sterilized (a typical case of the demographically dubious strategies encouraged by an ill-conceived scheme). Then there were the cases where tenants seemed to have outwitted their landlords by getting sterilized and thereby becoming the rightful owners of their landlords' properties according to the new regulations. These were classified as straightforward 'regularization' cases. Such people were not simply preserving their rights to continue living in the properties they rented; they were actually obtaining new rights of ownership through sterilization. Can it be said categorically that the DDA was 'forcing' sterilizations in such cases, even if the overall structure of the scheme was coercive? When I questioned the DDA staff of Welcome on this issue, one of the lower-divisional clerks responded: 'Some were sterilized by force (*zaberdasti se*) but actually, once it was known that you could get major benefits through sterilization, then many people chose to get sterilized out of greed (*lalchi se*)'. There then followed a conversation in which all officials present emphasized the value of the rewards and the greed of people wanting plots. Force or choice? Need or greed? The records tell us much, but can they really help us unpick the relationship between these apparently contradictory motivations on the part of residents?

One additional source of information in the files consists of letters relating to disputes over plots, written by or about residents shortly after the emergency. Such letters may not enable us to distinguish categorically, victims from agents and opportunists, but they can at least help us plot the perimeters of possible action. The slum department received several such letters in the period immediately after the emergency. Needless to say this was a period of bureaucratic turbulence. Documents bear witness to the fact that the slum department had been transferred from the DDA to the MCD at the end of the emergency and the executive officer of the zone, who had signed all the family planning allotment orders, had been replaced (perhaps transferred or retired, we do not know). The slum department was now faced with the mammoth task of clearing up the debris left behind by the hastily enacted policies of the emergency. Not only was it inundated with requests from homeless people who claimed to have got sterilized but had not been issued plots; it was also faced with desperate appeals from 'original allotees', absentee landlords and squabbling tenants, some of whom had lost their plots as a result of the family planning policy.

There is no space here for entering into the details of such cases. Instead I shall simply summarize one case in order to illustrate both the complexity of the situation and the problem of how to interpret the files. The case in question involved a dispute between a man who claimed to be the original allottee (I shall call him Ram) and his tenant who was a medical practitioner.

According to a letter written by Ram's solicitor and a report furnished by the executive officer of the DDA, Ram had been allocated a plot in 1965 in exchange for the demolition of his home in the infamous slum of Jamuna Bazaar in Old Delhi. By 1968, he had built a home and was letting out one room on rent to a medical practitioner who used it for seeing clients. When around 1970, Ram left Delhi 'to attend a wedding' (possibly a euphemism for living elsewhere), his tenant, who had left the medical profession owing to various charges against him, grabbed full possession of the plot, throwing out Ram's possessions. The medical practitioner then put three tenants on the plot, from whom he collected rent. Ram appealed to the DDA on several occasions and in 1976 was told that he could reclaim the plot by furnishing a sterilization certificate. On 24 September 1976, the plot was 'regularized' in Ram's name by means of an FP allotment order. It is recorded that he re-entered his home 'with the help of the police.' However, two months later, the ex-medical practitioner broke into the house 'with the help of some local persons', recaptured the plot for a second time and continues to rent it out.

There is a high level of consistency between the solicitor's letter and the DDA executive officer's report, both of which were written in 1977, and there is a fair amount of documentary evidence to support their version of the story, but a letter from the Deputy Director (Lease and Liquidation) addressed to the Deputy Vigilance Officer in 1982, reminds us that these are only paper truths, the veracity of which was still in debate some five years later. The letter claims that there is no concrete evidence that Ram was the original allottee in 1965 since his thumb-printed documents are on DDA-headed paper, but the slum department was still under the MCD in 1965 and did not transfer to the DDA till two years later. Furthermore Ram's FP allotment order is photocopied and therefore cannot be used as proof of regularization. The officer further points out that the medical practitioner is also claiming rights to the plot on the basis that he too got sterilized, although he also lacks sufficient evidence ....

And so a paper battle unfolds, with Ram's solicitor arguing that the DDA officer who appeared as a witness in court was in 'collusion' with the ex-medical practitioner and had therefore removed the original 1965 allotment order from Ram's file. Clearly, once we take into consideration the possibility that certain papers can be removed from the files by officials of the DDA, whilst others can be added at a later date, and yet others forged possibly with the incentive of bribes, we further confirm the difficulty of untangling truths from paper truths, as well as the difficulty of distinguishing suffering from opportunism or exploitation.

What, then, is the value of trying to understand the emergency through the files, given that one is constantly up against the limitations of the evidence— the fact that all official documents, including letters, are themselves nothing more than representations? Why did I not go straight to the colony and ask people about their actual experiences? This I eventually did, but I found beginning with the files essential to the larger project of my research for a number of reasons. First, as I have already indicated, it was the files that drew me in to my research, telling me of things I could not otherwise know and guiding me as to what questions I should ask when I did eventually meet the residents of the colony. Secondly, the files provided me, not so much with accurate data to be charted, as insights into how the bureaucracy itself did the charting at a critical, but forgotten, moment of Indian history. Thirdly, it goes without saying that the personal memories of those caught up in the DDA family planning allotment scheme are no more reliable than the files in terms of telling us precisely what happened during the emergency. They too have to be approached as representations, though they are representations of a different kind, charting human experiences and emotions, speaking of fear, suffering, pragmatism, opportunism, humour, ingenuity and pain—none of which have much place in bureaucratic archives. The value of these memories lies in helping us try to chart the truth as it was for the victims and perpetrators of the state regime.

Working in the slum department may not provide access to such phenomenological truths, but it can tell us much about the significance of official papers lying about in neglected heaps in places like Welcome, but which nonetheless represent a powerful resource for action, whether in the present or the future. The documents pertaining to the emergency demonstrate more clearly than most the extent to which people's fates did, and to a large extent still do, depend on the possession of a few flimsy pieces of paper. The documents in the files and the officials' interpretations of them also suggest that people's priorities may lie more in trying to obtain appropriate bits of paper than in living lives which correspond to what is written in those papers. In this sense, though the papers do not represent reality, the importance of official paperwork is such that reality is often taken to be—and in this sense *becomes*—what is written in the papers and thus forms a basis of action. (I am reminded of Alice Totless's observation that people say Picasso's portrait of Gertrude Stein does not look like her, to which the artist is said to have replied, 'But it will!')

Ultimately, however, the significance of working in the records room as an ethnographic terrain lay not so much in what the files revealed about the rules and regulations of the colony, as in what they revealed about the dynamics of people's relationship to those rules—by which I mean the relationship both of bureaucrats and ordinary citizens to the everyday bureaucratic structures within which they live their lives. Given that so many of us—not just evicted slum dwellers in India—live today in a world permeated with bureaucratic features, it seems to me that the relationship between people and papers is something that anthropologists cannot, or at least should not, ignore. Certainly, in my own attempts to come to grips with people's experiences of the emergency, understanding this relationship has been central.

Bureaucratic effacements

Having devoted most of this paper to tracing how slum department records provide a means to remembering the emergency, I would like to end by suggesting that they also provide insight into the process by which the emergency became a forgotten moment. For the files represent history in the process of being made, and in this sense, they embody all the different stages of the emergency—its emergence, its enactment *and* its forgetting.

I therefore want to end by examining three bureaucratic responses to the post-emergency confusion over the ownership of plots in Welcome. The first of these is dated May 1977, some six weeks after the new executive officer had come to power. He was clearly confused by some of the family planning documents he was receiving and wrote to his superior for clarification:

Some persons have come with allotment orders issued by Shri K. K. Nayyar, the then executive officer. The allotment order is made provisionally. I find the word 'provisionally' does not bear any material significance in this regard because once a person raises a structure over the plot there is no point in cancelling the same.

This was surely a very reasonable point. The new officer estimated that there were about one hundred cases of people with provisional allotment papers who did not yet have plots and asked whether such provisional allotments should be honoured or not. To this, the Deputy Commissioner replied that since the allotment orders were issued by a duly authorized officer of the DDA, 'we have no option but to honour them'. No attempt was made, however, to remove the term 'provisionally' from the allotment orders, with the result that these and some 900 other family planning allotments made in Welcome are all officially classified as 'provisional' to this day. This means that their owners are still living in the grey zone of uncertainty, well-placed for potential exploitation in the future should things turn critical again. By June 1977 (one month later), the lenient and reasonable attitude of the new executive officer was beginning to waver. In response to a request from a Muslim woman, who had 'motivated' her husband to get sterilized but had not yet received a plot, the executive officer came out with the curious statement: 'There was no such policy approved by the DDA that those who undergo sterilization will be allotted plots'. Nonetheless, he again passed the case to his superior, the Deputy Commissioner, who again said that 'there is no option but to allot a plot'.

By 1979, however, the slum department officials seem to have gone one step further in trying to wipe out the entire sterilization episode. Evidence of this is found in a circular, issued from the MCD headquarters on 7 July 1979 and addressed to all executive officers of the slum department. The circular refers to a meeting held some four days earlier in which item no. 98 for discussion was: 'the cancellation of allotment of plots/built up houses made during the emergency on the basis of sterilization'. In this meeting, a committee had decided to postpone the issue until provided with concrete examples for discussion. It therefore requested the executive officers to collect examples of sterilization allotments, regularizations and transfers for discussion in a meeting the following week.

What is revealed in the MCD responses to the sterilization issue is a gradual progression from tolerance to denial and finally attempted effacement. The MCD was contributing to the growing national trend, already fairly developed by mid-1979, of forgetting the emergency. What was to happen to the thousands of people who, only three years earlier, had been forced to adjust to the slum department's demand for sterilization certificates, often by losing their own fertility, we shall never know. Yet one shudders to think of their vulnerability as officials casually contemplated a reversal of the entire system. No information is available concerning the outcome of the second meeting. Probably once the scale of the phenomenon was realized, it was decided that cancellation of the family planning allotment orders would cause too much havoc. Better then to defer the issue, to leave the pending cases pending. It is no doubt for this reason that most of the requests in relation to family planning allotments still lie buried in a file marked 'pending cases'.

By 1980, the emergency had ceased to be a matter of national concern. In that year, Indira Gandhi returned to power and forgetting the emergency became a national duty.

Notes

1. The colony's official name is 'Seelampur phases 3 and 4', but it is locally known as Welcome after the Welcome Hair Oil Factory that used to dominate the landscape. It is situated in the Shahdara District on the eastern side of the River Jamuna which dissects the capital not only geographically but also socially. The phrase 'Trans-Jamuna' used to describe this part of Delhi reveals the 'west-is-centre' logic of the city.
2. Two recent volumes attempt to rewrite the history of partition though the voices of ordinary people whose lives were enmested in the event; see Butalia 1998; Menon and Bhasin 1998.
3. Marika Vicziany's work on the coercive nature of family planning in the period before the emergency is exceptional in treating the issue of sterilization within the much wider framework of inequality and relationships between citizen and state, cf. Vicziany (1982–3).

References

Ali, S. 1990. *Slums within slums: a study of resettlement colonies in Delhi*. Delhi: Har Anand/Vikas.
Amin, S. 1995. *Event, metaphor, memory: Chauri Chaura 1922–1992*. Delhi: Oxford University Press.

Butalia, U. 1998. *The other side of silence: voices from the partition of India.* Delhi: Viking.

Chib, S. S. 1978. *Nineteen fateful months.* Delhi: Light and Life.

Das, V. 1995. *Critical events.* Delhi: Oxford University Press.

Dayal, J., and A. Bose. 1977. *For reasons of state: Delhi under emergency.* Delhi: Ess Ess Publications.

Henderson, M. 1977. *Experiment with untruth: India under emergency.* Delhi: Macmillan.

Jagmohan. 1978. *Island of truth.* Delhi: Vikas.

Menon, R., and K. Bhasin. 1998. *Borders and boundaries: women in India's partition.* Delhi: Kali for Women.

Mistry, R. 1996. *A fine balance.* London: Faber and Faber.

Nandy, A. 1995. Emergency remembered. *Times of India*, 22 June.

Pandey, G. n.d. Nation and masculinity: some reflections on Gandhi and the partition of India. Paper at *Gandhi and his legacy* workshop, October 1995, Centre of South Asian Studies, SOAS.

Shah Commission. 1978. *Shah commission of enquiry*, third and final report. New Delhi: Government of India.

Selbourne, D. 1977. *An eye to India: the unmasking of tyranny.* Harmondsworth: Penguin.

Sinha, B. M. 1977. *Operation emergency.* Delhi: Hind Pocket Books.

Tarlo, E. 1995. From victim to agent: memories of the emergency from a resettlement colony in Delhi. *Economic and Political Weekly* 30: 2921–8.

——. n.d. *Unsettling memories: narratives of the emergency in Delhi.* London: Hurst, forthcoming.

Vicziany, M. 1982–3. Coercion in a soft state: the family-planning program of India: part 1, The myth of voluntarism; part 2, The sources of coercion. *Pacific Affairs* 55, 3: 373–401; 4: 557–93.

Dimensions of dominance: class and state in Uttar Pradesh

Craig Jeffrey and Jens Lerche

This essay explores the relationship between state power and class reproduction in the Indian countryside. The analysis focuses on the different relationships between low-caste rural workers and the local state, and Jat capitalist farmers and the local state in Uttar Pradesh. Access to certain forms of state power is shown to be closely circumscribed by the ability to mobilize material resources, and therefore by class position. This evidence goes against the projection of a simplistic state-versus-people contradiction, a perception common in most of the literature pertaining to state and civil society as well as in most post-structuralist writings.

The essay begins with a review of recent approaches to the state and society in India before focusing in particular on Akhil Gupta's model of rural discourse and the local state in north India. This provides a basis for an examination of the relationship between rural elites and local state bureaucracies in three parts of Uttar Pradesh. We examine the different balance of colonization, co-option and opposition that characterizes the relationship between dominant rural castes and local state officials and institutions. In the final empirical section of the paper, we refer to the rise of the Bahujan Samaj Party (BSP) in Uttar Pradesh and its impact on local class relations. We conclude by pointing to what we see as the most important limitations of Gupta's recent work, particularly his lack of attention to the scale and social location of local political privilege, and his inattention to class contradiction. We close by outlining certain implications for wider debate on state-society relations.

The state in India

The influence of state policies on class relations in rural India is widely acknowledged. State policies have reinforced economic inequalities based upon access to agricultural land during the past thirty-five years. The introduction of new agricultural technologies from the mid-1960s, and subsequent concessions to the rich-farmer lobby, have enhanced the economic position of surplus-producing middle- and upper-caste peasants relative to landless low castes (Byres 1988; Duncan 1988; Hasan 1989).

Within the political economy tradition, Pranab Bardhan observes that state policies towards low-caste rural workers are conditioned by the state's requirement for a sheen of legitimacy among the subalterns (Bardhan 1984). Bardhan does not explore, though, how class reproduction is related to the activities of various state institutions and officers. Nor does he attend to how discourses circulated by the state are reinterpreted by the public (cf. Gupta 1989).

Partly in response to the lack of such sensitivity in the standard literature on the political economy of India, a number of authors, writing from a broadly post-colonial perspective, have drawn attention to questions of public discourse. Sudipta Kaviraj, Satish Saberwal and Partha Chatterjee all argue that the core dichotomy in India today is between the modern discourse of the elite and its state, and a public 'community' or 'lower' discourse (Chatterjee 1993; Kaviraj 1984; 1991; Saberwal 1996). The modern elite and the dominant capitalist classes are not sufficiently strong simply to impose the modernity discourse on society. To Kaviraj and Saberwal, the discursive dichotomy exists even within the state, between a modern Weberian bureaucracy at a higher level versus the lower ranks of bureaucrats. This perspective appears to correspond rather well with reports of collusion between reactionary elites and the local administration, and common perceptions of local-level corruption (e.g. Herring 1983).

Opposed to more Foucauldian analyses claiming that the hegemony of the modernity discourse in the Third World is almost total (e.g. Du Bois 1991; Escobar 1995), Kaviraj, Saberwal and Chatterjee thus argue for the continuing existence of an important discourse, or set of discourses, disconnected in its source from the state. Hence, while the simple non-class-based state-society dichotomy proposed by this brand of Indian post-colonial writings is problematic, they usefully highlight the need to focus on public, as distinct from state discourses and practices.

Drawing on ethnographic fieldwork in a region of western Uttar Pradesh, Gupta (1995; 1997; 1998) has explored the nature of public discourses on the state. In an important article, Gupta (1995) examines how different sections of rural and small-town society have sought to penetrate, imagine and contest the local state. Through an analysis of the everyday practices of local bureaucrats and the representation of the state in local newspapers, Gupta argues that corruption is at the core of the discursive construction of the state (Ibid.: 376). This argument is based on the assertion that a common interest in improving accountability exists within rural society. For Gupta, differently positioned actors—lower castes, rich peasants, newspaper reporters—can be gathered together under the headings of 'subalterns' (Ibid.: 393), 'the public' (Ibid.: 392) or 'plebeians' (Ibid.: 394). A 'zone of cultural debate'—'public culture'—exists, which appears to be available to all rural groups and within which the discursive construction of the state is built up through the circulation of notions of corruption and accountability.

In his most recent writings, Gupta (1997; 1998) draws on his insights into public discourses on the state to identify two types of populism: the ruling Congress party and its leader Indira Gandhi's populism of the 1970s, and what he terms 'agrarian populism'. He argues that populism, especially agrarian populism, is the 'most important feature' of 'developmentalism' in India (Gupta 1998: 33–4). Agrarian populism has its roots among the modern-surplus producing farmers of the green-revolution belt of northwestern India (the states of Punjab, Haryana and western Uttar Pradesh) who have succeeded in constructing their own brand of populism, claiming to represent the countryside against the city, or *Bharat* against India. The main actors in this process were the peasant leader Charan Singh and, later, the farmers' union, the Bharatiya Kisan Union (Ibid.: 75). Agrarian populism was constructed chiefly on two levels. First, the state-sponsored development discourse was criticized for having failed to deliver the growth and welfare it had promised. As part of this, government corruption and mismanagement were criticized (Ibid.: 88–90). Second, a 'thoroughgoing critique of the industrial-centred model of development itself' (Ibid.: 91) was delivered, challenging the overall development discourse (Ibid.: 80ff). According to Gupta, agrarian populism was successful in bridging class divisions within the rural population, partly due to the immediate appeal of its criticism of government policies, and partly due to the common interests between different classes sketched above (Ibid.: 97).

Gupta's work therefore complements previous post-colonial works in a number of important ways. Its field-based evidence aims at substantiating what was previously only an assumption: namely, that a public discourse of the state, different from the discourse circulated by the state itself, exists in contemporary India. Moreover, Gupta seeks to demonstrate that the public discourse is truly public in the sense that it cross-cuts class divisions —a conclusion which he purports to back up with empirical evidence about the similarities among practices and discourses of various rural classes. Implicitly opposed to attempts by Bardhan (1984) and Kaviraj (1988) to distinguish between class interests and vertical populist organizational forms, Gupta uses his material to claim that horizontal and vertical interests and organizations have been conflated into agrarian populism in Indian villages. Hence, the primacy of the state-society dichotomy over class is no longer a postulate; it has been shown to be an empirical fact.

Gupta's argument will be discussed in the concluding part of this essay. Here, it suffices to point out that his empirical analysis of the rural population's efforts to obtain local state resources is concerned only with the state-society interface mediated by the *pradhan* (the local mayor). It is unclear why this is given primacy over other types of state-society relations which may be of equal importance for public discourse about the state and for the reproduction of rural social groups.[1] Serious omissions include the collusion between rich farmers and the police, and rich farmers' access to government jobs.

Unlike Gupta, we will argue that access to these forms of state power has become central in the reproduction of class advantage in the areas which we investigated in Uttar Pradesh. This will provide a platform for exploring under what conditions and to what extent this power may be undermined by less advantaged groups. Empirically, the class category is explored within caste (*jati*) groups, as both villagers and scholars commonly acknowledge that a rough class-caste approximation exists in this part of India. Class division within the caste group is primarily established by using land ownership as the proxy, followed by an assessment of non-agricultural professional employment and capability to influence local government institutions. While there are a number of minor problems with this methodology, it does give a good overview of social differentiation and its interlinkage with access to government resources.[2]

Class differentiation and the local state in Uttar Pradesh

Meerut District: working the fields

Our account of rich farmers' collusion with state officials draws primarily on twelve months fieldwork conducted by Craig Jeffrey in Meerut District, which forms part of the fertile Upper Doab region of western Uttar Pradesh.[3] The introduction of new agricultural technologies from the mid-1960s resulted in a sharp rise in agricultural productivity (Patnaik and Hasan 1995; Sharma and Poleman 1994). Meerut District is now characterized by highly profitable sugar-cane and wheat agriculture.

Jeffrey's research focused upon the economic, social and political strategies of members of four Jat kinship groups in the township of Daurala and the two villages of Masuri and Khanpur.[4] All these settlements are located within 25 kilometres of Meerut city. Interviews were also conducted with a random sample of fifteen Scheduled Caste (SC) male household heads, thirteen men from poorer Other Backward Castes (OBC) or Most Backward Castes (MBC), and two Muslim men.[5] In each of these interviews, broader information about lineages was sought. In each settlement, Jats constitute between a third and a half of the total population and own and cultivate over 90 per cent of the agricultural land. The Scheduled Caste population varies between 10 per cent in Khanpur and 33 per cent in Masuri.[6]

The research showed that there are clear differences within the Jat caste and between Jats and lower castes in access to land, lucrative non-agricultural employment and state power. Of the 250 households within the four Jat lineages, 66 per cent possess a claim to 6 acres of agricultural land or less, 22 per cent to between 6 and 12 acres and 12 per cent to more than 12 acres of land. Jats owning more than 12 acres typically employ 'permanent' labourers on contracts of between six and nine months. It is common for those cultivating more than 6 acres of land to employ temporary workers for the most labour-intensive agricultural activities. Of the seventy-three Scheduled Caste households in the sample, 33 per cent own agricultural land, either outright or in partnership. Only one of these households possesses more than 4 acres. Only 7 per cent of the seventy Most Backward Caste households, and 15 per cent of the Muslim households, within the sample own agricultural land. None of these households possesses more than 4 acres.

The reproduction of a class of rich Jat landowners is related to state policies and state institutions in a number of ways. It was this group that was the first to take advantage of the influx of green revolution technologies in the 1960s. Between 1965 and 1985, these cultivators intensified their agricultural production through investment in electric tube-well irrigation and tractors, the adoption of improved varieties of sugar-cane and wheat, and the application of chemical fertilizers. The resulting increase in agricultural yields, combined with favourable state procurement prices for cane and wheat, increased the rates of return from agriculture.

Rich farmers seek to spread economic risk and raise their social status through investing their agricultural surplus in efforts at acquiring salaried employment (usually within the public sector) or off-farm business for their sons.[7] A well-placed son is widely regarded as providing a Jat father and mother with long-term economic security. Public-sector employment is particularly favoured since it provides financial security, frequently offers opportunities to extract side incomes and entails minimal work. In contrast, semi-skilled or unskilled wage labour is regarded as insecure, burdensome and demeaning amongst Jats.

A few rich Jats diversified out of farming before Independence. Of the forty-nine Jat men born between 1898 and 1922 for which we have occupational information, thirty-two were farmers, seven entered the British system of local administration before 1947 and one became a politician after Independence. This privileged minority benefited from the spread of the Arya Samaj Hindu reform movement in western Uttar Pradesh (see Dutta 1997), colonial stereotypes stressing the honesty of the Jats (Stokes 1986), and the availability of secondary schools and tertiary education in Meerut. Six of the fifteen male descendants of this group have managed to enter higher professional employment.[8]

A second generation of Jats, born between 1922 and 1946, made a more dramatic shift out of farming. Of the sixty-three male Jats raised in households possessing more than 12 acres of agricultural land, 14 per cent entered higher professional employment, chiefly medicine and tertiary-level teaching, but also including law, engineering and senior administration. Rich young men who failed to obtain such prestigious employment have remained in agriculture or entered low-ranking professional or white-collar employment.

Since 1947, the move out of agriculture among richer Jats has continued. Of the eighty men born in households possessing over 12 acres of land, but not involved in higher employment or business, 11 per cent entered higher professional employment and 26 per cent entered low-ranking professional or white-collar employment. Of the thirty-one men born in higher professional households, 39 per cent entered higher professional employment and 32 per cent entered low-ranking professional or white-collar employment. A number of richer farmers have also sought to reduce economic risk through establishing off-farm businesses. These are usually small-scale concerns such as rural shops, agricultural processing units, educational institutions and transport or construction operations run through a contract with the government or a sugar mill. Only a single adult male descended from a richer farmer or higher professional has entered unskilled or semi-skilled wage labour.

Jats raised in households possessing 12 acres of land or less often face the more immediate threat of the subdivision of agricultural land and an attendant decline in their economic and social status. Opposed to the larger landowners, this group has found it difficult to obtain higher professional employment. Instead, they have been reasonably successful at securing low-ranking government, army, police, teaching, and factory employment during the past thirty years. Of the ninety adult male Jats born after 1946, descended from Jats possessing 12 acres or less, 35 per cent have entered these forms of employment. A small number of these households have also entered off-farm business, usually owning and running shops, small transport businesses or agricultural processing units. The smaller landowners have also had to find non-agricultural income sources from even less distinguished sources. Of the 190 adult men born after 1946, and descended from Jats possessing a claim to 12 acres or less, 18 per cent have moved into unskilled or semi-skilled wage labour, usually as private drivers or factory workers; 7 per cent maintained that they are *berozgari* (unemployed). The evidence of a shift into professional employment amongst the Jat elite and a very different, lower-ranking non-agrarian occupational structure among the smaller Jat landowners points to class differentiation within the four lineages and the caste.

Nevertheless, compared to other lower castes, Jats have been largely successful in reproducing their local economic advantage during the twentieth century. Of the 413 male Jats in the four-lineage sample, 10 per cent are presently in higher professional employment and 31 per cent are in low-ranking professional or white-collar work; the corresponding figures for 248 low-castes and Muslim males are 2 per cent and 12 per cent. Among low-caste and Muslim adult men, 69 per cent are presently employed as unskilled or semi-skilled wage labourers, compared with a figure of just 8 per cent for the Jats.

The success of the Jats in obtaining government employment is all the more remarkable in the light of their exclusion from reservations tailored towards improving the access of SCs and OBCs to public-sector employment. Differential access to public-sector employment is reproduced through an informal market in government posts. Corruption in the allocation of public-sector positions is particularly associated with the recruitment procedures managed by the Staff Selection Commission (SSC) (at the central level) and Uttar Pradesh Public Service Commission (PSC) (at the state level). State-level recruitment run through the Uttar Pradesh PSC is based upon a system of examinations and interviews. After the examinations, candidates are grouped by caste. Those performing best within each group are called for interview. Positions are then allocated on the basis of these interviews. Recruitment organized through the SSC follows a similar pattern, although physical tests are conducted for the police force and allied services.

Corruption occurs at various stages within the processes of recruitment overseen by these institutions. During group discussions held at

Meerut University, students referred to how many candidates pay large bribes to obtain examination papers before a public service examination. Nevertheless, most respondents claimed that money changes hands *after* a candidate has successfully negotiated the written examination, or written examination and physical test. A young Jat from a rich family in Daurala, claimed that in an interview for a clerical post within the Uttar Pradesh Roadways 'they won't even look at you' until you give Rs 60,000.

The widespread existence of such practices in the recruitment procedures overseen by the SSC and Uttar Pradesh PSC results in references to a 'market' in government jobs. Most Jats maintained that it is necessary to pay between Rs 40,000 and 75,000 to become a police constable, Rs 30,000 to 50,000 to enrol successfully as an army sepoy, Rs 20,000 to 60,000 to become a bus conductor in Uttar Pradesh Roadways, Rs 5,000 to 20,000 for a government or private-run factory job, and Rs 40,000 to 70,000 for a low-ranking clerical position within the bureaucracy. This market is said to have emerged in the late 1970s as a result of population increase and a rise in the number of graduates without a parallel expansion in the bureaucracy or sufficient growth in the industrial and service sectors. Prices are said to have risen as a result of the national extension of OBC reservations in 1991. A similar market has emerged in the reserved sector, where prices in Meerut District are generally said to be between one-half and two-thirds of the figures quoted for the Jats.

In this context, entry into public-sector employment depends upon access to money, information and contacts. A number of Jats claim to possess a 'link', 'source' or *jan paychan* ('known and recognized figure') within a government department. This may refer to an acquaintance within the bureaucracy, who is expected to ensure that a bribe reaches the right person or to someone trusted to represent the interests of the candidate more forcefully. In the latter case, the role of the contact may be to lobby officials so that a bribe proves unnecessary or to ensure an official's complicity following the payment of a bribe.

A range of clerks employed by the state act as intermediaries or dealers between Jat candidates and recruitment officers or more senior officials. For example, civilian clerks within the military take money from candidates in return for assistance in sepoy-level recruitment tests. A second type of dealer is not employed by the state. These brokers are referred to as being especially cunning, well-connected men: *ghumte phirte admi* ('the wandering men') according to a MBC male from Khanpur village. This category includes retired military or police officers operating between candidates and police or army recruitment officials. According to Jat students interviewed in Meerut, these men typically wait until a candidate has passed his medical and physical test before arranging a deal, but also leak test papers to candidates and bribe physical examiners.

The large bribes required to secure public-sector positions make it impossible for most SCs, and the poorest Jats within the four lineages, to obtain government posts. A number of Jat households which can afford to pay substantial bribes lack the necessary political clout and social status to establish effective links with reliable brokers or state officials. We heard a large number of references to dealers who had cheated SCs, MBCs, Muslims and poorer Jats. The case of Jaipal, a small Jat farmer in Masuri, illustrates one way in which such cheating occurs. Faced with the prospect of the future division of his 4 acres, Jaipal sought to arrange government employment for his son. He put his faith in a local policeman who claimed to have influence with the police bureaucracy. Jaipal gave this man Rs 20,000 and received an assurance that a police post would be forthcoming. The policeman then returned some months later, having been unsuccessful, and returned Rs 15,000. He claimed that Rs 5,000 had been spent on 'travelling expenses'. This happened three times before Jaipal decided to give up. After Jaipal had recounted his story, a rich Jat commented that the policeman would not have risked cheating on a village big-man (*bare bare admi*).

The economic success of male Jats in general, and richer Jat farmers in particular, has also been closely linked to their ability to secure other state privileges. In his research in Bulandshahr District, Gupta provides a model for understanding the superior access of the rural rich to state resources. Drawing on empirical research in a village and small town in this district, Gupta describes a form of political brokerage centring on the activity of upper class *pradhans* of the village *panchayats*. These officials channel government resources earmarked for development to their supporters in the village (Gupta 1998: 146).

Jats in Daurala, Khanpur and Masuri have been able to control the *pradhanship* of these settlements for most of the past fifty years. Nevertheless, by 1997, the *pradhans* in all the three settlements belonged to the low castes. These men had taken advantage of recent reservations in *panchayat* appointment and one individual had even managed to obtain considerable independence from the Jats. This reflects the fact that the ability to cream off state resources, through obtaining a formal position within the *panchayat*, has become less important for rural Jats in Meerut District than acquiring positions within public-sector employment and privileged access to police and judicial protection.

In defending access to a portion of agricultural land, Jats often require quick and decisive police or legal intervention. Police protection and legal judgments have become almost wholly privatized in the Upper Doab of western Uttar Pradesh (Brass 1997). Within these 'shadow states' in police and judicial assistance, transaction costs are high. As a former Member of the Legislative Assembly (MLA) argued, 'you cannot just walk into a police station and say "how much should I pay?"'. In this context, procedures are organized in networks built around key individuals. These usually involve a series of stages of authorization that are consistent with the desire or need amongst politicians and state officials to accumulate rental incomes from their posts.

Politicians are often intermediaries between the public and police officials, judges or magistrates.[9] A former Jat MLA living in Meerut, described the process as follows:

> The farmer will approach the MLA with a problem. The MLA will then phone or go to the police station or SP's (Superintendent of Police's) office. The police officer will either say 'Give me this much and I will get your work done' or it will just work with influence. The MLA will go back [to the farmer] and say 'he has asked for Rs 15,000', when in fact he only asked for Rs 10,000. So politicians have become like commission agents.

Jats identified certain individuals who possess a 'link' with a local MLA or MP. For the Jat member of the public, the 'link' translates into an expectation that the politician will assist as far as possible in 'getting work done' by ensuring the co-operation of state officials to accomplish an identified task. For the politician, the rural or urban Jat provides a means of effectively canvassing votes and raising funds before elections. We estimate that between twelve and nineteen Jat male household heads (between 5 and 8 per cent) within the four-lineage sample possessed a link with an MP or MLA.

The most important benefit of possessing such a political link is the enhanced bargaining power it delivers in interactions with local and district-level officials and other Jats within 'civil society'. District Magistrates (DMs), Sub-Divisional Magistrate (SDMs) and Senior Superintendents of Police (SSPs) usually seek to appease MLAs and MPs, whose co-operation is likely to increase opportunities to extract rental incomes from their posts. Senior state officials are also aware that politicians may punish or reward them through their influence on the transfer of officials (cf. Wade 1985).

Three or four Jats originating within each settlement, and possessing links with a politician, regularly assist friends, kin, caste members, and even people of other castes, in making contact with state officials. These

Jats may be viewed as lobbyists, or gatekeepers to the local state, for large sections of the rural population. They tend to be younger, better educated and more mobile than the large landowners who presided over land disputes and provided access to state officials before Independence. This mediating role may provide an opportunity to extract a rent, individually or in league with a politician. The lobbying role also occasionally provides a platform for a political career either inside the village or urban *mohalla* (neighbourhood), or at the district or MLA constituency level.

It is therefore possible to perceive a chain of negotiations associated with access to police and judicial assistance. A person may approach a lobbyist who is likely to take up the case at hand. The two men may then arrange a meeting with a local politician who will probably, but not inevitably, agree to lend his weight to the cause by accompanying them to meet a senior official.[10] If the senior official is persuaded by their arguments, they are likely to instruct local officials to take up the case or promise to issue a favourable judgment in a legal dispute. A powerful rich Jat farmer may be able to avoid seeking the assistance of lobbyists and politicians and contact senior police officials directly.

In this context, the ability of a rural Jat to secure state assistance is inversely proportional to the number of mediators through which he or she operates and the size of the bribe that the mediators claim must be paid in order to guarantee help. There is a striking correlation between land size and rural power thus conceived. Seventeen of the nineteen male Jat household heads whom we strongly suspected of possessing a link with a MLA or MP, like all the Jats acting as lobbyists, possessed a claim to over 12 acres of agricultural land.

Scheduled Castes, MBCs and Muslims lack the resources to build effective links with politicians. In the absence of political links, SC, MBC and Muslim men argue that they would have to pay large bribes in order to compete effectively with Jats in struggles over access to state officials in a dispute. Of the thirty SC, MBC or Muslim household heads, three claimed to have been the recent victims of Jat aggression related to land. During fieldwork we encountered many other references to such crimes. Low-caste people and Muslims are frequently afraid of naming Jats in reports made to the police and they are sceptical of their chances of obtaining fair decisions through the judiciary.

Muzaffarnagar District: Kisan raj

In other parts of western Uttar Pradesh, dominant landowners have adopted a rather different strategy in their relationship with local state officers and institutions. This may be illustrated with reference to Jens

Lerche's research in the Jat-dominated village of Mirpur (fictitious name) in Muzaffarnagar District bordering Meerut District to the north. This village was surveyed in 1993 by Lerche, and revisited in 1996 and 1998.[11] Of the 449 households in this settlement, 46 per cent are Jats and 23 per cent are Jatavs (SCs; called 'Chamars' by the Jats). The Jats own 95 per cent of the land. The village is fully irrigated by electric tubewells, and nearly everyone ploughs by tractor. The main crop, which covers about 90 per cent of the fields, is sugar-cane. About half of this crop is typically sold to nearby state sugar mills at high government prices.

Landownership among the Jats of Mirpur in Muzaffarnagar District is slightly less polarized than in the Meerut villages studied by Jeffrey. Of the 204 Jat households, 65 per cent own less than 6 acres of land and 5 per cent possess over 12 acres. The orientation towards non-agricultural occupations is stronger in the Muzaffarnagar case with nearly half of all Jat households (46 per cent) engaged in professional and public-sector employment. As in Meerut, those owning more than 12 acres of land are significantly better represented in higher professional occupations (27 per cent versus 4 per cent). Only 4 per cent of the 229 low-caste and Muslim households of the village own land. Historically, these groups found employment as craftsmen or agricultural labourers for the Jats. Since the late 1960s, however, a sizeable number of the male earners within these groups have entered slightly better paid non-agricultural occupations, such as brick-kiln work. A fairly high proportion has also managed to move into more lucrative low-ranking government employment (29 per cent).

The relationship between the Jats of Mirpur and local state institutions has been defined by the close involvement of this caste in the Bharatiya Kisan Union (BKU) farmers' movement. Mirpur is situated just 5 kilometres from the BKU's headquarters at Sisauli. The BKU is primarily a Jat organization based on strong clan ties among Jats. It is led by a traditional Jat caste leader, Mahendra Singh Tikait, who is also the *chaudhuri* (headman) of the Balliyan *khap*, the clan of the Mirpur Jats. In the late 1980s, the BKU managed to create a 'village republic' in its heartland around Sisauli. The historical juridical autonomy of the Jats—and their independent 'police force'—was revived in a Jat *kisan raj* ('farmers' rule'). Police and other government officials were barred from entering the villages, unless they obtained permission from Tikait or the Jat village councils. Tikait effectively controlled whether or not criminal cases were referred to the police and courts. He also tried to limit the power of officers within the official *panchayat* system of local government. More generally, Tikait and his powerful Jat supporters were able to police low-caste social activity in the village, forcibly preventing them from voting in elections and coercing them into supporting the BKU movement. For example, in Mirpur the local Jat council ruled that at least one person from each household of the village, including all low-caste households, was obliged to take part in BKU actions. Low-caste people were fined and abused if they did not oblige. In Mirpur, rich Jat control over state officers and institutions was therefore achieved through direct expressions of physical and organizational power, rather than through the more dispersed collusive methods employed by rich Jats in Meerut District.

Jaunpur District: Thakur hegemony

The third case study is of Deogaon (fictitious name), a village in Jaunpur District of eastern Uttar Pradesh, surveyed by Jens Lerche in 1992–3 and revisited in 1996 and 1998. Since Independence, upper-caste Thakur and Brahman control over landownership in Deogaon has been significantly undermined by the acquisition of land by former tenant farmers belonging to the middle-ranking Yadav caste. The agricultural labourers of the village belong to the Chamar caste who are Scheduled Castes, while village crafts and services are still done by designated service-caste households. The focus of the fieldwork was on the core Thakur and Brahman hamlet of the revenue village, Madhya Deogaon, and on the Chamar and Yadav hamlets (Station Par and Paradeipur).

The land belonging to the Madhya Deogaon households is almost fully irrigated by tubewells. Wheat is the main crop by value and area. Land distribution among the fifty-eight Thakur and Brahman households of Madhya Deogaon mirrors that of Muzaffarnagar village. Of these fifty-eight households, 72 per cent possess less than 6 acres of land and 12 per cent own 12 acres or more. As in Meerut and Muzaffarnagar districts, the large landowners have been particularly successful in entering high-ranking professional occupations, although the small sample prevents firm conclusions. Among Thakur and Brahman households, 47 per cent draw on incomes from low-ranking professional or white-collar employment. The Yadavs are small peasants owning on average 3 acres of land. Only 17 per cent are engaged in low-ranking professional or white-collar jobs. Of the eighty-six SC households, three-quarters own land but none possesses more than two *bighas* (1.33 acres); 26 per cent are engaged in low-ranking, public-sector professional or white-collar employment.

Like the Jats in Meerut District, the Thakurs of eastern Uttar Pradesh have negotiated privileged access to state benefits through acts of regular collusion with state officials. This is evident in the attempts of Thakurs to take advantage of irrigation programmes and of loans designed to assist small farmers. Many Thakurs have acquired cheap irrigation materials and other benefits associated with the irrigation programme by bribing or exerting influence on the local *patwari* (who keeps the land records), *gram sevak* (council officer) and *pradhan*. These state officials collude in falsely listing Thakurs as 'small farmers' entitled to be beneficiaries of the scheme. Thakurs have also been able to avoid being taken to court over cases of violence or theft perpetrated against low castes by bribing or exerting influence on local police officials. Compared with the Jats of western Uttar Pradesh, however, the Thakurs' hold over the local state is fragile. Their main competitors for power and land in the village are the OBC Yadavs who, for a period, managed to take over the *pradhanship*. But SCs have also openly defied Thakurs in Deogaon. For example, even though labour relations are not wholly free, SC agricultural labourers have negotiated wage increases every third year since 1972 by organizing strikes.

Emancipatory processes and the state

The role of the local state in class reproduction changed in a number of important ways in the mid-1990s. This was closely related to the coming to power in Uttar Pradesh of the low-caste Bahujan Samaj Party (BSP). The BSP can be seen as a party primarily serving the new SC middle classes, but it projects itself as representing all low-caste interests, and has been successful in mobilizing the low castes through fierce anti-high-caste rhetoric. Following the breakdown of the Congress(I)'s political hegemony in the late 1980s, the BSP became a junior partner in an anti-high-caste, middle-class-based coalition government in Uttar Pradesh in 1992–5, and BSP-led governments were established briefly in 1995 and 1997 under the stewardship of an SC woman, Mayawati.[12] While in charge of the government, the party targeted welfare programmes at SC groups and attempted to build a low-caste hegemony within the civil service through the allocation of key public-sector administrative posts to SCs. It also spearheaded a campaign against caste-based cultural violence, oppression and discrimination, symbolically centred around the installation of statues of the SCs' historical leader, Dr Ambedkar, across Uttar Pradesh.

The BSP was very successful in promoting emancipatory processes which were already under way among the SCs. The new assertiveness of low-caste people led to several clashes over social status, land and wages with middle and upper castes. The SCs' previously deferential behaviour *vis-à-vis* the landed middle and upper castes has been replaced either by open challenge or, where that is not possible, by a quiet knowledge of their enhanced position.

The low-caste people of the fieldwork villages assess these changes in a fairly uniform way. The SCs said they had acquired 'self-respect' or become 'confident' (*swabhiman*), 'zealous' (*utsah*) and 'courageous' (using the English term). In the Muzaffarnagar village, one SC man commented with a laugh on the newly-found state protection against caste-based violence: 'We are like 11,000 volt electrical wire—everybody has become scared to burn their hands'. In Meerut District, one SC man in Daurala claimed that Jats 'are a little afraid of us now'. A rich Jat in the same settlement argued that 'if an Ambedkar statue is put up in our fields we can do nothing'. In the Jaunpur village, a group of SCs started their explanation of the events during the 1993–6 period by saying 'everything had changed' in their relationship to the Thakurs, and the Thakurs had stopped referring to any SCs as 'our own' (*niji*).

Scheduled Castes generally linked their new confidence to changes that had occurred in the relationship between SCs and the state. In the Muzaffarnagar village, the increase in the confidence and assertiveness of SCs coincided with a decline in the BKU as a political force. These changes combined to end *kisan raj* and open up opportunities for SCs to influence local state officials. For example, during the first Mayawati regime, the SCs in the village complained to the District Magistrate about two Jats who had encroached on a cremation ground used by Banghi, Julaha and Jatav people. The local government administration's answer came promptly as the *tehsildar* (senior land-revenue officer) arrived in the village to investigate the issue. Moreover, in the atmosphere of political support for SCs, the Jat *pradhan* in Mirpur has accepted certain SC rights. On his instruction, beating up SC men and attempting to molest SC women, which were commonly done by drunken young Jats after the yearly Holi festival, have also come to an end since 1996. The *pradhan* has also secured certain government funds for the SCs, most importantly channelling money into the construction of a new communal hall for Jatavs worth Rs 80,000.

Scheduled Castes have also benefited from an increase in the stringency with which the Scheduled Castes and Scheduled Tribes (Prevention of Atrocities) Act (1989) has been implemented. The Mayawati government breathed new life into this legislation, which is formally directed at reducing caste-based atrocities and discrimination. Mayawati initiated fast-track investigation of any claims of abuse, jailed the accused while the case was investigated and awarded Rs 6,000 to assist with legal expenses to any victim of caste-based crime. In Deogaon, for example, two or maybe three cases were registered and followed up by the police according to the letter of the law. This signalled changes in the official attitude to high- and low-caste households in this area.

Where state assistance has been combined with some form of local SC political representation, the increasing flow of resources or access to protection has been especially pronounced. For example, in the summer of 1997, all three Meerut villages were constituencies reserved for low castes. Daurala and Masuri both contained a SC *pradhan* and there was an MBC *pradhan* in Khanpur. These low-caste *pradhans* have achieved a measure of independence from Jat farmers and were said to be fairly efficient, at least compared to previous *pradhans*, at channelling resources to low castes in each settlement.

This was especially clear in Masuri, a village which has been selected under an 'Ambedkar village' scheme initiated by the BSP. Under this scheme, one village in each block with a high proportion of SCs was earmarked for special government assistance. Although this scheme was running before the BSP came to power, it became the cornerstone of the 1997 Mayawati government's efforts at redistribution. Scheduled Caste respondents in Masuri maintained that the SC *pradhan* of the village had made significant moves to improve their living conditions and provide SCs with government loans and educational grants. Scheduled Castes in Deogaon, Jaunpur District, have also benefited from the Ambedkar scheme. Indeed, Deogaon received more than its official entitlement. For example, all eighteen eligible and two non-eligible households received Rs 16,600 each in house-construction grants.[13] In addition, all schoolgoing Chamar children from first to seventh standards received scholarships (Rs 25 to 40 per child per month), and most Chamars above sixty years of age received an old age pension (Rs 125 per month).

In Jaunpur, the access of SCs to state largesse or help has been associated with a form of local political brokerage. This has been focused around a Chamar woman, who is a BSP party member and has recently become part of the district-level BSP hierarchy. This local BSP leader won her first victory when the SC agricultural labourers went on strike in 1994. She filed a case with the police against the Thakurs, pointing out that the labourers (like practically all agricultural employees in India) were paid below the stipulated minimum wage. She also accused the Thakurs of breaking the Scheduled Castes and Scheduled Tribes (Prevention of Atrocities) Act by beating and abusing their SC labourers. In marked contrast to their traditional tolerance of such exploitation, the police arrested a few Thakurs and impressed on the rest that they were breaking the law, and made the Thakurs accept a 33 per cent wage rise.

Since 1993, the local BSP leader has acted as a political broker and now helps SCs to obtain loans and old age pensions, and file cases under the Scheduled Castes and Scheduled Tribes (Prevention of Atrocities) Act. In her interaction with state officials, this woman trades on the political clout of the BSP. Her success in ensuring the assistance of state officials is also said to be a result of her style of operation, which, she admits, only works because she is a woman. She simply confronts the government officials she has to deal with, scolds them and 'gets things done'. This direct approach has included a number of highly publicized cases, such as protecting polling booths through quarrelling and physically fighting with polling-booth officers at the 1995 assembly election, and heated 'negotiations' with the Sub-District Magistrate. The SCs of Deogaon have thus found a way of securing access to the local state which bypasses upper-caste brokers, including the *pradhan*.

This has not led to any changes in the basic property relations in Deogaon, however; neither has it improved the SCs' access to government jobs. Only one new Chamar from the core Chamar hamlet has obtained a government job during the last two years, and that was in time-honoured fashion, through paying the going rate for the position. Nevertheless, both Chamars and Thakurs find that the SC position within the local class system has improved. Contrary to the theory proposed by Gupta in 1995, this improvement was not seen to result from the actions of an impartial, non-corrupt regime inspired by good governance. The Mayawati government is widely acknowledged to have been the most corrupt ever seen in Uttar Pradesh, and the Deogaon SCs are eager to 'misuse' the government administration as much as possible. For example, low castes in this settlement openly boasted about gaining more than their fair share of government programmes and of exaggerating Thakur violence against them in complaints to the police.

In as far as change has occurred in western Uttar Pradesh villages, the improvements in the bargaining power and political purchase of SCs have provoked reactionary Jat violence and intimidation. Male members of the dominant caste typically register this degree of SC uplift in observations about the demeanour, style and movements of SC men. For example, in the Meerut villages, Jats frequently complain that while SCs formerly sat at some distance from a Jat gathering, 'now they will come and sit on the *sirana* (head) of the *charpoy* (rope bed)'. Jats seek to reinscribe caste difference through occasional acts of brutality or intimidation: the weapons of the strong, to adapt Scott (1985). In Daurala one rich Jat explained his friend's assault upon the SC *pradhan* of the village *panchayat* by pointing out that 'he became cheeky, so we punched out his teeth'. A number of Jats revelled in the fact that the *pradhan* was ultimately unsuccessful in obtaining police and judicial assistance, and was forced to come back and beg the forgiveness of the Jat aggressor.

Conclusion

The empirical evidence that we have presented raises questions about the dichotomous reading of the relationship between the state and society found in post-structuralist and mainstream literature. Akhil Gupta has gone further than other post-structuralists in arguing empirically for a dichotomy between the state and civil society, but our material makes it possible to identify two weaknesses in his analysis.

First, in building his theory of local politics and agrarian relations around a discussion of local government elections and the mutual interests between the rich and poor, Gupta fails to link his analysis of vertical relations to an awareness of oppositional class strategies and demands. The ability of many Jats to maintain their privileged position through co-opting and colonizing the local state is closely associated with the intimidation and harassment, rather than complicity, of the rural poor. Class conflicts and contradictions are also evident at the level of discourse, where the low castes and Jats seek to define each other in ways that increase their political leverage and opportunities for economic accumulation. Contradictions also come across at the level of daily struggles over government jobs, police protection and state arbitration. The recent rise in the BSP is a reflection of these, which operates to intensify class contradictions as well.

Second, as we argued in the introduction, Gupta's model of agrarian populism (1997) and public discourse (1995; 1998) are predicated on the notion that rural society articulates an alternative to the vision of development that is promoted by the Indian state and 'the West'. In demanding higher purchasing prices for key cash crops through the BKU, or complaining about the distribution of public-sector employment, the Jats and other castes are hardly espousing an anti-developmental position. Even when and where rural actors take a stand against the state bureaucracy, they are frequently demanding more rather than less state intervention and assistance. This is closely linked to common expectations of the state's behaviour. Rather than using discourses of corruption and accountability to construct the state and limit malpractice, we found that richer landowners and low-caste people more usually accepted that state institutions and officers are normally corrupt. Complaints typically focused on the distribution of gains, rather than on state organization and procedure.

Future research into the reproduction of inequality in north India could usefully build upon and learn from aspects of Gupta's finely-grained ethnography of state-society relations. There has been very little anthropological research regarding the strategies and discourses employed by police officers, bureaucrats, government teachers and administrators. Nevertheless, in abandoning an earlier tendency to defend a political economy approach (Gupta 1989), we believe that Gupta fails to account for the range of ways in which rural elites may co-opt and colonize the state. Moreover, his model does not allow for state action which may undermine such local political advantage. That is, he ignores what most SCs in the areas in which we worked have come to believe: that the state can and must be made to work in the interests of the rural poor.

Recent writings by Sudipta Kaviraj can serve as an antidote to this. His focus is not on all-encompassing discourses, but on differences based on social inequality. Kaviraj (1997) argues that the struggle for equality in India today has become a struggle for 'equality between caste groups', with 'caste' showing certain similarities to 'class', and that the fight for access to state power is the central element in low-caste emancipation. While this does not account for the differences in class reproduction *within* castes (for example, between poorer and rich Jat farmers), Kaviraj's understanding of realities on the ground enables him to develop a much more sophisticated analysis of the relationship between social reproduction and state power and discourse.

Gupta's position is symptomatic of much post-structuralist writing. The issue of class, the colonization of the state by local dominant classes, and the state as an actor in local class-based conflicts do not figure in their equations. Post-structuralists also tend to obscure how local discourses of the state partly reflect the class position of rural people and often operate to sustain and legitimate the wealth and power of the rural rich. The problem for studies which raised any of these issues has been the paucity of empirical evidence, and consequently the bluntness of analysis. The complex relationship between the state and social groups documented in our essay can help to correct this. We have provided evidence for at least some of the multiple ways in which the practices of public and state agents, interacting with political changes at the state level, act to reproduce, or more rarely undermine, class divisions in rural India.

Notes

1. Other recent works on the local state in India have included research into: the constitution and functioning of local government *panchayats* (Lieten 1996; Lieten and Srivastava 1999; Williams 1997; Webster 1992); the socially segregated access to government-run health and educational services (Jeffery, Jeffery and Lyon 1989); the significance of access to state officials and institutions in land, wage and social disputes (Lerche 1995; 1999; Srivastava 1999); the emergence of 'shadow states' in the provision of public services (Harriss-White 1997); discourses of and about the state circulating within civil society (Brass 1997); somewhat dispersed evidence of richer farmer colonization or co-option of local state officials (Attwood 1992; Bailey 1957; Bliss and Stern 1982; Breman 1985; Carter 1974; Gupta 1998; Lieten 1994; Singh 1992; Upadhya 1988); and scattered references to collusion between rich farmers and the police (Balagopal 1991; Brass 1997; Breman 1997; Chowdhry 1997).
2. The main problems of this way of looking at class differentiation can be listed as follows:
    a) It misclassifies households which are so strongly engaged in non-agricultural activities that they have sold their land. However, judging from the village data this appears not to be a problem in the villages surveyed.
    b) It equates land size with accumulation strategy. Utsa Patnaik has correctly pointed out that the 'choice' between a capitalist accumulation strategy and a 'semi-feudal' reproduction strategy does not rely on land size. What matters is surplus appropriation and whether or not the appropriated surplus is reinvested in the production processes enabling further accumulation (Patnaik 1971). However, the dividing line we have drawn between small and big landowners (12 acres) ensures that farmers classified as big landowners depend on agricultural labourers to a significant degree. Moreover, in the two western UP cases presented here, all landowning Jats capable of producing a surplus engage in capitalist agriculture. This may not necessarily be the case for all big farmers in the eastern UP village. However, in our study of this village, the main focus is not on class divisions within the landed castes but on differences between landowners and their low-caste workers.
    c) It only looks at class within various castes, not at class formation in general. This objection is correct, but hardly relevant for the cases presented here.
3. This fieldwork formed the basis for a doctoral dissertation (Jeffrey 1999). Craig Jeffrey acknowledges the support of the Economic and Social Research Council who funded this research and would also like to thank Dr O.P. Bohra for assistance in the field.
4. The genealogical tables for these groups stretch back at least ten generations and were constructed from the memory of respondents and the official

records of the village genealogist (*bat*) for each settlement. Two of these lineages originated in Daurala and one each in Khanpur and Masuri.

5. The caste classifications are the standard government categories. The caste hierarchy in Indian villages places SCs as the lowest-ranking group, perceived to be 'unclean' or 'untouchable' by other castes, even if the practice of untouchability is outlawed. The castes 'above' the SCs are often divided into 'backward' castes and 'forward' castes on the basis of their ritual status. The backward castes designated as 'Other Backward Castes' (OBCs) are distinguished from SCs. The 'Most Backward Caste' (MBC) category was introduced to distinguish poorer castes within the OBC category (usually formerly involved in craft or menial activity) from richer OBCs. In Uttar Pradesh, those owning enough land to engage in cash-crop agriculture are usually forward-caste or from upper sections of the OBC category. Agricultural labourers tend to belong to the SC or MBC categories.

6. The populations of the three fieldwork areas were: Daurala town 10,025 inhabitants, Masuri 4,373, and Khanpur 4,913, according to the 1991 census (Government of India, 1991).

7. As a result of the continuing strength of patriarchal forces within Jat households, very few female Jats enter salaried employment (see Chowdhry 1994; Jeffery and Jeffery 1997; Jeffrey 1999).

8. Higher professional employment refers to employment as a doctor, lawyer, engineer, tertiary-level teacher, Grade I or Grade II government administrator or senior army official. Conversations with Jats revealed that this employment is regarded as *thik-si naukri* ('good service employment') and valued above other professional and white-collar jobs.

9. As Robert Wade has argued in his study of corruption in South India, the enthusiasm amongst many politicians to extract rents is closely linked to the rising costs of contesting elections (Wade 1988). One well-connected Jat maintained that it currently costs between Rs 200,000 and 500,000 to obtain a ticket from a political party and about Rs 1 million to contest an election in Meerut District.

10. We did not encounter any examples of rural women acting as or through lobbyists. The gender implications of these networks and the significance of masculinity in the generation of affinity are explored in Jeffrey (1999).

11. During a twelve-month stay in India in 1992–93, Jens Lerche and two assistants conducted fieldwork lasting six months in two villages in Uttar Pradesh: Mirpur in Muzaffarnagar district and Deogaon in Jaunpur District. This was backed up by extensive touring of the districts where the villages were located. The research assistants were two sociologists: Mr Prakash Deo Singh and Ms Rajashree Ghosh. Mr Indu Shekhar (also a sociologist) joined the research team during the last two months. The follow-up visits in 1995–6 and in 1998, were both of a month's duration. During these visits, Prakash Deo Singh again joined in as a research fellow. Jens Lerche acknowledges the support of the Danish Research Council for Development

Research which funded the initial research, and the School of Oriental and African Studies of London University which funded the later visits.

12. The background for this development has been explored in some detail in Lerche (1999).
13. The magnitude of the grant becomes clear when compared to a daily wage in agriculture (Rs 30) and daily wages for the migrants in Bombay (Rs 50–75).

References

Attwood, D. 1992. *Raising cane: the political economy of sugar in western India.* Delhi: Oxford University Press.

Bailey, F. G. 1957. *Caste and the economic frontier: a village in highland Orissa.* Manchester: Manchester University Press.

Balagopal, K. 1991. Post-Chundur and other Chundurs. *Economic and Political Weekly* 26, 42: 2399–405.

Bardhan, P. 1984. *The political economy of development in India.* Oxford: Blackwell.

Bliss, C., and N. Stern. 1982. *Palanpur: the economy of an Indian village.* Oxford: Oxford University Press.

Brass, P. 1997. *The theft of an idol.* Princeton: Princeton University Press.

Breman, J. 1985. *Of peasants, migrants and paupers: rural labour circulation and capitalist production in west India.* Delhi: Oxford University Press.

——. 1997. Silencing the voice of agricultural labourers in south Gujarat. Unpublished Kingsley Martin Memorial Lecture, 7 November, University of Cambridge, Cambridge.

Byres, T. J. 1988. Charan Singh (1902–87): an assessment. *Journal of Peasant Studies* 15, 2: 139–89.

Carter, A. T. 1974. *Elite politics in India: political stratification and political alliances in western Maharashtra.* Cambridge: Cambridge University Press.

Chatterjee, P. 1993. *The nation and its fragments: colonial and postcolonial histories.* Princeton: Princeton University Press.

Chowdhry, P. 1994. *The veiled women: shifting gender equations in rural Haryana 1880–1990.* Delhi: Oxford University Press.

——. 1997. Enforcing cultural codes: gender and violence in northern India. *Economic and Political Weekly* 32, 19: 1019–28.

Du Bois, M. 1991. The governance of the Third World: a Foucauldian perspective on power relations in development. *Alternatives* 16, 1: 1–30.

Duncan, I. 1988. Party politics and the north Indian peasantry: the rise of the Bharatiya Kranti Dal in Uttar Pradesh. *Journal of Peasant Studies* 16, 1: 40–76.

Dutta, N. 1997. Arya Samaj and the making of Jat identity. *Studies in History* 13, 1: 97–119.

Escobar, A. 1995. *Encountering development: the making and unmaking of the Third World.* Princeton: Princeton University Press.

Government of India. 1991. *Village/town primary census abstract, UP 1991.*

Gupta, A. 1989. The political economy of post-Independence India: a review article. *Journal of Asian Studies* 48, 4: 787–96.

——. 1995. Blurred boundaries: the discourse of corruption, the culture of politics and the imagined state. *American Ethnologist* 22, 2: 375–402.

——. 1997. Agrarian populism in the development of a modern nation (India). In F. Cooper and R. Packard, eds, *International development and the social sciences: essays on the history and politics of knowledge*, pp. 320–44. Berkeley: University of California Press.

——. 1998. *Postcolonial developments: agriculture in the making of modern India*. Durham: Duke University Press.

Harriss-White B. 1997. The State and informal economic order in South Asia. Paper for Moscow School of Social and Economic Sciences Colloquium on Exploratory / Informal Economies: Substance and Methods of Study (9–12 January).

Herring, R. J. 1983. *Land to the tiller: the political economy of agrarian reform in South Asia*. New Haven: Yale University Press.

Hasan, Z. 1989. Power and mobilisation: patterns of resilience and change in UP politics. In F. R. Frankel and M. S. A. Rao, eds, *Dominance and power in modern India: decline of a social order*, vol. 1, pp. 133–203. Delhi: Oxford University Press.

Jeffery, R., and P. Jeffery. 1997. *Population, gender and politics: demographic change in rural north India*. Cambridge: Cambridge University Press.

Jeffery, P., R. Jeffery, and A. Lyon. 1989. *Labour pains and labour power: women and childbearing in India*. London: Zed Books.

Jeffrey, C. 1999. *Reproducing difference: the accumulation strategies of rich Jat farmers in Meerut District, western UP*. Ph.D. dissertation, Cambridge University.

Kaviraj, S. 1984. On the crisis of political institutions in India. *Contributions to Indian Sociology (n.s.)* 18, 2: 223–43.

——. 1988. A critique of the passive revolution. *Economic and Political Weekly* 23, 45–7: 2429–44.

——. 1991. On state, society and discourse in India. In J. Manor, ed. *Rethinking Third World politics*, pp. 72–99. Harlow: Longman.

——. 1997. Democracy and social inequality. Paper for conference on Democracy and Transformation, Centre for the Advanced Study of India, University of Pennsylvania, Philadelphia, at India International Centre, New Delhi, India, November.

Lerche, J. 1995. Is bonded labour a bound category? Reconceptualising agrarian conflict in India. *Journal of Peasant Studies* 22, 3: 484–515.

——. 1999. Politics of the poor: agricultural labourers and political transformations in Uttar Pradesh. In T.J. Byres, K. Kapadia and J. Lerche, eds., *Rural labour relations in India*, pp. 182–243. London: Frank Cass.

Lieten, G. K. 1994. On casteism and communalism in Uttar Pradesh. *Economic and Political Weekly* 29, 14: 777–81.

——. 1996. *Development, devolution and democracy : village discourse in West Bengal*. New Delhi: Sage.

Lieten, G. K., and R. Srivastava. 1999. *Unequal partners: power relations, devolution and development in Uttar Pradesh*. New Delhi: Sage.

Patnaik, U. 1971. Capitalist development in agriculture: a note. *Economic and Political Weekly*, 11, 39: A123–A130.

Patnaik, U., and Z. Hasan. 1995. Aspects of the farmers' movement in Uttar Pradesh in the context of uneven capitalist development in Indian agriculture. *In* T. V. Sathyamurthy, ed., *Industry and agriculture in India since Independence: social change and political discourse in India, structures of power, movements and resistance*, vol. 2, pp. 274–300. Delhi: Oxford University Press.

Saberwal, S. 1996. *Roots of crisis: interpreting contemporary Indian society*. New Delhi: Sage.

Scott, J. C. 1985. *Weapons of the weak: everyday forms of peasant resistance*. New Haven: Yale University Press.

Sharma, R., and T. T. Poleman. 1994. *The new economics of India's green revolution: income and employment diffusion in Uttar Pradesh*. Delhi: Vikas.

Singh, J. 1992. *Capitalism and dependence: agrarian politics in western Uttar Pradesh 1951–1991*. Delhi: Manohar.

Srivastava, R. 1999. Rural labour in Uttar Pradesh: emerging features of subsistence, contradiction and resistance. *In* T.J. Byres, K. Kapadia and J. Lerche, eds, *Rural labour relations in India*, pp. 263–315. London: Frank Cass.

Stokes, E. 1986. *The peasant armed: the Indian revolt of 1857*. Oxford: Clarendon Press.

Upadhya, C. B. 1988. *From kulak to capitalist: the emergence of a new business community in coastal Andhra Pradesh, India*. Ph.D. dissertation, Yale University.

Wade, R. 1985. The market for public office: why the Indian state is not better at development. *World Development* 13, 4: 467–97.

———. 1988. Politics and graft: recruitment, appointment and promotions to public office in India. *In* P. Ward, ed., *Corruption, development and inequality: soft touch or hard graft?* pp. 73–109. London: Routledge.

Webster, N. 1992. Panchayati raj in West Bengal: popular participation of the people or the party. *Development and Change* 23, 4: 129–63.

Williams, G. 1997. State, discourse and development in India: the case of West Bengal's Panchayati raj. *Environment and Planning A* 29, 12: 2099–112.

Talking dirty about politics:
a view from a Bengali village

Arild Engelsen Ruud

Politicians of various statures, operating at different levels, play a large role in Indian society. These village, caste or clan leaders, local *panchayat* representatives, party activists, ward representatives, town mayors, elected members of legislative assemblies, or members of parliament all serve in an intermediary, translational role between the state and society. There is some agreement that the language and values that apply to the state are not readily appreciated in local society, both villages and towns, and vice versa.[1] The two, admittedly very schematic, spheres of state and society each have their own agendas, aims, rules and concerns. The politician is a man (and rarely a woman) who is capable of engaging in both spheres, with a lucid understanding of how both of them work. He represents the one in the other, and mediates, mobilizes resources and supplies contacts. In a village the leader-politician receives and often assists people who ask for his intervention, deliberates in disputes, gives voice to majority sentiments, represents the village outwards and the state inwards, mobilizes voters to ensure maximum turnout, and in the whole process he establishes his own position as a man of value and power.

It is the contention of this essay that this man and the activities that he represents are viewed with ambivalence by most non-politicians. The high voter turnout in India coexists with a deep cynicism about how politics 'really works'. The attitudes that ordinary villagers exhibit towards politics as an activity are of interest to several basic questions

I wish to thank Pamela Price, Kathinka Frøystad, Øivind Fuglerud and the editors for excellent comments and suggestions on earlier versions of this essay. All errors of interpretation are mine.

about the Indian polity. India is the world's largest democracy, with a regularly higher voter turnout than the United States, and yet politicians are viewed as crooks, corrupt and self-seeking, unprincipled and devoid of ideological commitment. The Indian electorate seems strangely unconcerned about the moral standards of its representatives. A parallel riddle has to do with Gunnar Myrdal's famous characterization of India as a 'soft state', one that is unable to ensure that its laws and regulations are adhered to (Myrdal 1970). The Indian democracy seems to enjoy a high degree of legitimacy and entrenched solidity after fifty years, which is quite a record in the Third World; nevertheless, the citizenry seems rather undemanding about either the implementation of laws which it elects representatives to design or the moral standards of those representatives. My aim here is to investigate this ambivalence and to try to come closer to an understanding of the puzzle represented by cynicism coupled with participation. The ethnography is from a village in West Bengal, in the Dakshin Damodar area of Burdwan district, gathered over some years in the mid-1990s, and it describes a situation of 'everyday politics', where there is no revolt, no upheaval and no large looming questions. This essay cannot answer all the riddles, but I hope to gain some insights which will allow us to understand more closely what people expect from their 'leaders' or 'representatives', and how that affects the lubricating effect which politics has on state-society interaction.

The high moral ground

Going over my fieldnotes, I found that the notes of the first month or so were filled with peoples' statements about the state of politics in India or West Bengal, or more often about politics in general. These statements were almost invariably negative. One term that was often used is 'dirty' (*nungra*). Politics was referred to as being dirty, meaning unprincipled, as something unsavoury that morally upright people would not touch, a sullied game of bargaining and dishonesty. Another term that was frequently employed to describe this foul game was 'disturbance' (*gandagol*). Politics, it was held, represented a continuous social disturbance that caused unease, brought disharmony to society, and ruined its elaborate design and calm stability. The reason for this, I was told, was that politics thrived on instances of trouble, or 'rows' (*jhamela*). These could be outright fist-fights (*maramari*), or abusive exchanges (*galagali*), drawn-out quarrels (*jhagra*), or just general animosity and hostility (*hingsa*). This type of 'trouble' was presented as the sustenance of politics. A slightly different rhetoric was also heard quite often. Politics, it was held, filled society with 'poison' (*bish*). People only accepted this situation because of 'fear' (*bhay*); fear of the dangers involved when getting in the way of powerful politicians or on the wrong side of them. Disturbances kept people in a state of fear and in line. Overall, the general drift was that the misery that is India's, is the work of politicians, all of them corrupt and unscrupulous.

Reading my early notes more closely, however, there appears to be another strand to this. Certainly, there were the personalities themselves, the individual politicians, who could be corrupt, and ambitious bullies and all that. But more than that, it was the game itself that was considered 'dirty'; it was inherently so and sullying to those that participated in it. Unprincipled people certainly made politics 'dirty', but politics also made politicians 'dirty'. With few exceptions, the very logic of the game, it seemed, would sully even principled actors. Merely by choosing to be engaged in politics, anyone was almost bound to be tarnished by unsavoury decisions, shady actions and odorous alliances. A suspicion always tarnishes the reputation of anyone involved in politics, a suspicion that there is necessarily something shady in their dealings. It was said of one politician, who I thought was 'clean' because of the importance of his position and the modesty of his living standard, that 'if he were [clean] he wouldn't be where he is'. One simply cannot, it was implied, become powerful and important by being principled and clean. The statement was made by a minor businessman who may have held a particular grudge against politicians as a class, although it probably conveyed a more general sentiment. Only by dealing behind closed doors, fixing deals and breaking rules, does one become powerful, seems to be a commonly-held view. One of the first sayings in Bengali I came across was 'He who goes to Lanka becomes Ravana'.[2] It means that whatever you may have been earlier, once you have reached the land of Lanka you become like Ravana, the demon-king residing there. The saying is used to explain something about politics. Commonly, it refers specifically to the dominant political party in the state, the Communist Party India (Marxist) (CPM) is the dominant partner of the ruling government coalition, the Left Front, which has been in power since 1977. Implicitly, the saying suggests (and this I believe to be a widespread opinion) that the CPM used to be a party of good, honest, hard-working people dedicated to something they believed in. Now that the party has come to power it has changed, it has become 'dirty', it has become just like the Congress used to be, it has become Ravana. The perspective often also includes the Congress, which used to consist (in popular imagination) of dedicated nationalists, but which deteriorated into a den of scheming, plotting, unprincipled individuals soon after coming to power after Independence. The saying alludes to the efforts people in power engage in to stay in power, that is, to the unprincipled actions aimed at securing votes, money and resources, as well as positions for oneself, and one's allies and friends. By implication it seems to suggest that initially politics does not have to be 'dirty', since both Congress and the CPM are held to have consisted of people who joined for ideological or moral reasons. The implication, however, is that the activity of politics itself causes degeneration of the actors.

The desire to distance oneself from the unsavoury game of politics was not a general gesture aimed at a visiting foreigner; it could equally be made at home or in other social contexts. Indeed, the closer to the concept of 'home', the more reluctance and unease people exhibited in talking about politics and the more they abhorred measures that breached a certain code of conduct. It was not popular to have outsiders know about the kind of internal problems 'we' have in 'our' group, locality or family.[3] This distancing from political action came out in how one young woman referred to her father. He was locally a major political figure, who went under the name Munsi-saheb. The woman's brother, who lives elsewhere, asked her how their father was doing, using the term *abba*. This is the affectionate term used by Bengali Muslims to refer to their fathers, which these siblings also used. In answering, however, the daughter referred to him not as *abba*, but as Munsi-saheb ('Munsi-saheb is in trouble again'), using the name employed by most people in the village. Immediately afterwards, in a different context, she used the term *abba* as she would normally do. This suggests that the term Munsi-saheb was used to refer to him as a political figure, even by his daughter, who thus made that aspect of him somewhat separate from the father to which she was emotionally attached. This leads me to the interpretation that in doing so, she distanced herself—and perhaps also her father—from the nastiness of his political moves. At the time, these included actions which she felt were unsavoury, particularly his efforts to befriend a long-time opponent whom she much detested.

Politics, then, at least among ordinary people, seems to be very much about measures that cannot easily be defended within the values of family life, and the norms and morality of kinship which also apply to village social life. The ideal village society is one free of quarrels, characterized by one of dignified behaviour and living, and ordered respect. This sentiment grows out of basic kinship values that are extended to include each person's social surroundings, captured in the phrase *atmiya-swajan* (literally 'family and one's own people').[4] The basic rule for order is respect for seniority, whether of age, gender, caste, or kinship (which means that the father-in-law is always senior, even if he is younger and poorer than his son-in-law). Ties between landowners and labourers, between lenders and givers, and the less clearly defined ones between political patrons and their clients and supporters, are all constructed (ideologically) within the same pattern, as exemplified by the use of kinship terms among unrelated patrons and clients.

Political manoeuvres, quarrels, disputes, 'groupism',[5] and compromises with opposing groups spoil the image of the harmonious whole, which is the ideal state for a group or a village. Politics is associated, rightly or wrongly, with unnecessary disturbances and undignified quarrels among people who belong to the same family or caste, or to the same neighbourhood or village, and who ideally should be friends and treat one another with respect. It involves actions that spoil this image, and it was from these that Munsi-saheb's daughter distanced herself by referring to her father by his political name, rather than the intimate *abba*.

The ideology of order has a quality which does not leave room for the client to question the patron, because just as a son should not question the wisdom of his father, so also a client submits to the will of the patron. The intimate terms of address which are used evoke the whole pathos of family life, including the emotional and moral bonds that constitute a family. As in most of India, these terms of address are not reserved for close blood relatives only, but are used in a variety of contexts, including strategic political relationships. Village leaders are called 'elder brother', 'paternal' or 'maternal uncle', or just 'brother', depending on relative age and status. In this evocation of kinship through terms of address lies an evocation of a broader set of norms which are never the less complex and even cynical. No one expects these terms to measure up to the expectations of actual relationships. When a poor man in a difficult spot goes to a local big man and calls him *dada* (elder brother), he symbolically expresses submission and loyalty, and pledges to act as a younger brother, which brings into focus the notions of obedience to the elder, protection of the younger, and the younger's dependence on the elder.

Just how deep runs this ideology? An ideology, understood as a set of norms and values attached to formulated ideals, may well preclude the formulation of opposing sets, but it will rarely be strong enough wholly to preclude alternative interpretations of reality.[6] In many cases notions of mutuality may carry real expectations and even guide actions. But expressions of a need to distance oneself from a patron and appear as someone who has entered a strategic relationship with eyes open are also present. Normally, in rural Bengal, a client-position is not something anyone would brag about; on the contrary, it is widely perceived as humiliating and embarrassing (unless it represents an unusually advantageous asset). The desire to express a certain distance from the patron is quite common, particularly among friends and relatives. Stories which characterize local politicians, patrons, money-lenders or landowners in negative terms are not unusual. The desire to show that one has retained moral standards, in spite of what may outwardly seem to be classic clientship, comes out in the case of my friend Hanubhai. His patron was my host in the village, a CPM village leader of some stature and an active patron of several labourers. The relationship with Hanubhai dated back to the days of his father, who had died a decade earlier, leaving his widow and three minor children in the hands of this patron. Hanubhai addressed his patron using the term *mama* (mother's brother), a kinship term that evokes the intimacy and love supposedly held by maternal uncles (living far away) rather than the sternness of paternal uncles (living in the same household). In return for work and benevolence, Hanubhai could be counted on to make up numbers at meetings called by the leader, participate in rallies, and do odd jobs at odd hours—such as driving the visiting anthropologist in a bullock-cart to pick up guests. On these trips he would pour out his heart.

The reverence had become irreverence, as I listened to how the leader while young had used low-caste women for his sexual pleasure, how he still behaved in relation to subordinates like his zamindar grand-uncle before him, how he did not know anything about cultivation and how easily he could be cheated, how his son had once been involved with thieves, how he had vomited when trying to eat pork (this Communist leader was a Muslim), and many similar stories. Hanubhai was not the only one to tell such stories, nor was that leader the only one about whom such stories circulated. But the outpouring of spite negated the submission and obedience exemplified by Hanubhai's willingness to do odd jobs. No one held it against him that he treated the big man as his patron and chose to show him respect in the manner he did, as a benevolent and respected member of his family. Yet his irreverence in private aimed to prove the opposite, that he was not subject to the leader. Indeed, the irreverence seemed to prove that Hanubhai was an independent actor, who knew the environment in which he was moving (as the stories about his employer showed), and thereby presented himself as a clever strategic player—the opposite of a willy-nilly supporter-cum-client.

Perhaps my friend Hanubhai's outpouring of spite against his *mama-*patron was exceptional, particularly since his patron was also my host. What we often find is that people actively oppose the actions of their patrons or village leaders, although not in public. If the fieldnotes on which the above is based were exemplary, they might have been construed as revealing the 'hidden transcript' of a subaltern consciousness (Scott 1990; cf. Haynes and Prakash 1991). However, these are not unusual notes, but ones based on information and opinions that villagers readily and at times eagerly volunteered. Nonetheless, I believe they point to something interesting about the context in which people enter into (political) relationships and the motives which guide them. In a word, people enter, or want to appear to enter, into political ('patron-client') relationships with a handkerchief over their mouths due to the perceived odour. In the case of Hanubhai, who had received real patronage and had every reason to be known as grateful and submissive, the need to distance himself from his patron and appear as someone who had entered a strategic relationship with his eyes open was clearly present. Even to call a *fictitious* kinship relationship a *kinship* relationship is to miss out the fact that, at the edge of the realm of blood-kin, the moral bonds of kinship start to weaken fast. In the present context, what appears most salient in an act of submission among non-kin is that it is strategic. The poor man who approaches a rich or powerful man does so with an eye to win something, to obtain what he does not have, be it money or protection, or to make a prudent move against future mishaps. The employment of kinship terminology diminishes neither the strategic aspect of the act, nor the desire to see the relationship as strategic.

When not reinforced by close ties of blood (or emotion), the patron-client relationship, for all its pathos in evoking kinship terminology, is very much constituted by the exchange of goods and services that takes place within it, and it may not even be so strong. In his monograph on Bengali village life and politics, *Rank and rivalry*, Marvin Davis (1983) characterized patron-client relationships as 'transactional', that is, as binding on the two parties only to the extent that there was a mutual benefit. The clients felt free to switch to other would-be patrons if they thought such a move to be pertinent and profitable. In most cases, the poor may not have much of a choice, but that does not diminish the perception of a strategic element. On the contrary, lack of choice may augment the client's need to see the relationship as strategic. Bonds may be of a close and personal kind, depending on intimacy and individual histories, but in cases where they are not—and to many villagers dependency is an inescapable fact of life—real or make-believe patronage will always remain an insufficient coating that cannot hide the humiliating and degrading position of being underneath in a hierarchically-conscious society. Only by understanding the relationship as wholly strategic—even when fictitious kinship terminology is employed—can the client retain his own stature and standing *vis-à-vis* friends and peers.

In their discourse therefore, villagers distance themselves morally from politics, yet at the same time many are in fact involved in it in one way or the other. This is embarrassing and there is a tendency to be ambiguous about one's own involvement, but the embarrassment is mitigated by viewing the involvement as strategic. I shall use the case of a political village meeting which I attended to elaborate further on these points.

A village meeting

In the village where I lived, I attended a meeting called by activists of the dominant political party, the CPM. The party has instituted something called the *gram sabha* or village committee, a village-level body of elected representatives, which is supposed to act as the villagers' platform for discussing and formulating local demands which were then forwarded to the party or the *panchayats*.[7] This particular evening saw the second annual election to the village's *gram* committee. It may be worth mentioning here that the CPM had not only held the chief ministership and been the dominant partner of the Left Front government for nearly twenty years at the time of this meeting, it had also won the majority of elected positions in both this and the neighbouring districts. Indeed, Burdwan District is jokingly called 'the red fortress', and the CPM is simply referred to as 'the party' (while the Congress is 'Congress').

An audience of some 150 people was seated to watch the show at this particular party election meeting. The number was surprisingly high, considering that a live broadcast of a world-cup cricket match between India and the West Indies in Calcutta was on television that very night. Two 'VIPs' (a *jela parishad* member and the *gram panchayat* chairman) and the six most senior village leaders and activists were seated on chairs on the podium under the canopy. It was a late autumn evening and there was a slight humidity in the cool air. The audience was seated on the mats and blankets in front of the podium, wrapped in shawls and smoking *biris* (country cigarettes), and patiently listened to the speeches. Around the podium the junior activists fluttered, bringing in tea and messages and ensuring that everything was in order.

The big men present made speeches, some short and some long.

The *gram panchayat* chairman made a particularly long speech, lasting close to an hour, on topics ranging from the importance of the *gram* committee as a 'democratic' initiative taken by the CPM, exemplified by all the good work done by the *panchayat* and the CPM volunteers, to the bad things that would happen if the central government accepted the Dunkel proposition.[8] He also encouraged villagers to use this opportunity to tell the party activists present, local or non-local, including himself, what was still wrong, what they wanted done and how relations could be improved, as well as any matter of interest to villagers that the *gram* committee could help with. The *gram* committee and its annual meeting were—he asserted—a 'democratic' (*ganatantrik*) meeting-place for the party and 'ordinary people' (*sadharan manush*), where grievances could be ventilated and the activists would have to listen, in front of the entire village society (*puro gramer samaj*). Those present were also asked to propose their own candidates for the board and chairmanship of the new *gram* committee, since there would be a democratic election (*ganatantrik nirbacan*). The *gram panchayat* chairman, a very important figure in the local political set-up, had thus not only spoken about a few general political positions that the party advocated, but he had also emphasized the democratic nature of the meeting, making it clear that this was an exercise in democracy, in people's participation in decisions. In a sense, it was an exercise which brought the conventions and manners of democratic institutions right into the middle of the village and its affairs. What he promised was real elections and real influence.

It was quite late by the end of his long speech, about nine in the evening, the time people normally have dinner in the winter season. Many started leaving, although it was clear that the programme was still far from over. The announced elections, for instance, had not been held. But the 'debate' (*alacona*), in which villagers would come forward with their propositions and grievances, still kept some back. Altogether, six people ventured forward to speak into the microphone and suggest candidates. Five of them were young party activists, each of whom made speeches lasting for five to twenty minutes. They all started with a 'red salute' hailing the red flag, and proceeded to praise the party for taking the initiative to form the *gram* committee or for its good work. They remarked on the consequences of the Dunkel proposition for the village, 'as explained to us by the honourable [*gram panchayat*] chairman'. Then they went on to suggest to the party leaders or *panchayat* representatives present that the village really did need that road planned for so long, that school extension, or that well in the northern end of the village. Or they suggested that the water-sharing procedures be improved. Two of the speakers proposed candidates for the board, from among the reasonably senior party activists of the village.

During these speeches of various lengths, people in the audience entertained themselves. An occasional snide remark could be heard from the podium, but most of the time the only noise that could be heard was muted laughter, cheerful chattering and a few whispered quarrels. Some of the more daring and wittier among the audience made much fun of the speakers or of what was being said, particularly of the junior speakers. Remarks such as 'Hey, be quiet, our leader [*neta*] is trying to talk' caused muted rounds of laughter when the young man who had tried to organize the village labourers made a stuttering speech. In general, at least at the beginning of the meeting, the atmosphere was mirthful and merry, and even the quarrels were friendly.

Only one of the six speakers was not an activist, but a poor hot-headed peasant with a grievance against one of his neighbours (who was an activist). Propped up by friends, he ventured a short rambling speech about how the *gram* committee should ensure that there was no quarrelling in the village and that those who stole land from others were to be punished. And then he proposed himself as a candidate for the board. He himself was rather embarrassed at his poor performance, but many laughed encouragingly during his speech, and there was much laughter and applause afterwards.

Many left after his speech. Three more party activists then made speeches, which took another half-hour. By that time there were only ten or twelve people left to form the audience, and there were as many or more people on or around the podium, including the young activists. The level of activity behind the stage had also been steadily increasing. At any one time, one or more of the local party leaders stepped down from the podium and went into the shadows behind. There, in relative obscurity, in smaller or larger groups, they smoked and discussed in low tones, sometimes for quite a long while, after which they returned to the podium. The leaders discussed matters of importance with one another or occasionally with individual villagers, who had problems to which they wanted someone powerful to lend an ear. The leaders' backstage discussions were long deliberations on various topics, and one of them was the leadership of the new *gram* committee.

Towards the end of the round of speeches, Harinath, a senior local activist who was still fairly young, engaged several of the main party leaders in discussion. As I understood it, Harinath was fighting for his political survival. Until quite recently, he had been a man of importance in the village. He was the *panchayat* member for two periods totalling ten years and had held several other posts. But Harinath had become increasingly corrupt; he had been taking 10 per cent off each Integrated Rural Development Programme (IRDP) loan that he granted, and finally he had embezzled Rs 18,000 from the cooperative society. For that he was almost universally condemned in the village, and was dropped by the party and stripped of his positions. Harinath now aspired for the chairmanship of the *gram* committee. As support and proof of his popularity, he brought some friends from his own community, who were members of the crucial Bagdi caste. This group had, for a long time provided strong support to the party, including a crucial capacity for violence that had been used during the early stages of CPM rule in the state. There was some disorganized opposition to Harinath's endeavour by a few Muslims from one part of the village (the eastern neighbourhood), who felt that they too had supported the party for a long time and that it was now their turn to be its representatives. Two men from the eastern neighbourhood led the opposition to Harinath, but after some bickering, behind-the-scene negotiations went in favour of him.

Finally it was announced that the election was going to be held. The party—that is, the representatives present—proposed a list of candidates. Out of eight names, three were new: Harinath was proposed as chairman and two others as ordinary members. The hot-head who had proposed himself was not included; it was later explained to me that, according to democratic principles, one could not propose one's own name. A senior party activist of the village read out the list and asked for 'the community's approval' (*samajer anumati*). By that time, only five people were left to represent the community. They grunted 'yes', and the chairman of the meeting ratified the decision as 'unanimous' (*ekmat*).

The meeting ended, the remaining spectators went home, and the young activists were left to dismantle the equipment. The VIPs were invited insistently to spend the night in the village; they cordially declined, but spent another half an hour smoking *biris* and discussing matters without being disturbed before they took off on their two-wheelers.

Politics as usual

There are several interesting aspects to this meeting. One is that it did not seem to amount to a democratic meeting at all. The leaders who had been present gave different explanations for this. One held that the meeting had indeed been democratic, since people could have participated if they had wanted to. Another said that: 'It is very difficult to get people to participate in such things, because they are not used to it. Debate, election, it all takes time. And they are more worried about their dinner'. A more lucid leader, a party member and one of the two senior leaders of the village, made it clear that although the *gram* committee is formally open to everyone and all can participate, everybody still knows that it is an organ of the party, not the state, and only with the party's support can it be effective. The committee only has the power that the party allows it to have.

The party is very dominant in this area, and retains full control over the local government institutions (*panchayats*), as well as an effective control over the district bureaucracy and the police. Allocations of money, projects, priorities, selection of IRDP recipients, patronage of various kind to groups or individuals, are all controlled by the party. The lucid leader's account of the realities of local politics made it clear that the composition of the *gram* committee leadership was a matter that the party leaders would have to take upon themselves. They had to ensure the introduction of the right people, by getting the equations right. If the committee was not composed of people whom the party could trust, the party would be unable to work with it.

We may still wonder why the party bothered to put on a show of democracy and consultation. If the party invests the *gram* committee with whatever potency the latter has, why does it resort to this kind of charade, a make-believe free debate and election? Could the party not institute a local body, appoint its local activists to it, and announce that it would be given such and such tasks? I did hear—through reliable contacts—of villages where real debates did take place and real elections were fought over seats in the *gram* committees. But these were rare cases. In the main, the annual meeting of the *gram* committees constituted a theatrical performance, whose value lay not in enhancing participation or democracy, but in instilling in villagers the notion of the might and ideology of the party. If I am to venture an explanation, it would have to be in the following vein. The performance of the *gram* committee meeting displayed the language and vocabulary, the personnel, and the trappings and mechanisms of the state and those in power, in codes that were culturally constituted. It had the state's formal rules and procedures, and represented its imagery, in a setting of different political realities. The trappings quite probably had a legitimizing effect in that they linked the acting politicians to a larger political entity, by referring to the norms of the modern state. And they also said something about knowledge and command over institutions with linkages to the state apparatus.

The motives of the party are one thing, the motives of the audience are another. They are a very interesting aspect, because 150 people turned up at a meeting with a comparatively poor entertainment factor.[9] There is no reason to believe that anyone expected it to be an open meeting, with a free debate followed by an open-ended election. Behind-the-scene manipulations were expected, as a natural part of any political proceedings or deliberation, as found in any show of this kind. 'What are they talking about in the shadows there?', I asked one of the audience during the meeting. 'They are doing politics' (*marali karche*), was the answer, the term used for 'politics' being an ironic twist of the term for 'headman'. The next day, when I talked to people about the absence of any real election, some dismissed the question as unimportant, as something that really did not matter: 'So what?'. Others held that it was always like this, and that 'the big leaders' would always behave like this, unfortunate though it was.[10]

People seem to have shared the lucid leader's understanding that if the party did not get its way at the meeting over the constitution of the *gram* committee, then this body would lack the party's collaboration and hence be powerless. The committee was an extension of the party, not a representative body of the village. No one was fooled about this except perhaps for a while the anthropologist! This was not something new or unusual. No one mentioned it beforehand, nor did they have to. It was widely accepted that this was how the world functioned.

Why did people bother to show up, then, at a completely impotent and only somewhat entertaining meeting on a chilly autumn night? And why did they not grab the opportunity to turn the *gram* committee even a little notch in a more representative or deliberative direction? As to the first question we may note that there was no coercion, yet it would have been noticed if anyone who was expected to attend the meeting did not do so, and conversely if anyone who was not expected to attend the meeting actually did so. Such stories get around in these small communities. However, in this village of some two thousand inhabitants, a lot of people did not attend. It is not my privilege to know the hearts and minds of those that formed the audience. Their innermost motives—which might be unclear even to the individual participants—cannot be fully known. It is however a well-known fact in village politics and life that the number of people mobilized for such meetings reflects the standing of the local leaders. The attendance is indicative of a leader's capability as the party's local man, and is something that the party (through the invited VIPs) will take note of. Others too will notice it, such as rivals or villagers in general. A poorly-attended meeting reflects very badly on a local leader, who will be most embarrassed, whereas a well-attended meeting reflects well on him, and keeps him in a good mood and in the party's good books, and may contribute towards keeping him in power.

At this particular meeting, however, the village party leaders were not up for election—they never are. The meeting was about the *gram* committee, composed of very minor local politicians or party activists. Yet there was no effort from among the audience, save one hothead, to render the meeting more democratic, to raise the level of the debate, or to 'tell' the party leaders what one felt. Some of those who did attend the meeting did so because they came as loyal clients, and did not wish to embarrass the local leaders. At the same time, the chatting, occasional joking and laughter, which took place during the meeting and the fact that most left quite early, seem to suggest that most people did not understand their role as clients in a completely self-effacing manner. Instead they can be understood to have kept their distance from the whole gamut of deliberations ('politics') that went on behind the stage, and indeed from the proceedings as a whole.[11]

There is, however, more to this laid-back attitude to the outcome of the show. A cynical saying 'He who has power owns the land' (*Jor jar muluk tar*) seems to capture the mood of such meetings. Local gossip about politics point to the fact that only the powerful are leaders. That is, the arrow of causation here is from power, might or 'strength' (*jor* is the capacity to enforce), to leadership and lordship over the land. In other words, those who become 'leaders' are already powerful. Power yields more power, which fits well with observed village behaviour. The saying also underlines the importance of reputation—reputation for power, clout and influence—and the importance of the show, which is being seen with the right people and knowing the right ways, such as meeting procedures. But not the least, the saying also points out that a pre-existing basis of clout or influence is necessary for people to seek someone's intervention. In other words, one of the qualities needed in a leader is an ability actually to use his power, and connections. Otherwise he is not of much use. By implication, those who do not have power, such as the ordinary villagers, are ineffectual and unable to turn the course of events.

A surprising feature is that if a leader is able to deliver, then his unsavoury characteristics are sometimes overlooked. Let us briefly consider what happened to Harinath, formerly considered corrupt and very much the politician you kept your distance from, but now elevated to the (admittedly minor) post of chairman of the *gram* committee. References to his corruption and embezzlement became increasingly infrequent in local conversation. Only the Muslims of the eastern neighbourhood, who had been overruled by the party in the selection of the *gram* committee chairman, continued to harbour ill feelings against him. In other parts of the village, people ceased to talk about Harinath. 'No one talks about Harinath any longer', I was informed. Increasingly, however, he could be seen in the company of the village's two elected *panchayat* members, and when two members of his (extended) family were given IRDP loans, it was evident that Harinath was getting back into the good books of the party again. When he married several months later, the grand feast he hosted was well attended by people from the main village. He was no longer shunned. And where I had previously been told that he was 'a totally corrupt man', I was now told that 'as a person he is not bad'.[12] His influence and contacts were again obvious and, the negative aspects of his past were no longer emphasized.

That 'influence' excuses unacceptable (political) behaviour is a somewhat oversimplified interpretation. Personal appeal, as well as norms and values, are elements that contribute towards the making of leaders. Yet I believe there are valuable lessons to be drawn here about the realities of village politics. One is that ordinary people will participate in meetings, elections, and so on, because their presence in good numbers is important to the local and not-so-local leaders, rather than to the process or to the participants themselves. Another lesson is that people tend to leave the selection of their leaders in the hands of the already powerful, along with political deliberations and other difficult questions. People sit back, uninvolved, and wait for the outcome, which they will eventually deal with.

What took place after the meeting was a process of general acceptance of the result that had been reached. Once Harinath was back in the warmth, a favourable reassessment of him took place, making him increasingly acceptable to a majority of the villagers. The criticism which had been widespread only months earlier was replaced by a certain quiet and pragmatic acceptance of his political acumen and stature— which in itself seemed to legitimize the acceptance. His ability to manoeuvre himself back into the network of powerful men in the area, from where he could again start acting as patron and middleman for villagers who required intervention, was sufficient for people with compelling or not-so-compelling problems to turn to him. A realistic assessment of his position and influence told individuals that in order to get a particular problem solved, they could seek Harinath's help and intervention. He would probably be willing to help, since he needed to build his stature further. Anyone seeking his help would become vulnerable to his manipulations—morally dubious yet beneficial. To retain a distance (in private) might be important, but increasingly difficult as well, since one would have to visit him regularly and address him in kinship terms.

With kin who are not fairly closely related, the norms of family loyalty lose their strength, and a starker reality of calculating actors exists under the rhetoric of kinship. In this context kinship becomes a shroud, which covers a relationship that depends on material or political exchange for maintenance. But not entirely. The rhetoric of kinship has meaning in that it publicly legitimizes and solemnizes a relationship, and in this respect, of course, it has some weight in forming the relationship. When first employed, kinship terms of address establish (or seek to establish) a closer and more solemnized relationship. But once established and accepted, the fictitious kinship terminology seeks to bring in the might of kinship morality— the whole array of scruples, mutuality, loyalty, and so on. It is difficult and morally suspect to be too outspoken and critical about someone you have a reasonably close relationship with and call 'elder brother' or 'maternal uncle'. Even if—in your heart—you consider your relationship to him to be wholly strategic, a certain decorum has to be maintained.

Those able to deliver become leaders. What keeps them in position is their ability and capacity to get things done. There is a singular absence of emphasis on the moral requirements of a leader. In the general appreciation of the rules of this game—a game most people realise they cannot escape when serious problems arise—lies not only the cause of embarrassment, but equally an understanding of politics as an activity that entails its own legitimacy. People have to compromise their standards of morality. Few of them are independent and self-sufficient enough to be able to live wholly apart from the more powerful and to avoid being entangled in politics, even locally. They are also too cautious to take the chance of trying to do so. To be entangled means to engage in or derive benefit from a sort of activity that goes uneasily with widespread public standards of moral conduct. What the ethnography suggests is that the audience at the meeting evidenced signs of discomfort which could derive precisely from the problematic fact that they were present. The implicit acceptance of this pursuit of material interest is but a wider appreciation of the compulsions that move the individual. Yet it sits uneasily with people's moral standards and self-images. Villagers all turned up at the meeting, laughed in embarrassment and jested to salvage their dignity, and they then went home early realizing that their obligation ended with being simply present at the meeting. They all knew this about one another, and all took part in a reciprocal act of absolution.

Subaltern autonomy, Indianization, or shamefaced acceptance?

This essay does not draw firm conclusions, but suggests some lines of interpretation based on existing theoretical frameworks. Is it an autonomous subaltern consciousness that is revealed every now and then in the small cracks, such as in Hanubhai's exasperated outpouring or in the jesting at the political meeting? Is it possible that the embarrassment of the audience, its reluctance and distancing at the meeting are evidence of an ineffectual yet real opposition? If we let ourselves be guided by the work of James Scott (1985; 1990) and the Subaltern Studies group, we could suggest something along the following lines.[13] A (semi-)conscious awareness of being exploited does exist, but the exploitation is perhaps not so much economic as political and ideological. Yet it is nonetheless real; it keeps some out of power and others in it, and sustains an unjust system that has delivered some goods but leaves much to be desired. Ordinary people's awareness would then be what caused the reluctance of the audience and, their desperate efforts to salvage their dignity. At the same time, this awareness could be seen to exist together with a realization that they are poor and are subjects of the local political players operating in the midst of the maze of a massive state apparatus. Ordinary villagers are and possibly understand themselves to be largely powerless, so they reluctantly play along, hoping to derive some benefit while not exposing themselves.

This line of reasoning, which gains its inspiration from studies on Indian colonial history and contemporary Malaysian peasant society, is not entirely satisfactory. West Bengal is a reasonably open and free society, with opposition parties, newspapers, and free elections. At the state level, the opposition gains more votes in total than the ruling parties, which have been kept in power for more than twenty years by the election system and the first-past-the-post rule. Admittedly, there is a certain amount of violence in some areas. But even the village I studied had its Congress activists (although they were not very active) and the neighbouring village had an active and quite a large Bharatiya Janata Party group, which almost managed to win the 1993 *panchayat* election there. Moreover, the merits and demerits of parties and individual politicians are openly discussed with gusto in many informal gatherings in village society. I would also argue that in contemporary West Bengal, the rule of the strong and powerful is effectively limited by the secret ballot.

It is also useful to derive some inspiration from what we may call 'modified subalternism', as represented by Dipesh Chakrabarty (1989), although this line of thinking finds its avatars in many other models too (Ruud 1999). We could then argue that it is not so much the crooked politicians who corrupt the Indian polity, but the values of society which creep in to 'Indianize' a political model that was really a misfitting transplant. Organized interest groups, civic values and civil society, representative democracy: these were forms that did not fit the Indian reality. Instead we now see the contours of political forms that are at least in part 'Indian', and in that respect, rallying around big men who can act as patrons and distribute state resources according to particularistic principles makes a lot of sense.

This 'Indianization' model is very inspiring. Its advantage is that it allows for an acceptance of the essential openness of the Indian political system, but may also account for the idiosyncratic manner in which it functions. Rallying around strong men may be a mode of politics in tune with the particularistic values of local Indian society. However, the model leaves one aspect unaccounted for. At the level of practice, if politicians to an increasing degree act according to norms shared by society, why do people 'talk dirty' about them, and why is their behaviour not applauded? In a modification of the 'Indianization' model, I propose a slightly different understanding of the normative universe in which attitudes towards politics are formed in a village, generalizing from the Bengali example. This universe contains a deep ambivalence towards politics (or the pursuit of worldly interest, *artha*) and because it is ambivalent, it does not give rise to simple moral guidelines.

This approach is inspired by a strand of anthropological literature. From his close reading of Mayer's ethnography (1960), Dumont (1980) points out that power in some cases can interfere with the working of the principles of ritual ranking. The Rajputs of Mayer's village followed an outward lifestyle of exceptional carefreeness and solidarity with other castes, the so-called 'allied castes' forming the basis of the political position of the Rajputs in the village. The Farmer caste of the same village followed an entirely different lifestyle, of vegetarianism, frugality and ritual purity, but although such a lifestyle is more Brahmanical and ritually superior to that of the meat-eating Rajputs, the Farmers only barely rivalled the Rajputs in ritual rank. Dumont concedes the point that power here complicates the principle of ritual rank, but declines to view this as a demonstration of parallel ranking systems. Instead he argues that 'one could indeed isolate a "Kshatriya model" alongside the Brahman model, but it is an underlying model, in some way shamefaced' (Dumont 1980: 91). *Artha*, the realm of the pursuit of worldly interests, is inferior to *dharma*, the higher religious principle. But, as Dumont puts it, 'in an actual situation, power may victoriously offset purity' (Ibid.: 89).

It is not the purpose of this essay to address issues relating to ritual rank or the implications of politics for caste purity. Yet in Dumont's reading we find a parallel story of how politics, and the ranking of individuals which emerges from within the game of politics, influence and upset higher norms and ideals. In a word, power contributes towards ranking, in very real and tangible ways, but it remains morally dubious, shamefaced and in some ways inferior. In the language of Indology, power is *artha*, which is not necessarily opposed to *dharma*, but is distinct from it. In contemporary Bengali villages, politics is perceived as a shamefaced but very real field of activities with its own rules and logic, which are normally, albeit not invariably, in conflict with moral ideals governing social conduct. People seek to keep their distance from such a morally dubious activity, yet they find it compelling nonetheless, because politics is about power and the material aspects of life and society, on which most people depend. This necessary involvement is troublesome and even one's own strategic manoeuvring becomes problematic when it involves close relationships with people of poor reputation. When coated in kinship terms, which carry their own moral weight, the relationship becomes still more difficult.[14]

Why then are politicians so easily considered less than pure and less than morally upright, and yet accepted as leaders of society? In Mayer's central Indian village, it is the commensality among castes (or rather, the Rajputs' lack of restrictions on their commensality with other lower castes), which contributes towards the Rajputs' power and position. They share food or enjoy the *hookah* with a large number of castes which are described as their 'allied castes', and they stand together in village affairs. In a word, Rajputs compromise their ritual purity but are rewarded with political support. This is not an explicit agreement but a social mechanism that rewards closeness, in spite of the fact that such a mechanism has a hard time finding cultural legitimation. With reference to the contemporary Bengali situation, I would argue along slightly different but parallel lines; in their daily activity, (local) politicians have to compromise on their principles, occasionally default on old obligations, and to be everywhere, being agreeable to all and sundry. Such activity may in the eyes of most people, jeopardize moral standards and entangle politicians in activities that are not ideal. Being in politics—which is often conceived of as a separate activity—entails an expectation that one must compromise on standards. Compromises, alliances (sometimes with old enemies), deals and power equations rather than principles, are the *sine qua non* of building political positions and they are what politics is reckoned to be all about. Politics does and will always mean getting involved in an activity that is less than absolute and pure, but which has its own fascination and attraction because it is about real and tangible issues.

If there is a general understanding that politics—the pursuit of worldly interest, *artha*—is almost invariably shamefaced and morally dubious, then it is easy to see how this can have a compounding effect. The understanding that politics is about power and not morality sets the broad limits for people's expectations about what can be gained through involvement in politics. What can be achieved and what is possible are constrained not by moral considerations, but mainly by the right circumstances and by power, clout, influence and contacts.

Notes

1. See, for instance, Chakrabarty 1989; Kaviraj 1991; 1992. The same idea is also found in abundance in the somewhat older literature dealing with Indian administration: see Potter 1996.
2. *Ye yae lankae se habe raban,* which constitutes another way of saying 'power corrupts'—so nothing specifically Indian here.
3. Or to have outsiders interfere in our problems. One good example of this is the two very different village leaders in Hitchcock's 1959 article, both of whom emphasized the need to keep the police out of their village.
4. Bengali kinship ideology, and its implications for kin and non-kin ties and for notions of social order, are discussed by Inden and Nicholas (1977); Greenough (1982); Davis (1983).
5. A novel term much used in contemporary Bengal; the older term was *daladali,* known in English as 'factionalism'.
6. Material relating to this line of reasoning can be found in Ruud (1999).
7. 'The *panchayats*' is a generic term for the three-tier system of local-level representative bodies with statutory powers: the *gram panchayat* covers ten-fifteen villages, the *panchayat samiti* normally covers a development block, and the *jela parishad* is the representative body at district level.
8. This was the time of the central government's negotiations with the World Bank, and the 'Dunkel proposition' was derided on every wall and in every political speech in West Bengal.
9. India's victory in the cricket match later that evening was celebrated with much merry-making and in one neighbouring village with fire crackers.
10. The term being used for 'big leaders' was *bara netara,* again somewhat ironic since village leaders rarely qualify for the rather grand term *neta*.
11. I discount the junior activists' labours and speeches, which were pretty clearly a training exercise for party favours and future positions.

12. The first statement was in English, the second was *'manushik dik theke [se] kharap nay'.*
13. The contributions of Sulbaltern Studies scholars (Guha 1982–9) are very diverse and a short summary cannot give due credit to their diversity. However, I believe most contributors would recognize at least some of their ideas in my discussion.
14. To apply Dumont to contemporary Indian society is a problematic exercise and my aim is not to suggest ahistoric trajectories. The interest of his model lies in its ability to yield insights into this particular ethnographic conundrum. Whether or not the ranking of *artha* below *dharma* was also found in ancient India and represents something quintessentially Indian is an altogether different debate that is not relevant in the present context.

References

Chakrabarty, D. 1989. *Rethinking working-class history: Bengal 1890–1940.* Princeton: Princeton University Press.

Davis, M. 1983. *Rank and rivalry: the politics of inequality in West Bengal.* Cambridge: Cambridge University Press.

Dumont, L. 1980 [1970]. *Homo hierarchicus: the caste system and its implications.* Chicago: University of Chicago Press.

Greenough, P. R. 1982. *Prosperity and misery in modern Bengal: the famine of 1943–1944.* New York: Oxford University Press.

Guha, R., ed. 1982–9. *Subaltern studies I-VI: writings on south Asian history and society.* Delhi: Oxford University Press.

Haynes, D., and G. Prakash, eds, 1991. *Contesting power: resistance and everyday social relations in South Asia.* Delhi: Oxford University Press.

Hitchcock, J. T. 1959. Leadership in a north Indian village: two case studies. In Richard L. Park and Irene Tinker, eds, *Leadership and political institutions in India*, pp. 395–414. Princeton: Princeton University Press.

Inden, R. B., and R. W. Nicholas. 1977. *Kinship in Bengali culture.* Chicago: University of Chicago Press.

Kaviraj, S. 1991. On state, society and discourse in India. In J. Manor, ed., *Rethinking third-world politics*, pp. 73–99. London: Longman.

——. 1992. The imaginary institution of India. In P. Chatterjee and G. Pandey, eds, *Subaltern Studies VII*, pp. 1–39. Delhi: Oxford University Press.

Mayer, A. C. 1960. *Caste and kinship in central India: a village and its region.* London: Routledge and Kegan Paul.

Myrdal, G. 1970. Corruption as a hindrance to modernization in South Asia; Corruption: its causes and effects (extracts from *Asian drama,* 1968). In A. J. Heidenheimer, ed., *Political corruption: readings in comparative analysis*, pp. 229–39 and 540–5. New York: Holt, Rinehart and Winston.

Potter, D. C. 1996. *India's political administrators: from ICS to IAS.* Delhi: Oxford University Press.

666666666

66666666666

6

Ruud, A. E. 1999. The Indian hierarchy: culture, ideology and consciousness in Bengali village politics. *Modern Asian Studies* 33, 3: 689–732.

Scott, J. 1985. *Weapons of the weak: everyday forms of peasant resistance.* New Haven: Yale University Press.

——— . 1990. *Domination and the arts of resistance: hidden transcripts.* New Haven: Yale University Press.

The return of king Mahabali: the politics of morality in Kerala

Filippo Osella and Caroline Osella

General theories of the state often rest upon a dichotomy between a supra-local 'state' and some other, local, particularistic realm: family, tribe, caste. 'Civil society' has then necessarily been drawn in to theorize the great mass of social and political life which actually falls between these two extremes, and to stand as a buffer zone mediating the dichotomy (cf. Hann 1996). This concept is used both by those who evaluate the local and particular negatively, and emphasize the integrative power of the nation (for example, in discussions of communalism), and by those who celebrate the local (for example, the 'grassroots' organization) as the locus of resistance to state domination. Mainstream anthropological analyses of the relationship between citizens and the state in India have also been dichotomous, appealing either to a problematic transition from the particularism of the 'traditional' to the universalistic ideals of modernity and democracy (e.g. Singer 1972), or to an underlying opposition between the morality of 'traditional' values, and the amorality of modern-day society and the state (e.g. Dirks 1987; Dumont 1980; Inden 1990; Guha 1982; 1983; Kaviraj 1992).

In this essay, we want to move away from such dichotomies in order to see the state as multilayered and pluricentric, and as it is encountered at a local level in the form of specific officials and representatives. Then,

We have received generous financial support for various periods of fieldwork and writing-up between June 1989 and September 1996 from the Economic and Social Research Council of Great Britain, the London School of Economics, the Leverhulme Trust, the Nuffield Foundation and the Wenner-Gren Foundation. We would like to thank Gilles Tarabout, Joel Kahn, Geert De Neve and Yasushi Uchiyamada, as well as participants in departmental seminars at SOAS, Sussex and Goldsmiths, for comments on earlier drafts.

both 'state' and 'people' become ambiguous, 'fuzzy' agents which resist characterization in essentialist terms. We shall suggest this through an ethnographic consideration of specific local discourses on morality in which the south Indian Kerala state and its citizens constitute themselves as legitimate political agents within a relationship of intimacy. By Kerala state we mean elected politicians and bureaucratic state officials brought together under the local term *sarkar* (government). Our focus will be the annual festival of Onam, when ordinary people, politicians and state representatives alike oppose the pervasive immorality of every day to a lost golden age, when Kerala was ruled by the mythical Mahabali, a just king who looked after the well-being of his subjects and kept the population well-fed and happy. Our ethnography will unsettle two more dichotomies, in this case local essentialisms which are often (falsely) elided: morality versus amorality and *dharma* versus *adharma*. Importantly, good king Mahabali was a demon—a creature of *adharma*, a state of existence outside the 'proper' socio-cosmic moral order—who eventually lost his kingdom to Vamana, an incarnation of the god Vishnu, who restored proper *dharmic* rule and yet brought along with *dharma* all the shortfalls of current life.

Building on recent work on the anthropology of postcolonial states (e.g.Bayart 1993; Chatterjee 1993; Ferguson n.d.; Yang 1994), which questions the explanatory value of analytical models built on a dichotomy, and possible antagonism, between 'political superstructures and local socio-political forms of organisation' (De Boeck 1996: 95), we will suggest that through Onam, in an apparently shared narrative of a lost golden age which highlights a specific Malayali identity, 'state' and 'people' construct relationships of political intimacy with each other (Herzfeld 1997), embedded in familial idioms of moral responsibility, reciprocity and patronage. On the one hand, the familial intimacy between patron and client provides the state government and bureaucracy with a justification for its interventions in and demands on people's lives, and on the other hand, it confers on people, as clients, specific moral claims, rights and degrees of political leverage sometimes denied to them as citizens of a democratic state.

Our data are drawn from three separate periods of fieldwork, totalling three years between 1989 and 1996 in Valiyagramam, a mixed-community rural *panchayat* in south Kerala's rice-producing area. As the dominant economic activity, agriculture has been gradually giving way over the last fifty years to paid employment, small business and migration. As in other parts of Kerala, the population has benefited from legislative and social reforms resulting in (albeit limited) land redistribution, literacy, healthcare, and so on, but inequalities have been considerably exacerbated by the recent impact of migration to the Persian Gulf and by economic liberalization. The area is characterized by a rapidly expanding middle class, a small and declining elite, and a substantial and increasingly impoverished working class, comprising many who work precariously as casual day-labourers.

Onam

Onam is Kerala's most important festival. It is the Malayali New Year (falling between mid-August and mid-September) and it is celebrated equally by Hindus and non-Hindus as a time when the unity of the family and kin group is particularly emphasized. Wherever possible, migrant workers return to the village and families are re-united; among lower castes, ancestors return to visit on this day.[1] In front of houses, children build *athapukolam*—circular geometrical designs made of flowers—to welcome and seat the visiting Onam deity, *onattappan* ('Onam father'). On the main day, *thiruvonam*, heads of families distribute presents (usually clothes) to family members and a sumptuous meal is prepared by the women of the house. This ideal pattern is followed, of course, only by those who can afford it, but even in the poorest families a special effort is made to celebrate.[2] At Onam, patron-client relations are also reiterated: on the day before *thiruvonam*, permanent labourers and members of artisan and service castes working for a particular landlord arrive at his house bringing small presents in kind, tokens of their trade. Landowners' return gifts include items necessary for the workers' Onam feast—paddy, rice, coconut oil, tamarind, mango pickle and bathing oil, as well as cloth and a small amount of money.

For ten days there are festival events, family visits, feasts and games. In the state capital, Onam is celebrated by government-sponsored 'cultural activities', focusing on the performance of 'traditional' Malayali art forms (Zarilli 1996), and ending with a pageant, including a parade of floats from various government departments and trade associations, marching bands, and military and paramilitary units. While these pageants are replicated on a lesser scale in most major towns across the state, in villages a plethora of events are organized by schools and various cultural organizations.[3] In villages, Onam is also the occasion for sporting events: from country-football and *kabbadi* (a sort of 'tag' game) to boat races (*vallam kali*). In all these events, the emphasis is on competition, which is particularly heated for sports; prizes are distributed to the best performers and winning teams by 'authorities', local dignitaries or 'VIPs', who are asked to preside over and judge competitions.

Mahabali and Vamana

Onam celebrates and recreates the lost golden age of the mythical king Mahabali, when nobody cheated or lied and all lived in harmony. Mahabali is a prototypical just king, known across India (cf. Chambard 1996); Kerala's popular narratives of the Onam myth echo pan-Indian stories. Here is a version collected in Valiyagramam:

In old times Kerala was ruled by a king, Mahabali, who was a demon (*asura*). It was a time of happiness and plenty: there were no quarrels, no cheating, no robbery and no gossip; there were no castes and everyone was equal. The gods saw all this and, jealous, they went to complain to Vishnu. They said: 'Do something about this demon king'. Vishnu agreed and transformed himself into his *avatar* [incarnation] Vamana, the dwarf Brahman, and went to visit Mahabali. Vamana asked Mahabali, 'Give me some land as *danam* [gift], because I want to settle in your country'. Seeing that the petitioner was a Brahman, the good-hearted king agreed, telling Vamana that he could have land anywhere he wanted in Kerala, as much as he could cover with three strides. The dwarf Vamana immediately became the giant Vishnu and in two steps covered the whole of Kerala. He returned to the king to ask for his third step, as there was no land left. Mahabali said, 'I have nothing left, you took everything. You can take me, but you must grant me a boon; my people are now happy and well and I want to come once a year to visit them and to see that they are all right'. Vamana agreed and Mahabali lowered his head. Vamana stepped on Mahabali's head with his right foot. The earth opened and Mahabali was pushed underground. Once a year he comes back; at that time, his happy kingdom is recreated.

'On one level, this myth is a straightforward narrative of the victory of the socio-cosmic order of *dharma* over the rule of *adharma* and demons. The demon-king surrenders himself to the gods, in an act of complete sacrifice. Mahabali, meaning 'great sacrifice', loses his whole kingdom and is banished to the underworld, his devotion rewarded by the promise of eventual redemption (in a Brahmanical reading).[4] In pre-colonial times, rulers of central Kerala competed to acquire the right to attend and make Onam offerings at the Trikkakara temple near Kochi, owned by a Brahman king, Edapalli Raja (Menon 1965: 104ff; Tarabout 1986: 444–7). At Onam, the kings assembled at Trikkakara and each sponsored one day of the twenty-eight day festival. The kings, by submitting themselves and their powers to the rule of *dharma* as embodied by the temple deity Vamana/Vishnu, recreated the sacrifice of the mythical demon-king and legitimized themselves as rightful *dharmic* rulers. The Trikkakara festival also held an explicit political dimension: through allocation of ranked rights of worship, it constructed and reiterated a political hierarchy among rulers. Onam, as well as the Malayali New Year, coincides with the paddy harvest and is considered a time of plenty and happiness. By participating in the festival, local kings associated themselves with the periodic renovation and regeneration of the cosmos, bringing fertility and well-being to Kerala and its inhabitants (cf. Tarabout 1986: 442–7).

For the kings, the focus of Onam was not Mahabali's annual return, but the annual re-enactment of his sacrifice and the reconstruction of *dharmic* rule by the intervention of Vishnu. In a similar 'orthodox' reading, local Brahmans explained to us that what they celebrated at Onam—as, they insisted, was the case in the past for the whole population of Kerala—was not the return of Mahabali, but, on the contrary, his defeat by Vishnu and the establishment of *dharma* (cf. M.N. Sivan 1977: 30–2). For Brahmans, it is Trikkakarappan (i.e. Vamana), who is seated at the centre of the *athapukolam* in front of people's houses, so that when demon Mahabali visits he will see his former subjects now worshipping divine Vamana, restorer of *dharma*, and will return to the underworld. At the same time, Brahmans complained that since Kerala became part of the Indian Union, both Communist and Congress-led governments had distorted 'egalitarian' interpretations of the Onam myth for 'propaganda purposes'.

Constructing political identities

It is not clear whether local Brahmans are right to suggest that the focus on Mahabali is a recent development; songs associated with the festival appear to be old, while in neighbouring Tamil Nadu there are similar celebrations for the return of Mahabali, albeit at a different time of year (Reiniche 1979: 24). And Trikkakara temple is the *only* temple in Kerala dedicated to Trikkakarappan; poignantly, the temple is said to be built upon the ruins of Mahabali's royal palace. What is beyond doubt however is that, for the vast majority of people, Onam now celebrates the annual return and rule of the demon Mahabali; among non-Brahmans, it is decisively the tragic hero Mahabali who is greeted and offered flower decorations, while Vamana is the villain of the tale. Even in this case, however, there are multiple interpretations of the myth, determined partly by informants' social position (caste and class) and political allegiances, and partly by Kerala's political history since the turn of the last century. As we shall see, Onam is central to the construction of political identities and agency.

One reading of the myth has a clear anti-Brahmanical flavour, drawing on the rhetoric of the struggles in the 1930s for political reform and democratic rule, which included demands for the removal of

Brahmans from government bureaucracy, then dominated by this small community to the exclusion of local elites. Here Mahabali gets identified as a Dravidian, autochthonous king who loses his kingdom thanks to the trickery and bad faith of a non-Dravidian Brahman. Mahabali's defeat is connected to an alleged loss of power, land and status by local, 'Dravidian', landed elites to north Indian Brahman immigrants. Proponents of this reading are, of course, usually Nayars, members of the local non-Brahman landed elite. Conservative sections of this elite, often connected to Hindu fundamentalist organizations, shift the focus from the moment of usurpation to an earlier point. They like to stress the lost golden age of Mahabali as an epoch when people worked 'sincerely'. Then the sons-of-the-soil argument recedes in favour of an underlying discourse of vehement criticism of trade union militancy and left-wing policies which have granted labourers and low-caste communities some degree of protection and rights. The golden age's famed sincerity (*atmarthata*) becomes shorthand for the times before land reform, when labourers were at the beck and call of their patrons and employers.

Members of low-caste communities have different perspectives on Mahabali. He remains a Dravidian king, a tragic local hero whose piety resulted in his own downfall and the establishment of *dharma* in Kerala which, it is stressed, has brought nothing but misery and oppression to lower castes. Importantly, in most popular understandings of Onam, the festival is about the annual reconstitution of a particular moral order and is akin to other religious festivals such as goddesses' festivals in Kerala (Tarabout 1986) or Dasara across India (Fuller 1992: ch. 5); unlike those other festivals, however, morality here is embodied in Mahabali and his rule, and associated with *adharma* and demons, whereas immorality, unfairness and misery become hallmarks of *dharma*. The fact that Mahabali is a demon is not in itself a problem; after all, as low-caste Malayalis often stress, Brahmans have always branded deities worshipped by the low castes as demons. The emphasis in popular readings is on the rule of Mahabali as an egalitarian time, when people were *onnupole* ('like one', 'equal') and there were neither caste nor class differences.[5] This interpretation uncovers the contingent nature of caste and class differences, and explicitly links differentiation to high-caste exploitation of the innocent and sincere.[6] Inequality is de-naturalized and linked to a primordial act of cheating, such as that of Mahabali by Vamana. This strongly egalitarian reading of the Mahabali myth connects at one level with the development of militant caste associations among the lower castes and with long-term campaigns against caste discrimination, and at another level with the success of Communist parties and left-wing trade unions. At both levels, Mahabali is celebrated as an anti-establishment figure, his rule being portrayed as a time of natural castelessness, while left-wing rhetoric describes it as an original instance of primitive communism, so that communism itself is rooted in primordial, autochtonous practices.[7] Albeit to a lesser degree, the Congress party has also tried to take up Mahabali's egalitarianism, linking it to Gandhian notions of self-respect, anti-untouchability and self-rule (*swaraj*). The golden age of Mahabali is then generally seen as a historical antecedent and legitimation of current political projects; at the same time, Malayalis are widely endowed with a sense of justice stretching right back to mythical times and rekindled every year during the Onam season.

Onam, national identity and public morality

Linking Mahabali's mythical rule to the Malayali character reflects a wider role that Onam has come to play in the construction of a specific regional identity. Although the idea of a 'United Kerala' had been strongly advocated by the Kerala Communist party since the early 1940s (Hardgrave 1993: 197), Kerala has been a unified state only since 1956. The Communist party, elected for the first time in 1957 and then periodically returned to office as the main partner of Left coalitions, set itself the explicit task of establishing 'an appreciation for and a preservation of a "purely Malayali Kerala"'(Zarilli 1996: 85), asserting a collective identity in which all Malayalis, regardless of caste, religion and region, could recognize themselves. Central to this project of constructing an 'imagined political community', in Anderson's words, has been the sponsoring of state-wide Onam celebrations. At one level these pageants, through the performance of 'traditional' art forms, stress the cultural specificity of the state and the richness of its cultural traditions; at another level they seek to construct an image of overall unity and amity. Importantly, pluralism and social tolerance are represented, together with equality and justice, as defining the Malayali character, found in Mahabali's golden rule as well as in present-day Kerala where, according to official rhetoric, diverse communities coexist amicably without communal conflict, unlike the rest of India.[8] Kerala's well-known social reforms and progressive policies become not just the result of specific political projects, but are naturalized as the expression of a distinctive character and will: compromising, adjustable, flexible and fair.

Onam, the time when these collective moral values are heightened and renewed, then becomes a platform to engage in criticism of the perceived immorality of present-day life. Specific moral flaws in certain sections of the population are considered prime obstacles to development of the state economy and to amelioration of the population's general well-being. Recent targets of annual reprimands, in the press and in speeches by politicians and state officials during the Onam season, are Gulf migrants and the emerging middle classes, both accused of greed and selfishness, because instead of investing in productive activities, they engage in conspicuous consumption of expensive goods and services (cf. F. and C. Osella 1999). Moreover, their taste for foreign-imported goods and styles is presented as corrupting the integrity of traditional cultural and moral values, making them agents of current processes of 'neo-colonialism' and cultural decay. In recent years, these groups stand accused of transforming Onam, by introducing new and more expensive gifts, into a consumerist extravaganza which, highlighting inequalities, undermines the festival's egalitarian spirit. More state intervention is then justified by the moral failings of the migrants and middle classes. While these groups represent emerging (and competing) social agents, this kind of censure within the sphere of public culture is not new; during the 1970s and 1980s, a group singled out for similar condemnation was the tenant-cultivators who lost interest in political mobilization when—thanks to land reforms—they had gained full ownership of the land they previously rented (cf. Herring 1983; Oommen 1985; Tornquist and Tharakan 1996: 1847–58).

In recent years the left-led state government has moved towards an even more 'intimate' (Herzfeld 1997) relationship with its citizens, initiating an ambitious programme of economic and social development, the 'People's Campaign for the Ninth Plan', based on devolution of some state planning and substantial budgetary resources to local bodies. The campaign, which follows a critical reappraisal of the 'Kerala Model', has several objectives, but it has in particular set itself the task of redressing popular disenchantment with state-sponsored developmental programmes (Tornquist and Tharakan 1996). Under the slogan 'Planning for Empowerment', the campaign aims at recreating that spirit of popular participation and mobilization characteristic of the 1950–70 struggle for land reform. By promoting grass-roots participation and establishing direct links between local *panchayats* and the State Planning Board, the planners hope to cut down the corruption, red tape and 'inefficient' middle-level bureaucracy which have thwarted recent development policies (Isaac and Harilal 1997).[9] The whole programme has a strong moral and voluntaristic dimension: in the State Planning Board's words, 'we should be able to break the atmosphere of cynicism that exists among the people today and instil in them a new sense of optimism and direction

... it should be possible thereby to tap monetary, material and labour resources at the local level for the implementation of the plan' (qu. in Bandyopadhyay 1997: 2452). It is hoped that the process of mass mobilization and consciousness raising fostered by the campaign will be such that allocations from the state 'would be supplemented by voluntary contribution of labour, materials or money' (Isaac and Harilal 1997: 57). Here Onam criticisms of Gulf migrants and nouveaux riches go hand in hand with wider ideological efforts to reverse recent trends of 'petty-embourgeoisement' in rural areas and to supersede current individualistic ideals 'of how one could and should make a fast buck without too much hard work and without engaging in tiring attempts at solving Kerala's socio-economic and political problems' (Tornquist and Tharakan 1996: 1854–5). This then is what the 'state' demands of its 'people'.

State and patronage

The rhetoric of the 'developmental' state, articulated and embodied in the practices of its elected representatives and bureaucracy, goes beyond merely presenting current policies as promoting and preserving specific moral values associated with Mahabali's golden age and a specific Malayali identity or character. The *sarkar* or government seeks identification in its morally-concerned endeavour with Mahabali's just rule, while, by sleight of hand, political leaders take on the mantle of Mahabali himself, becoming the embodiment and repository of cherished national values. Onam spectacles are performed by and in front of the population, but they are viewed and judged—from the grand pageants of the state capital down to village boat races—by politicians, state representatives and a variety of 'dignitaries'. The form and structure of these celebrations cannot but remind us of annual temple festivals in Kerala and throughout south India (cf. Fuller 1992: chs 5–6), which bring together whole neighbourhoods or villages in the celebration and reconstruction of a deity's rule over a specific territory, while simultaneously allowing patrons to participate in the royal attributes of the deity itself, for both patrons and deities offer protection, help and support to their constituencies. This is of course the stuff of Hindu kingship; recent studies in Tamil Nadu show that kingly practice remains a powerful tool in the hand of caste leaders, rich entrepreneurs and politicians seeking to constitute themselves as patrons and leaders of wider communities (De Neve 2000; Mines 1994; Price 1996).

Onam festivities therefore offer political possibilities to would-be big-men. Elsewhere we have argued that gifts given at Onam by village landowners to permanent labourers seek to couch exploitative labour practices in idioms of kinship and patronage: while labourers interpret gifts as a specific right, employers present them as a gesture of munificence, simultaneously transforming labourers into clients (F. and C. Osella 1996). 'At Onam everyone should be celebrating the return of king Mahabali by feasting', one of Valiyagramam's biggest landowners told us; 'Onam is a time of plenty and no-one should go without a proper celebration. So I give my labourers the items necessary for a feast'. But it is not just village big-men who use Onam to constitute themselves as patrons; ruling parties and politicians follow similar strategies. This becomes particularly explicit in two well-established policies: the first is the allocation of annual cash bonuses to government employees in the Onam wage-packet, and the other is the sponsorship of 'Maveli/Mahabali Stores', government-run shops selling at controlled prices an array of goods necessary for preparation of traditional Onam meals and for presents. What are perceived by many people either as hard-earned rights or as nothing but the fulfilment of electoral promises are transformed into acts of munificence and concerned benevolence. In return for its patronage, the state government then demands commitment to its developmental programmes, for example through voluntary participation in the 'People's Campaign for the Ninth Plan', where release of state funds is explicitly linked to donations of money, materials and unpaid labour towards local development projects.

If the invocation of Mahabali's rule and the celebration of Onam serve to constitute relationships between the state government and its citizens—which are embedded in idioms of moral responsibility and patronage and entail specific rights and duties on both sides—they also do so for the relationship between Kerala and the central government. This relationship is an ambiguous one, partly depending on which political parties are in power in Kerala and Delhi. Almost every year, the Kerala government has to enter into negotiations with the centre before Onam to get extra supplies of rice at controlled prices to meet internal demand. These requests are usually met, although when the central government is in the hands of a hostile party, negotiations may be protracted and the quantity of rice released less than originally requested. Negotiations and haggling between the state and central governments are followed in the press and are hotly debated. Crucial to the discussions is the relative strength of personal links between Kerala's chief minister and officials in Delhi; a well-connected chief minister can mobilize contacts and call back favours to ensure that enough rice is delivered to Kerala to stack up the shelves of ration shops and Maveli/Mahabali stores in time for Onam. In other words, the central government is also constructed as a powerful—albeit distant—patron to whom local politicians must turn in order to fulfil their own obligations towards their clients.[10]

But during Onam, the central government may also be constructed as the epitome of the Brahman Vamana's rule: distant, indifferent, corrupt and blocking Kerala's path to social and economic development. It goes without saying that such accusations are less forceful when the central government is directly or indirectly supported by Kerala's ruling parties.[11] In any case, Onam celebrations become a platform for criticisms of the centre, political corruption being a major theme. In 1989, at the height of widespread allegations against the then Indian prime minister Rajiv Gandhi, accused of having received millions in bribes from a Swedish defence contractor, floats paraded across Kerala during Onam were used to portray and publicly denounce the corruption. Giant models of guns and effigies of the prime minister holding dollar bills were among items seen on floats. Then, critiques of the prime minister's corrupt practices—together with his lavish life-style, foreign-born wife and taste for expensive imported goods—were set against the moral values embedded in Onam, of which the state government made itself champion, while the prime minister's accumulation of personal wealth was directly related to his reluctance to release financial resources to boost Kerala's ailing economy.

The amorality of everyday life

Criticisms of the perceived immorality of post-golden-age everyday life are deeply embedded in the rhetoric of Onam. From the perspective of the 'state', we will now switch to that of Valiyagramam's villagers, who invariably cited a passage from a popular folk song: 'When Mahabali ruled the land, all were extremely good and not a single corrupt or cruel person was to be seen; people only used good gold to make jewellery; thieves and cheats were unknown, measures and measuring rods were true' (cf. Panikkar 1983: 90ff). Everyone drew our attention to the alleged absence of cheating during Mahabali's rule, while complaining about the difficulties and stress of living in times when cheating (*chadi*) is perceived to be normal practice. Villagers complain about ration-shop owners who sell rice mixed with stones and give short weight by using irregular measures; they complain about affines who refuse to pay promised dowries in full; they complain about relatives who borrow money, but never return it; they complain about brothers who refuse to split inheritances in equal parts; they complain about 'travel agents' who take money in the promise of a Gulf job before disappearing. The list of instances of cheating is endless, covering incidents as mundane as being sold second-quality vegetables at the market, to losing all of one's hard-earned savings in the hands of a corrupt state official; cheating is so widespread as to be at the centre of the gossip, arguments, angry exchanges and even fights which we witnessed almost daily around the village.

Moncy is the youngest of five brothers, all of whom have been working in Muscat for several years where they run several successful shops. In the late 1980s, Moncy was still unmarried and was living in Valiyagramam together with his parents and the wife of Manu, one his migrant elder brothers. In 1990, Manu returned from the Gulf unexpectedly and, within a few hours of his arrival, a major row started in the house, just a couple of hundred yards away from where we were living at the time. We joined the large crowd of neighbours who, attracted by the shouts and screams, had begun to congregate outside; suddenly the door was flung open and Manu appeared on the doorstep throwing Moncy out of the house. Moncy had been beaten up by his brother and, while friends sheltered him from more blows, it became clear that Manu had found out, through a phone call from his mother, that his wife was having an affair with her brother-in-law, Moncy. Later it emerged that Moncy had had affairs with the wives of his other brothers, and that he had been found out and beaten up on each occasion—which is why his other brothers had taken their spouses away to the Gulf. To make things worse, Moncy had also spirited away a large amount of money which Manu had sent back towards building a new house. Eventually Manu had to return to Muscat, but, like his other brothers before him, he took his wife with him. When we returned to Valiyagramam three years later, Moncy had married but was refusing to join his brothers in Muscat. He said that his wife Sheena was too 'innocent' (*pavam*); she could be misled too easily and because the village was full of cheats and tricky people, he had to be with her the whole time to protect her. To everyone it was clear that Moncy feared that his brothers would repay him in kind during their regular visits from the Gulf.

The general perception is that cheating is part and parcel of everyday living. Cheats (*chathiyanmar*) are everywhere, even within close family members. People must therefore protect themselves by being distrustful of everybody and by being on their guard the whole time. While villagers complain that today cheating is on the increase, directly related to increased economic differentiation brought by Gulf migration, they by no means see it as an exclusive feature of modern living.[12] Nowadays as much as in the past, honest people who behave with 'sincerity' (*atmarthata*) are considered rare, because there is very little to be gained by being sincere.

Although it is an essential moral quality, sincerity leaves you vulnerable to other people's recklessness and bad faith, the sad ending of Mahabali being a most telling case.

To some extent, the behaviour of the 'sincere' who dutifully discharge obligations is actually subject to condemnation; while publicly praised, they are privately ridiculed as *pavangal* (pl. of *pavam*). A *pavam*, in the vernacular sense, is a highly moral person of good intentions and behaviour, who does no harm to anyone; he is also an innocent and gullible person who, because of his good qualities, can be taken advantage of. Spoken by one man of another, the word *pavam* is often accompanied by a smirk, implying that the speaker is more competent and worldly-wise (F. and C. Osella 2000).[13] While people believe that in an ideal world, such as during Mahabali's golden age, sincerity should be the prevailing quality, the predicaments of everyday life force everyone to be a bit of a *kallan* ('thief'). But it is here that we must tread carefully, because—as we might already expect from Malayalis' unexpected take on the values of *dharma* and *adharma*—these local discourses on the pervasive immorality of everyday life do not stand in any simple relationship to external ones about 'corruption'.

Corruption and lack of sincerity

The recognition that there is a complex, shifting and ambiguous relationship between sincerity and cheating, and that several types of relationship mediated by goods and cash can be identified, informs villagers' perceptions of what constitutes corruption (*azhimati*). Briefly, three different types of payments are commonly made, in different contexts, to 'get things done'. First, there are gifts (named in Malayalam as *sammanam* or, in English, as *presentations*) made to create 'flows' of goodwill between giver and recipient cementing a *bandham*, a relationship of mutuality constructed in a kinship idiom (F. and C. Osella 1996). Secondly, *donations* (always named as such in English) consist of substantial sums of cash explicitly and openly requested by recipients, commonly to oversubscribed private schools or colleges to ensure admission over and above normal criteria. While management may well take a cut from *donations*, the amount is widely understood as going towards the running costs of the institution. Thirdly, straightforward bribes (referred to in Malayalam as *kaikkuli*, literally 'cash for the hand') are paid, via intermediaries who know current rates and take a cut, to government servants to circumvent rules and regulations or to smooth the passage of straightforward requests. In small amounts like the Rs 10 given to the government hospital compounder who dresses a wound, *kaikkuli* is often referred to as 'tea money', acting like tips to supplement the wages of the poorly-paid.

These various payments are attributed different moral evaluations. Gifts are unproblematic; they are part and parcel of *bandhukkar* reciprocity or patron-client relationships, they cement and reiterate moral and affective kin-like bonds, they are necessary where mediation and personalization domesticate and democratize relationships which would otherwise be distant and bureaucratically anonymous (cf. Herzfeld 1992; Yang 1994). *Donations* are investments in the future: what a person has to give in order to get ahead, given the entitlements and constraints allowed by society and social position. They obviously reinforce existing social and economic inequalities; thus, a low-caste Pulaya science graduate like Salomon, unable to pay Rs 50,000 to secure a job at a private school, works for just Rs 300 per month as a temporary remedial teacher in a tutorial college, and supplements this meagre income as a labourer during paddy harvest. By contrast, the emerging middle classes, especially Gulf migrants, pay *donations* willingly and with pride; investments in children's education are part and parcel of long-term family-oriented mobility projects, but are also public demonstrations of wealth and status (F. and C. Osella 1999). Bribes or *kaikkuli* are most widely bemoaned as part of the widespread amorality of everyday life. Unlike *donations*, bribes are a means to achieve something to which one is not entitled.[14] But condemnation of *kaikkuli* is qualified. Little stigma attaches to the person who gives bribes; the knowledge, contacts and cunning required in bribing someone are a demonstration of the giver's *buddhi*, that intelligence or power of discrimination which distinguishes adults from children (Gupta 1995; F. and C. Osella 2000).

The common understanding is that politicians and state officials are inherently corrupt; that even potentially upright individuals end up as corrupt once involved with politics and government; and that in order 'to get things done' ordinary people have no alternative but to satisfy the greed of rapacious officials. While in everyday discussions *sarkar*— government and state—is essentialized as an inherently corrupt and corrupting structure, at the same time it is also recognized that local state employees, officials and politicians—low-level representatives of *sarkar* with whom villagers have to deal in their everyday life—are just like everyone else; they all have families to feed, daughters to marry out and children to send to university, and to do all that takes money. Babu the contractor explained that Susie, the young public-works engineer, readily accepted bribes not because of any inherent moral fault on her part, but because 'her family had to spend so much in *donations* and *kaikkuli* towards her education and getting her the job; it's natural that she would try to get some of that money back'.

This recognition that people are basically *onnupole*, like each other, provides an explanation—albeit not an apology—for corrupt practices, and acknowledges that those accepting bribes have, like everyone else and by virtue of shared common humanity, specific familial duties. Thus politician, bureaucrat, contractor and labourer alike are brought into the same social space and distances are dissolved. What receives unmitigated scorn is not receiving gifts or cash per se, but the behaviour of those who, having accepted bribes or *donations*, fail to stick to their side of the bargain: in other words, cheat. Cheating is problematic when bribes or *donations* have been paid because—unlike gifts—they are not embedded in longer-term social relationships, but tend to be one-off transactions dictated by purely economic interests, akin to market exchanges, so that whoever makes these payments can expect a positive outcome (cf. Yang 1994:202). Villagers praised the newly elected Congress Member of the Legislative Assembly, who discreetly accepted bribes but was judged 'sincere', because he never failed to arrange telephone connections or shop licences for those who sought his help; by contrast, they found the behaviour of the previous office-holder, who did not take bribes but continually asked for party contributions in return for promises for help that never materialized, to be utterly reprehensible. While it is recognized that in order to deal with the predicaments of everyday life people should use *buddhi* (intelligence) to look after their interests and behave with a touch of *kallan*-ness (sharpness) to avoid being swindled, at the same time indiscriminate *chathi* (cheating) is condemned as representing a breakdown of reciprocal trust and obligations, as going against the sense of 'fair play' essentialized (and highlighted in Onam) as a Malayali quality.

Discourses on sincerity and cheating are embedded in wider notions of mediation and compromise in which personalized relationships allow for a great degree of bargaining and flexibility, expressed by the Malayalam idiom '*adjust cheyyam*' (an adjustment can be made) indicating that, with proper connections and social competence, a satisfactory compromise can always be found and negatively valued conflicts avoided.[15] But if adjustment and compromise can be found because villagers and *sarkar* representatives are held to be *onnupole* (like each other), recognized as sharing a common humanity and being linked by a multiplicity of personalized ties, there are sometimes cases in which connections are lacking, bureaucratic distance prevails and adjustments are impossible. Where citizenship is constructed in the familial idiom of patronage, instances of inability to gain access to channels of mediation deny not only the possibility of reaching 'adjustments', but also one's sense of belonging to an 'imagined community' constructed in the idiom of being *onnupole*. Here a person who might justify the corruption of sympathetic officials by reference to pressure of familial duties will revert to uncompromising condemnation of public corruption.[16] Then the criticism expresses a failure to break through the 'bureaucratic indifference' of those powerful people who might also be neighbours, fellow caste members or relatives (Herzfeld 1992). What becomes important is not the system per se, but one's own place and leverage within it, and the behaviour—helpful or obstructive—of those in a position to help. Willingness to reciprocate and perceived sincerity are then the key issues.

The state held hostage

Sincerity, together with equality and justice, are values periodically mobilized by the state in efforts directed, via reference to a unique sense of diffused morality and national unity, to the legitimization of political projects and developmental policies. But at the same time, these same values form the moral yardstick against which people in Valiyagramam and Kerala at large evaluate, at Onam in particular, the behaviour of kin, fellow villagers, patrons, elected representatives and the state government. It is not surprising to find that at the time of year when such values are enhanced and reiterated, it is conflicts and disputes, rather than peaceful harmony, which actually come to dominate celebrations (cf. Spencer 1990: 235–41).

We have mentioned earlier the organization of Onam sporting events in every village and town across Kerala. These competitions, undertaken in the spirit of fair play and 'sincerity' characteristic of the festivity, almost invariably end up in altercations, disputes and even open fights. The most important Onam competitions in Valiyagramam are boat races. Attracting large crowds, these races take place in the river crossing the village's extensive paddy fields, and they attract crews and boats from Valiyagramam and neighbouring villages. Boats, divided into different categories according to length and number of rowers, are sponsored by local sports clubs or wealthy patrons. The boats are manned by crews of 'expert boatmen'—a euphemism indicating that rowers are almost invariably low-caste labourers. Races are watched and refereed by a variety of local dignitaries who enjoy the competition from a stage erected on the river bank near the finishing line; on stage sit *panchayat* members, current and past local Members of the Legislative Assembly and their entourages, the superintendent from the town's police station, priests from local churches, *sannyasis* representing well known local *ashrams*, school headmasters and so on.

The atmosphere at these races is both good-humoured and light-hearted as well as charged with tension, partly because crews and many spectators drink heavily. In 1990, when we first went to see the races, the programme began with drunken youths paddling decrepit boats and dinghies or sitting astride old tyres and occasionally pushing each other into the water, while singing aloud the latest popular hits or vulgar 'boat' songs, drawing large cheers and laughter from spectators. As the qualifying heats (in which boats race in matched pairs) began in earnest, the trouble started. Before the qualifying race, the captain of one of the bigger boats went to complain to the VIPs on stage that he should not have been matched, at this early stage of the competition, with such a strong opponent and that the latter had been cheating by hiring expert crew members from distant villages. The captain was eventually persuaded to rejoin his boat and the race started.

At the end of the mile-long run, the two boats crossed the finishing line almost together, but the *panchayat* president, having consulted with other VIPs on stage, declared the crew which had already been accused of cheating as the winner. Immediately, the other crew jumped down from their boat and waded through the water, oars menacingly in hand; they climbed up on to the stage, knocking to the floor whoever tried to stand in their way and, shouting '*chathi, chathi!*'('cheating, cheating'), tried to attack the *panchayat* president. The imposing presence of the police superintendent eventually brought back some calm and, to diffuse the tension, the two boats were declared joint winners and both passed to the second heat. The aggrieved crew left the stage triumphantly, singing a well-known drinking-song. But when they reached the nearby bridge they drew catcalls from supporters of the other boat, and immediately a fight erupted; to put an end to the fighting the police, by then assembled nearby, resorted to a *lathi*-charge, indiscriminately beating up whoever came within range of their sticks. When calm appeared to have been restored on the bridge, a menacing crowd began to surround the police; one man, covered in blood and crying, detached himself from the group to clamber on to the stage, where he began to shout, between sobs, to all those present: 'The police have beaten up my elder brother, what a shame, what a shame (*nanam*), he's like a father to me. He's always been a good man, honest, hard-working and he never drinks. He's innocent and was beaten up by the police for nothing; you must do something'. There and then, the *panchayat* president turned on the police superintendent and extracted a reluctant and embarrassed public promise to hold an enquiry and take action against the policeman responsible for the beating. The crowd eventually dispersed, but the boat race was brought to an early end. On the following day, the *panchayat* distributed leaflets, in which the police apologized for the indiscriminate beatings and said that one policeman on duty the previous day had been temporarily suspended.

What these incidents indicate is that while people might be willing or forced to tolerate some degree of cheating and injustice in their everyday life most of the time, at Onam—the time when social morality is constructed as an essential attribute of Malayali-ness and proper personhood—cheating becomes intolerable. To be the subject of cheating and injustice denies one's own *manam* (moral and social worth), that sense of being *onnupole*, of being equal to everyone else, which entitles people to the respect and 'sincerity' of others. The assertiveness of the participants and crowds at the boat races invariably leads to confrontations and fights; we could read the races as a straightforward 'ritual of rebellion', which eventually strengthens social cohesion, or as part of a Bakhtinian carnival in which normal power relations are temporarily suspended and reversed (cf. Spencer 1990: 91–3). After all, the *panchayat* president later dismissed the day's events by telling us: 'This is nothing, these people [i.e. low-caste villagers] always get drunk and fight. It's in their nature to do so'. But his dismissive words barely match up to the worried concern with which earlier on he had hastily and publicly intervened at the highest level, turning openly against his fellow VIP, the police superintendent, to redress the wrongs allegedly suffered by some of 'these people'.

On occasions such as boat-race disputes, what is at stake is the reputation and power of patrons: a wrong decision might lose them credibility, clients and—in the case of politicians—concrete support and votes. Landowners who fail to feast and give presents at Onam are openly criticized by permanent labourers and clients, and in the long run end up losing them to more 'sincere' employers and patrons. Similarly, one local patron and politician, who had been a *panchayat* member uninterruptedly since the 1950s, refused to intervene in a land dispute between two brothers—which at one Onam ended up in a bloody street fight between their respective families—by saying to the person who ran to him for help : 'They are always fighting like this; let them cook in their own broth'. Within a few days, widespread gossip accused him of being unconcerned and arrogant, in a deliberate campaign of character assassination which in the following year lost him the local elections. What takes place at Onam is not just, in James Scott's words, a 'moment of madness' disclosing hidden transcripts where normally 'public action by subordinate groups is pervaded by disguise' (Scott 1990: 182). Public criticism of the performance of patrons at Onam is no empty ritual, but has a direct and immediate bearing on wider social relationships for the rest of the year.

At Onam, politicians, big-men and landowners alike not only present themselves as munificent patrons—as modern-day Mahabalis—but they are also constructed as such by their potential followers, who give them deferential gifts and put them on stage as VIPs during celebrations. We are reminded of Alfred Gell's analysis of the royal ritual of Dasara in the kingdom of Bastar; at Dasara, the *raja*, having been imprisoned by his subjects, was worshipped, but his political power was also neutralized. Following Appadurai, Gell argues that the festival is 'an instance on a mass scale' of 'coercive subordination'; 'coercive subordination, or ritualized coercive deference, are techniques through which the subordinate so flatters the superior that the superior must accede to the inferior's demands or risk loss of status' (1997: 436). At Onam, by virtue of their enhanced position of moral authority as representatives or embodiments of Mahabali and the values associated with his rule, patrons are immediately called upon by their constituencies and clients publicly to exercise and test their fairness, goodwill and magnanimity, and to uphold Mahabali's egalitarian values in defending the self-respect of even the lowest member's of society against the most powerful. Here we are not claiming that the complexity and vitality of Kerala politics can be reduced to relationships of patronage alone; nor are we suggesting that patronage is wholly innocent. Rather, we argue that when everyday political relationships, often characterized by social distance and indifference, are explicitly reconstituted in the idiom of patronage and thereby personalized, 'coercive subordination' enables political subjects to express their will and agency as clients.

Conclusions

Satish Saberwal identifies the roots of India's current political crisis in a lack of fit between the cultural premises of western-style democratic state institutions and those of people's traditional institutions and practices—based on family, caste, village, little kingdom and so on. As a result, the institutional demands put on citizens are in conflict with people's needs and inclinations (1996: 17ff). While Saberwal may be right about the relationship between the national government and its citizens—although better ethnographies of the state might add complexity to the picture—

we hope to have shown that, at least at a regional level, a common political language does exist. In Kerala, through Onam and the Mahabali myth, the state government and citizens alike struggle to constitute themselves and each other as legitimate moral agents, in a relationship constructed in familial idioms of patronage and connectedness.

James Ferguson, suggesting that oppositions between state and society are 'built on an illusion', invites us to consider states as 'not in opposition to something called "society", but as themselves composed of bundles of social practices, every bit as "local" in their social situatedness and materiality as any other' (n.d.: 15). In a similar vein, Bayart has argued that relationships between the post-colonial state and society in Africa are mediated by a rhizome of personal networks which, via patronage, 'link the "lowest of the low" with the "highest of the high"' (1993: 219; cf. De Boeck 1996). Mayfair Yang argues that in China, in a situation in which the state redistributive apparatus dominates, *guanxi* networks allow people to obtain what is not available through the market via a web of personalized relationships based on idioms of 'connectedness, familiarity, obligation, reciprocity, mutual assistance, generosity and indebtedness' (1994: 305). In India, Akhil Gupta (1995) and Barbara Harriss-White (n.d.) have shown that in practice boundaries between the state and (civil) society are fuzzy, making it difficult to draw hard and fast lines between public and private interests and moralities. While Harriss-White identifies an intermediate class in Tamil Nadu, which enriches itself by mediating between the formal (state) and informal economies, Partha Chatterjee (1998), Dipesh Chakrabarty (1984) and Arild Ruud (1996)—from different perspectives— have identified patronage as a prevailing instrument of mediation and political representation. While current practices might appear to resemble 'traditional' patron-client relations, Chatterjee warns us that these are not 'primordial loyalties' at work, but that they 'are enmeshed in an entirely new set of governmental practices that are a function of the modern state in the late twentieth century' (1998: 282; cf. Sivaramakrishnan 1995: 405). Important here is to stop comparing *theories* of the state—which characterize essentialized northern European, developed or first-world states as rational, impersonal, bureaucracies—with *ethnographies* of southern, developing or third-world states (cf. Piot 1999: 20–4). A failure to draw upon ethnographies of the 'rational, modern' states of the first group, and an interpretation of ethnographies from the second group against the backdrop of meta-theory, have led to pernicious and caricaturing dichotomies (van der Veer 1999). This lopsided analysis has also consistently propped up outsider discourses on 'corruption'. It is therefore dangerous, both in terms of the distortions it produces in wider representations and because these representations feed directly into public policy and translate into calls for intervention (cf. Piattoni 1998; Wade 1982).

Whether we see middlemen and patrons as 'obstacles to development' or as an essential component of a 'third space', in Kerala, as elsewhere in India, personalized relations and patronage connect people and the state through a combination of mediated relationships and shared cultural practices. They remind us that the state is composed of people, and that analytical models which start from dualistic categories are bound to posit distance and overlook the quotidian intimacy of the state. This intimacy in turn allows for a reciprocal critical engagement, through which existing political and social relationships are periodically scrutinized, evaluated and redefined. Ruud rightly suggests that clients are not mere blind followers: 'in actual practice the leaders stand the constant risk of losing followers' (1996: 276). As relationships with the state and its political representatives are personalized in a myriad of ties of patronage which establish a *bandham*, a connection or tie, between patrons and clients, they become the site for political struggle and the assertion of individual and collective rights (cf. Sivaramakrishnan 1995: 406). At the same time, mutuality and patronage, as political practices which blur boundaries between 'state' and 'society', between public and self-interest, become instruments for mediation and resolution of conflicts that are negatively valued by all sides (cf. F. and C. Osella 1996: 60–3).

Kerala ethnography suggests that relationships between state and citizens might be characterized, following Herzfeld (1997), by intimacy and closeness, rather than separation and distance, which calls into question the validity of analysing such relationships in terms of dualistic, static oppositions. Especially problematic is the dualism of morality and amorality, which often leads towards arguments reminiscent of Banfield's much-criticized 'amoral familism' (1958). Recent work by Ferguson (1997) shows how, in the Zambian Copperbelt, early popular criticisms of the amorality of urban life were replaced, following a decline in the urban economy, by accusations of selfishness directed in reverse towards the rural population and the 'Zambian' in general (see also the critical discussion of 'amoral familism' by du Boulay and Williams 1987). In Kerala, contradictory articulations among various popular and governmental discourses of morality, immorality and amorality express the unfolding of similarly complex political relationships. Sometimes, 'state' and 'people' are essentialized and reified, and sometimes they are desegregated and brought into a condition of immediacy; finally both 'state' and 'citizen' are simultaneously moral and amoral, in a world where ultimate moral values are embodied by a mythical just king who is also a demon.

Notes

1. Yasushi Uchiyamada tells us that among untouchable Parayans, the important *vavu* ancestors' day is celebrated during Onam.
2. There is a saying in Malayalam, '*Kanam vittu Onam unnanam*', which means 'We should have the *thiruvonam* lunch even if we have to sell all our properties'.
3. Schools organize children's competitions and sports; cultural associations put on plays, parades by mimics, and poetry and singing contests.
4. In the textual myth, Mahabali receives the double promise to return once a year to earth and to be reborn as Indra, the king of the gods (Chambard 1996: 237).
5. A popular Onam song begins with the line '*Maveli naduvanidum kalam manusharellarum onnupole*' ('When Maveli [Mahabali] ruled, all men were equal').
6. The kingdom of Mahabali is usually opposed to Swami Vivekananda's description of turn-of-the-century Kerala as a 'madhouse of caste'.
7. In the 1990 Onam supplement of the *Indian Express*, we read that, 'the era [of Mahabali] seems to have anticipated the communist ideals of our times. By some foul play rendered possible by his religious credulity such a magnanimous emperor was sent out of his empire which began to feel his absence all the more when misery faced it during the succeeding generations'.
8. While this is, of course, rhetoric and communal tensions do exist in Kerala, it is also true that (so far) such tensions do not generally erupt so frequently or violently as in many other states.
9. Bandyopadhyay, an enthusiastic supporter of the programme, writes that 'disinterest, apathy, cynicism and alienation follow sequentially with some measures of overlapping. If the masses could start thinking as if they were the live subjects of development ... [their] latent creative energy would burst asunder the mould which suppressed it so long. This is not a fairy tale' (1997: 2452).
10. In a newspaper article printed during the 1990 Onam season, we read that 'today's Mahabali is the central government which sends down extra thousands of tonnes of rice to Kerala, so that the public distribution system does not fail, and at least there is one square meal for the family during Onam'.
11. It is Left parties which tend to be more critical of the 'centre'; since 1957, a succession of left-led coalition governments have been dismissed and replaced by direct rule from Delhi.
12. 'Cheating' also occurs in conversations about land reform and property partitions; cf. Hansen (n.d.) on the rise of discourses on cheating in times of crisis and change. Perhaps 'cheating talk' is a general way of dealing with new economic inequalities and those who have a good situation and are resented for it; 'cheating' denaturalizes economic inequalities and denies legitimacy to those doing well .

13. The ambivalances and tensions expressed here find parallels in other complex societies; Yang's study of Chinese *guanxi* relationships of mutual help and patronage refers to the category *laoshi* as being both 'honest' and 'reliable', but also 'malleable', 'obedient' and 'mindless' (Yang 1994: 64ff).

14. We thank Geert De Neve for pointing out the relationship between entitlement and non-entitlement.

15. This is similar to the Zairean *l'arrangement* (De Boeck 1996: 99) and supports Partha Chaterjee's assertion that, 'the self is open-ended; adjustment and compromise are ethical norms' (1998: 278; cf. F. and C. Osella 1996).

16. The issue of corruption was dealt with in the movie, 'Indian'/'Hindustani', released at the height of widespread discontent over the blatant corruption of both the Tamil Nadu and Kerala chief ministers. The hero, 'Indian' (Kamal Hassan), is a veteran freedom fighter who took up the struggle against the British colonialists, and now resorts to a campaign of murderous vengeance against various public figures (doctors, policemen, politicians). Violent, prevaricating British colonialists are equated to modern-day corrupt officials, both dealt in the same way by 'Indian'. The film tries to set out a clear opposition between the morality of traditional Indian values—honour, reciprocity and sincerity located in rural life, family and caste—in the name of which the struggle for independence was taken up, but which remain unfulfilled in post-colonial society, and the amorality of modern society and the state—revolving around the city, greed and western styles—as an extension of colonial endeavours.

References

Bandyopadhyay, D. 1997. People's participation in planning: the Kerala experience. *Economic and Political Weekly*, 32: 2450–4.

Banfield, E. C. 1958. *The moral basis of a backward society.* New York: Free Press.

Bayart, J.-F. 1993. *The state in Africa: the politics of the belly.* London: Longman.

Breman, J. 1985. *Of peasants, migrants and paupers.* Delhi: Oxford University Press.

Carrier, J., and J. Heyman. 1997. Consumption and political economy. *Journal of the Royal Anthropological Institute* 3, 2: 355–72.

Chakrabarty, D. 1984. Trade unions in a hierarchical culture: the jute workers of Calcutta 1920–50. In R. Guha, ed., *Subaltern Studies III*, pp. 116–52. Delhi: Oxford University Press.

Chambard, J.-L. 1996. Les trois grand dieux à la porte du roi Bali. *Purusartha* 18: 229–72.

Chatterjee, P. 1993. *The nation and its fragments: colonial and postcolonial histories.* Princeton: Princeton University Press.

——. 1998. Community in the East. *Economic and Political Weekly*, 33: 277–82.

de Boeck, F. 1996. Postcolonialism, power and identity: local and global perspectives from Zaire. In R.Werbner and T. Ranger, eds., *Postcolonial identities in Africa*, pp. 75–106. London: Zed Books.

160 • *The Everyday State and Society in Modern India*

De Neve, G. 2000. Patronage and 'community': the role of a Tamil 'village' festival in the integration of a town. *Journal of the Royal Anthropological Institute* 6, 3:501–19.

Dirks, N. 1987. *The hollow crown: ethnohistory of an Indian kingdom.* Cambridge: Cambridge University Press.

du Boulay, J., and R. Williams. 1987. Amoral familism and the image of limited good: a critique from a European perspective. *Anthropological Quarterly* 60, 1: 12–24.

Dumont, L. 1980. *Homo hierarchicus: the caste system and its implications.* Chicago: University of Chicago Press.

Ferguson, J. 1997. The country and the city on the Copperbelt. *In* A. Gupta and J. Ferguson, eds., *Culture, power and place,* pp. 137–54. Durham: Duke University Press.

——. n.d. Transnational topographies of power: beyond 'the state' and 'civil society' in the study of Africa. In G. Schwab, ed., *The forces of globalization,* forthcoming.

Fuller, C. J. 1992. *The camphor flame: popular Hinduism and society in India.* Princeton: Princeton University Press.

Gell, A. 1997. Exalting the king and obstructing the state: a political interpretation of royal ritual in Bastar District, Central India. *Journal of the Royal Anthropological Institute* 3, 3: 433–50.

Guha, R. 1982. The prose of counter-insurgency. *In* R. Guha, ed., *Subaltern Studies II,* pp. 1–42. Delhi: Oxford University Press.

——. 1983. *Elementary aspects of peasant insurgency in India.* Delhi: Oxford University Press.

Gupta, A. 1995. Blurred boundaries: the discourse of corruption, the culture of politics and the imagined state. *American Ethnologist* 22, 2: 375–402.

Hann, C. 1996. Introduction: political society and civil anthropology. *In* C. Hann and E. Dunn, eds., *Civil society: challenging western models,* pp. 1–26. London: Routledge.

Hansen, T. B. n.d. Bridging the Gulf: migration, modernity and identity among Muslims in Bombay. Paper at *Narrating mobility and identity* conference, 30 August-1 September 1997, Copenhagen.

Hardgrave, R. L. 1993. The Kerala communists: contradictions of power. *In* R. L. Hardgrave, *Essays in the political sociology of South India,* pp. 189–262. Delhi: Manohar.

Harriss-White, B. n.d. Rural infrastructure, urban civic spaces and the micro politics of governance. Paper at *The anthropology of the Indian state* workshop, May 1998, LSE, London,.

Herring, R. J. 1983. *Land to the tillers: the political economy of agrarian reform in South Asia.* New Haven: Yale University Press.

——. 1989. Dilemmas of agrarian communism: peasant differentiation, sectoral and village politics. *Third World Quarterly* 11, 1: 89–115.

Herzfeld, M. 1992. *The social production of indifference.* Oxford: Berg.

——. 1997. *Cultural intimacy: social poetics in the nation-state.* London: Routledge.

Inden, R. 1990. Imagining India. Oxford: Blackwell.

Isaac, T., and K. N. Harilal. 1997. Planning for empowerment: people's campaign for decentralised planning in Kerala. Economic and Political Weekly, 32: 53–8.

Kaviraj, S. 1992. The imaginary institution of India. In P. Chatterjee and G. Pandey, eds, Subaltern Studies VII, pp. 1–39. Delhi: Oxford University Press.

Menon, S. 1965. Kerala district gazetteers: Ernakulam. Trivandrum: Government Press.

Mines, M. 1994. Public faces, private voices: community and individuality in south India. Delhi: Oxford University Press.

Oommen, T. K. 1985. From mobilisation to institutionalisation: the dynamics of agrarian movement in twentieth-century Kerala. Bombay: Popular Prakashan.

Osella, F., and C. Osella. 1996. Articulation of physical and social bodies in Kerala. Contributions to Indian Sociology 30, 1: 37–68.

———. 1999. From transience to immanence: consumption, life-cycle and social mobility in Kerala, south India. Modern Asian Studies 33, 4: 989–1020.

———. 2000. Money, migration and masculinity in Kerala. Journal of the Royal Anthropological Institute 6, 1: 117–33.

Panikkar, T. K. G. 1983 [1900]. Malabar and its folk. New Delhi: Asian Educational Services.

Piattoni, S. 1998. Virtuous clientism: the southern question resolved?. In J. Schneider, ed., Italy's 'southern question': orientalism in one country, pp. 225–42. Oxford: Berg.

Piot, C. 1999. Remotely global: village modernity in West Africa. Chicago: University of Chicago Press.

Price, P. G. 1996. Kingship and political practice in colonial India. Cambridge: Cambridge University Press.

Reiniche, M.-L. 1979. Les dieux et les hommes: études des cultes d'un village du Tirunelveli, Inde du Sud. Paris: Mouton.

Ruud, A. E. 1996. State and civil society interaction: without a 'civil society' or a 'public sphere'? Some suggestions from rural India. Forum for Development Studies 2: 259–85.

Saberwal, S. 1996. Roots of crisis: interpreting contemporary Indian society. Delhi: Sage.

Scott, J. C. 1990. Dominance and the arts of resistance: hidden transcripts. New Haven: Yale University Press.

Singer, M. 1972. When a great tradition modernizes. Delhi: Vikas.

Sivan, M. N. 1977. The Mahabali myth: a study in the sociology of religion. In K. Thulaseedharan, ed., Conflict and culture, pp. 25–54. Trivandrum: College Book House.

Sivaramakrishnan, K. 1995. Situating the subalterns: history and anthropology in the subaltern studies project. Journal of Historical Sociology 8, 4: 395–429.

Spencer, J. 1990. *A Sinhala village in a time of trouble.* Delhi: Oxford University Press.

Tarabout, G. 1986. *Sacrifier et donner à voir en pays malabar: les fêtes de temple au Kerala (Inde du sud): étude anthropologique.* Paris: EFEO.

Tornquist, E., and M. Tharakan. 1996. Democratisation, and attempts to renew the radical political development project. *Economic and Political Weekly* 31: 1847–58, 1953–73, 2041–5.

van der Veer, P. 1999. The moral state: religion, nation and empire in Victorian Britain and British India. *In* P. van der Veer and H. Lehmann, eds., *Nation and religion: perspectives on Europe and Asia,* pp. 15–43. Princeton: Princeton University Press.

Wade, R. 1982. Politics and graft: recruitment, appointment and promotions to public office in India. *World Development* 13, 4: 467–97.

Yang, M. M. 1994. *Gifts, favors and banquets: the art of social relationships in China.* Ithaca: Cornell University Press.

Zarilli, P. 1996. History, kingship and the heroic: kalaripayattu, the 'Kerala heritage' and state formation. *In* C. Bratel, ed., *Performing arts of Asia: the performer as (inter)cultural transmitter,* pp. 79–105. Leiden: I.I.A.S. Working Papers Series 4.

Irrigation and statecraft in zamindari south India

David Mosse

In his recent book, *Seeing like a state,* James Scott (1998) vividly illustrates an expansion of state capacity to find out about society in the nineteenth and twentieth centuries. States, he argues, transform social and natural landscapes through projects of administrative re-ordering. Whether through censuses or surveys, maps or mono-cropping, scientific farming or forestry, states produce simplifications which order, regulate and render an otherwise illegible social life 'legible' to the state, and therefore subject to rational management and control. The colonial state in India could be regarded as the epitome of Scott's modernizing, centralizing state. After all, by the close of the nineteenth century the state had enumerated and classified the population of the country, and produced a carefully mapped and surveyed 'village India', which was ordered and productive of revenue. As David Ludden puts it, the state's 'oriental empiricism' had produced a body of knowledge woven into the fabric of administration and law (1993: 226).

Scott's is representative of a type of Foucauldian analysis which plays on a dichotomy between state and society, modernity and tradition, or which portrays an antipathy between the state's modernizing project of 'development' and the knowledge and institutions of community which it overrides (Chatterjee 1995; Escobar 1995; Ferguson 1994). The same dichotomy occurs in the development policy commentary of the 1980s on the over-extended state, and its market or community-oriented

The research on which this paper draws was undertaken with support from an ESRC Research Fellowship (L/320/27/3065) under the Global Environmental Change Programme. Thanks to Chris Fuller and Véronique Bénéï for helpful editorial suggestions.

programmes to 'roll back the state', as well as in more recent debates on state and 'civil society'.

Like other essays in this volume, this one argues for a blurring of this state-society boundary and a re-incorporation of 'the state' into a broader analysis of society, which includes study of the relationships through which the state and its citizens are mutually constituted in regionally and historically specific ways. My particular focus is on a south Indian region—the former kingdoms and zamindaris ('estates') of Ramnad and Sivagangai—where the penetration of the modernizing colonial state was relatively late, intermittent, shallow and, at different levels, resisted; a region with a high degree of 'illegibility' to the British government, where the institutions of a pre-colonial 'state' order continued in a strange hybrid form, although rendered progressively dysfunctional by a centralizing colonial power.

Any abstract unifying concept of 'the state' has to be abandoned here. My focus is on a 'state' which is multilayered and decentered, and popularly understood and experienced as overlordship of a wide variety of kinds—of kings or warrior chiefs, of zamindars and their agents, of regional caste leaders or village headmen, of trader-banker 'owners' of villages, or of the British government. Rather than deal with ideas of the state, I will describe a set of material and symbolic transactions and resource flows through which overlordship and the power of the 'state' were constituted, dispersed or resisted.

The transactions on which I focus concern irrigation—a public resource which, as much as any, invokes a domain connecting the state with the community. Indeed, the study of irrigation provides a unique perspective on the relationship between centralized power and local lordship, on the articulation of state bureaucracy and community institutions, on competing logics of governance and rule, and the imposition of and resistance to colonial policy. Moreover, it is possible not only to appreciate the peculiar contradictory forms of 'state' which characterised south Indian zamindaris, but also to see their ecological and economic effects.

Irrigation and the state

Two influential scholarly constructions of irrigation have dominated debate for over a century. The first, proposed by Marx and elaborated by Wittfogel (1957), proclaims a link between the management of hydraulic irrigation and the centralization of power, organized bureaucracy and extractive land revenue most characteristic of 'oriental despotism' (cf. Heitzman 1997: 13;

Lansing 1991: 37; O'Leary 1989). The second, contrasting, historiographical construction of irrigation systems stresses the autonomous role of small 'village republics' and their assemblies. Irrigation technology from this point of view has mostly been simple, requiring only earthwork organized locally without involvement of the state.

Both constructions—state and community—have expressed contemporary ideological agendas. Wittfogel's 'hydraulic despotism' was a thinly disguised and politically understood warning about the dangers of state socialism and modern totalitarianism (O'Leary 1989: 244). The idea of autonomous 'village republics', while initially evoked as part of the discourse of imperial government, has more recently gained popularity as a critique of the modernizing development strategies of the centralized state and the dominance of 'western' technical engineering over indigenous community perspectives in irrigation (Agarwal and Narain 1997; Gadgil and Guha 1992; Sengupta 1993; Shankari and Shah 1993).

These polarized notions of 'state' and 'community' leave little possibility for understanding irrigation in India as a *shifting* 'nexus of community and land which links society to the state' (Gilmartin 1994: 1133; cf. Heitzman 1997: 12). It is precisely the role of irrigation in the articulation of 'state' and 'community' in south India—not as transcendent ideas but as historically produced and variable ones (Kaviraj 1997)—which is my theme. The focus is not on large-scale riverine or canal systems, which became (and remain) the centre of concern for the technical irrigation bureaucracy, but rather the decentralized network of reservoirs and channels which comprise tank irrigation systems, especially extensive in the agriculturally marginal dry plains districts of the Tamil country. It is the position of these systems at the margins of state control which makes them a useful lens through which to look at the shifting boundary between state bureaucracy and community institutions, and the intermingling of state power and local authority at different historical moments.

What is known of these systems in the pre-colonial period sustains neither the 'oriental despot' nor the 'village republic' model of irrigation development. Rather, irrigation tanks appear as constructed and operated through a state power which is decentralized (or 'segmentary') and redistributive. The colonial state, consolidated in south India after 1800, brought about complex changes in this resources system. Two themes call for attention, both related to changed state-community relations. The first (discussed in Mosse 1999) concerns the establishment of a centralized irrigation bureaucracy and the invention of community 'tradition' which followed. Briefly, as the public works administration of the Madras government came into being (in the 1860s–70s), extending the state's proprietorial rights over irrigation works in most of the region, so the government became aware of the cost of maintaining highly decentralized irrigation works and (for this reason) became newly interested in 'community customs' and 'traditions' of irrigation management and fearful for their decline. Indeed, the period from the 1870s to 1890s witnessed unprecedented moves to identify, document, codify or invent village 'traditions' of *kutimaramat* ('villager works') and even to enforce them through legislation. Custom and 'community management' can be seen, here, as the corollary of the extension of centralized state power rather than its reverse.

The second theme, the subject of this essay, concerns a different articulation of state power and community institutions, namely the persistence of old-order 'state' institutions and earlier forms of state-craft under British rule and their growing contradiction with the colonial state. Since political relations were often articulated and transformed through the medium of land and water, irrigation and paddy cultivation provide an apt lens though which to view the changes which preceded the emergence of the post-colonial 'development state' in one part of south India. They also draw attention to the persistence of older forms of patronage and 'redistribution' concealed behind the contemporary state's instruments of irrigation development, and its neo-'orientalist' constructions of community. This is a theme addressed at the end of the essay.

The ethnohistory of irrigation in a south Indian warrior state

In the southern Tamil plains districts of Sivagangai and Ramnad, heavy run-off from concentrated rainfall is captured, stored and controlled in a large number of reservoirs or 'tanks', formed by taking advantage of the natural depressions of the relief and erecting crescent-shaped earth dams across the drainage flow. Stable settlement in this semi-arid region would not have been possible without the storage of water in tanks (cf. Sengupta 1993). These have characterized this region from Pandya and Chola times (c. 750–1300) and they were precursors to the development of riverine canal irrigation in the eleventh century (cf. Heitzman 1997; Stein 1980: 94).

Today, in Ramnad (Ramanathapuram) and Sivagangai, there are over 10,000 tanks, irrigating an estimated 530,000 hectares.[1] The absolute and relative contribution of tanks to irrigation in these districts is far higher than elsewhere in Tamil Nadu or India more generally, where alternative irrigation sources (canals, wells) have been available, and where tank irrigation declined from 1968–9 onwards, particularly in relation to well irrigation (MIDS 1986; Vaidyanathan 1992). Tanks are intensively interlinked through drainage flows, often forming chains or 'cascades' broadly oriented to follow the gentle south-easterly slope of the land from the western hills to the eastern coast and capturing the maximum amount of run-off for irrigation (Sengupta 1993: 61).

Tank systems in this region were developed 'in a cellular segmented manner: similar, allied but staunchly independent units were merely added as the population and irrigated acreage increased' (Ludden 1979). In Ramnad and Sivagangai, this expansion was closely linked to the rising profile of Maravar caste warrior chiefs and the militarization of the plains area of south India under the Vijayanagara empire (fourteenth to sixteenth centuries) (Baker 1984). Maravars were organized into micro-regional clan and (loosely) territorial institutions or *natus*, which constituted domains of authority of the Maravar chiefs or *nattampalars* (heads of the *natu*) and the lesser domains of the Maravar village headmen (*ampalars*) within the larger warrior polity.[2]

There is evidence that irrigation itself contributed to the building of these political domains. For one thing, if *natus* defined domains of influence and power of local Maravar warrior leadership, they did so because they were the primary units of social and agrarian organization based upon links established through both kinship and drainage (Stein 1980: 59, Subbarayalu 1973: 36). For another, tank construction was itself part of a political process in which rival chiefs extended and maintained their own local domains of authority. In some instances warrior chiefs organized the construction or repair of tanks and protected cultivating communities in return for the right to a share of the produce of the land (Dirks 1987: 148, 153; Granda 1984: 31, 293).

It is the combination of strong clan-based territorial control and linkage into an overarching political authority which characterized the political economy of irrigation in Ramnad and Sivagangai from the fourteenth century. The creation, protection and repair of irrigation structures provided the means by which Maravar and Kallar *natu* chiefs and local headmen pushed the frontiers of cultivation forward and created nodes for the collection of revenue and military recruits, and thereby forged upward linkages, securing titles, honours and political legitimacy from reigning kings and overlords.[3] At the end of the eighteenth century, tank-digging was associated, not only with regional chiefship, but also village-level headship and hereditary titles such as *karana ampalar* (village headman), which went along with shares in the village harvest and rights to rent-free lands (*maniyam* or *umpalam*).[4] Some titles, such as the 'channel men driving *maniyams*' (*vaykkal al otti maniyam*), also explicitly recognized local command over labour.[5]

As is now well-established, regional temples were focal institutions integrating the 'loose domains of authoritative control' described by Stein (1985) as a 'segmentary state' (cf. Appadurai 1981; Dirks 1987; Price 1979a; 1996). It was through the control of symbolic honours and titles focusing on the temple, rather than administrative control, that the kings established their own sovereignty. While Maravar chiefs carved out domains for themselves by extending or repairing irrigation systems, they also thereby acquired from the king 'honours' in regional temples, which symbolized both rights and underwrote their authority over a local territory by linking it to that of the sovereign. Local histories of Maravar *natu* chiefs establish a persisting link between systems of temple honour and public irrigation works in the articulation of authority at village and regional level (Mosse n.d.).

Local water rights (*tannir urumai*)—for example, the right to draw water from a shared channel—are understood as in the gift of Maravar kings. Moreover, the gifting of water resources (like land) and the patronage of public works (temples and tanks in particular) were a necessary means of constituting royal authority and rule itself (Dirks 1987; Price 1996). In consequence, the state dispersed rather than concentrated its resources and authority. By the nineteenth century, 64 per cent of all tanks, villages and associated water rights in Sivagangai kingdom had been granted to royal kinsmen, warrior chiefs, temples or Brahman communities, and the state had given over its right to a fiscal share of the produce in a large part of the kingdom.[6] Moreover, on the remaining land there was very little by way of extractive revenue. Instead a 'share' (*varam*) system allocated or 'redistributed' the produce from irrigated fields to the king (recipient of the 'upper share' or *melvaram*), to the cultivator (recipient of a 'lower share' or *kilvaram, kutivaram*), and to various caste-specific village officers and servants. This system (in some form dating back to the Pandyas) brought the interests of state deep into individual villages, linking local irrigation systems to a transactional system which extended beyond the village to the palace, and also ensured that a significant proportion of the surplus notionally extracted by the state was fed back into irrigation maintenance and agricultural production (Washbrook 1988: 63–4).

Tanks in early Company years

By the late eighteenth century, however, the ecological consequences of the political logic just described appear to have been uncertain. The officers of the East India Company invariably described the irrigation systems they found in Ramnad and Sivagangai as in serious disrepair. As one early Collector put it:

[I] had opportunity, as I progress though the country, of witnessing the wretched state in which they [tanks] are at present—most of them could not have been repaired for many many years and the consequence has been that large tracts of land have remained uncultivated for want of a regular supply of water. The inhabitants of every village I passed begged that I would look at their tanks and asked how it was possible for them to increase the cultivation, or indeed to cultivate at all, in the condition in which they then were.[7]

Early nineteenth-century surveys classed up to 30 per cent of tanks as 'unusable' (Lardinois 1989: 24–5, 38–43). They reported 'sluices decayed, banks worn to almost nothing' and 'unable to withstand the slightest pressure', such that 'during the [last] monsoon scarcely one tank in the Zamindari [could hold] the quantity of water which came into them'.[8] Because of the ruinous state of tanks in a chain, many breached and swept crops away in the flood.

Company officers were convinced that ancient irrigation systems, far from being protected by warrior chiefs (*poligars*), had been much damaged by their military conflicts and the arbitrary oppression of inhabitants, who were forced to abandon cultivation and migrate, leaving many tracts 'excessively bare of inhabitants'. Indeed, they read the collapse of the region's irrigation system as visible demonstration of the moral and administrative disorder of the regimes they had come to replace. As Captain J. C. Caldwell, the first superintendent of tank repairs (northern districts), put it in 1801:

the state of the tanks in this place exhibit melancholy proof of the ruinous effects of an uncontrolled native management, under which the appropriation of funds towards the preservation of the country appears to be totally out of the question, so much so that a regular and progressive decay of all the ancient works which are the sources of cultivation and revenue takes place.[9]

In common with later nationalist and environmentalist commentators, Company officers viewed the decline of community as the recent undermining of ancient tradition by an exploitative state (cf. Mosse 1999). It may well be, however, that what they described was not a recent collapse, but closer to the normal condition of tank irrigation. The expansion of agricultural settlement during the eighteenth century was likely to have been far from orderly and peaceful (cf. Washbrook 1988: 67), and the irrigation systems produced were neither stable nor particularly well-adapted ecologically. The political incentives to invest in new irrigation works was always greater than to maintain them (Ludden 1985: 144–7) (and in this they resembled recent politically motivated state investments in irrigation). At any historical point, therefore, a significant proportion of tanks would have been in disrepair or abandoned, although this may have been exaggerated by the escalation of military conflict in the immediate pre-colonial period.

But a period of escalating conflict 1750s to 1790s may in fact also have been a time of extensive tank works—the digging and repair of tanks, or the construction of new branch channels—just as it was also a time of patronage of temples, the granting of *inams* (tax-free land grants) and other forms of royal gifting. Most of the folk-historical accounts of great irrigation works by Maravar chiefs come from this period. The political system which generated military conflicts, the ruinous effects of which so struck Company officers, also required continuous investment of state resources as largesse in tank works to ensure the mobilization of warrior support and the expansion of military commands, so as to resist the incursions from Mughal and later British forces. Warfare and tank building were two elements in the same mode of statecraft. The substitution of revenue systems and bureaucratic rule for plunder and largesse under *pax Britannica* had important consequences for the functioning of these systems (cf. Dirks 1987: 48).

Pax Britannica, permanent settlement and public works

British rule in the southern Tamil region was consolidated after the suppression of *poligar* resistance in 1801. Warrior chiefs and their kin who had supported the British campaign were established as zamindars: that is, holders of proprietary estates based on a combination of eighteenth-century English ideas about landholding and the pre-colonial institutions of Bengal. This form of 'permanent settlement' survived as the mode of land-revenue administration for one third of Madras Presidency (including Ramnad and Sivagangai), even though, as policy, it rapidly lost ground to Thomas Munro's ryotwari system, which brought government into direct contact with the owners of individually-assessed plots of land.

In 1803 the rajas and ranis of the two kingdoms of Ramnad and Sivagangai ceased to be sovereigns of military domains. The institutions of military rule—armies, forts, countryside protection and policing (*teca kaval*)—were dismantled as the former rulers were reconstituted (ideally) as gentlemen-farmers, landlords, influential friends of the British and spokesmen for rural society (Government of Tamil Nadu 1977: 428). A Court of Wards was set up to supervise estates during times of difficulty, sickness, minority or failures in estate treasury, and the integrity of the estates was later protected by a legal right of primogeniture to prevent dismemberment of the principalities of the former aristocracy. As Dirks puts it, the permanent settlement channelled segmentary political relations into 'the new domain of proprietary law', and kingly lordship into legal ownership under the British Raj (1986: 313). It defined an economic rather than a political role for zamindars, and in this role the upkeep of tank irrigation as the productive base of the zamindaris had a central importance.

Two principles underlay the permanent settlement: clear property rights in land, and a fixed revenue demand from the colonial government. The regulations of the permanent settlement resolved 'to grant to Zamindars ... and their heirs and successors a permanent property in their land in all time to come';[10] as the collector wrote of the new Ramnad zamindarini, 'however extensive might be the fruits of her own good management and industry, no increase would be demanded from her or her children'.[11]

The British fully expected these new landowners to profit from secure property and fixed rent, both sorely lacking, in their view, in earlier regimes. In particular it was believed that zamindars would invest in irrigation works and thereby profit from the extension of paddy on which share revenue was paid, as well as guard against inundation and drought. To this end irrigation tanks (along with forests and 'wasteland') were given 'in perpetuity' to zamindars, even though, towards the end of the nineteenth century, the government attempted to extend its claim over irrigation sources, as it had done in *ryotwari* districts.

Patronage, law and zamindari 'rule'

The evidence from nineteenth and early twentieth century Ramnad and Sivagangai suggests, however, that the permanent settlement did not produce a radical break with indigenous political life and modes of statecraft (Baker 1984; Price 1979a; 1996). Zamindars resolutely refused to define for themselves an entrepreneurial role. As Price has clearly shown, rather than profiting from efficient management and the expansion of paddy cultivation, they continued to pursue strategies to maintain royal status by vanquishing enemies and dispersing estate resources through patronage and redistribution. The 'gifting' of land and water resources remained central to this form of 'statecraft'. But while nineteenth-century zamindari rule did indeed perpetuate a diffusion of power, it did not achieve the pattern of re-investment in irrigation and production which had characterized earlier regimes. The strategies of kingly 'rule' were profoundly changed by the new institutions of British India in ways which disturbed earlier resource flows and circuits of investment (cf. Stein 1985: 412).

As Price has cogently argued, the systems of courts established by the colonial government provided new arenas in which Maravar royalty could challenge adversaries in 'battle'—arenas which also required demonstrations of power and influence in mobilizing resources for legal 'warfare' (1979b: 212). Legal adversaries were mostly contenders to the royal title in succession disputes. But as the Maharaja of Bobbili commented, unlike warfare, expenditure on litigation had little or no pay-back: 'in battles the conqueror ... annexes the enemies' country, or secures certain commercial privileges. But in litigation, except in very few instances, the winner gets nothing' (Price 1996: 79). Indeed, the president of the Board of Revenue noted in 1871 that 'the greater part of the resources of the Zamindari [of Ramnad]' has been devoted to legal conflicts' (qu. in Price 1979a: 231–2). Complaints about 'ruinous litigation' became the litany of the Court of Wards correspondence on both Sivagangai and Ramnad estates. In short, in the nineteenth century, investment in the protection of the zamindari title made more urgent demands on the estates' resources than investment in the protection of its productive base (which might anyway only enrich competitors).

Even if not protected, the estate's land and water resources could still be gifted, and so deployed by Maravar zamindars (and their managers) to legitimize royal title, and to preserve their political position as generous lords 'munificent in gifts of food, alms and in building chattirams [pilgrim houses]',[12] thereby manifesting *vallanmai* ('charity', 'liberality'), an attribute of dharmic rule (cf. Price 1996). There were, however, significant changes in the nature and consequences of gifting as a mode of 'statecraft' in colonial times. After the first years of the permanent settlement, the most common form of 'gifting' land was not endowing Brahmans or temples with villages, but *leasing* estate villages and tanks to individuals at favourable rates. Such leases, known as 'cowles' (*kavul*), transferred the *melvaram* ('upper share') rights to the lessee.[13]

These leases were made variously to royal family members, to charitable institutions, and particularly to Nattukottai Chettiyar bankers in connection with loans taken to finance expensive royal succession litigation. Indeed, at the end of the nineteenth century, Nattukottai Chettiyars (from the 'Chettinad' area) controlled massive capital, had become the chief merchant-banking caste of south India, and 'monopolised important components of the credit, banking and agrarian systems in Burma, Ceylon, Malaya and the Madras Presidency' (Rudner 1989: 423–4; 1994). Through their banking activity, they had also, unintentionally, become zamindar overlords of leased villages comprising a large part of the Ramnad and Sivagangai estates (Price 1996). Chettiyars not only held estate villages, but also took over Devastanam and Chattiram villages granted for the maintenance of temples and pilgrim houses respectively. Thereby the Chettiyars established themselves as principal 'royal' patrons and donors of major regional shrines by paying for the main processions or rites of the most important ten-day festivals, at which they received 'first respect' (*mutal mariyatai*) along with the raja and regional Maravar chiefs. Like the zamindars, Chettiyars also held private (*pannai*) land in villages, and appointed local Maravar headmen as munsifs (village revenue officers) and receivers of the 'upper share'.

So despite efforts by the colonial government to extend its own rule through new forms of legal property right and the economy of estate management, the gifting of village land and irrigation structures remained 'the traffic of the political process' (Dirks 1986: 324). Zamindars continued to treat productive resources (land and water) as political assets to *rule*—to gift, disburse and redistribute—in order to acquire religious merit, cement political alliances, secure credit, or reward services, in the court-room rather than on the battlefield. They refused to give up 'ruling' and continued to display kingly authority, understood as the 'power of allocation' involving a 'diffusion of power and a scattering of resources' (Price 1979b: 209, 211).[14] In consequence, the power and authority of the (colonial) state continued to be experienced as fragmented into a multitude of lesser landholding domains created through royal gift and privileged tenure superimposed upon the impartible zamindari estates.

Local overlords, Chettiyar bankers and others, were not only gifted the zamindar's rights to the 'upper share'of wet-land produce, but also acquired the rulers' function and obligation to invest in maintaining community irrigation systems, temples and other 'public goods'. This was recognized in the receipt of a *kulavettu* ('tank-cutting') grain share and honours in local temples. By the mid-nineteenth century, however, it was clear that the logic of an earlier political system linking local overlordship to investment in community resources no longer operated. Failure to redirect resources into tanks was the rule rather than the exception, and (despite the absence of war and migrant populations as disrupting factors) reports on the state of tank irrigation at the end of the century repeat and amplify the descriptions of decay and collapse given at its start. Surveys indicated a majority of tanks with embankments breached or washed away, beds and channels silted, or weirs broken, and most irrigated less than half their ayacut.[15] This crisis in ecology and agriculture, I venture, was itself witness to a fundamental shift in the logic of kingly rule under colonial government.

The crux of the problem was that while irrigation systems remained, political institutions incorporated into political strategies of rule, after 1800 zamindars had little real political power to disperse—their crowns were hollow (Dirks 1987). While they continued to disperse resources and create subordinate landed domains, they lacked the power to integrate these politically. Zamindari society operated as if state power was dispersible (as it previously had been), but within the colonial state it was not. The ecological and economic consequences of this were serious. In the absence of political rewards, obligations to invest in irrigation could only be established by law—for example, by writing them into the cowle lease agreements. 'Royal gifting' produced not a set of domain holders (*inamdars, cowledars*, etc.) integrated into the articulation of a warrior-state, but a landscape of complex and insecure property rights and obligations to invest, which were underpinned by law and contested in the courts.

Disputes over investments in tanks generated profuse litigation about obligations to maintain, repair or contribute to improvements. Indeed one-third (39) of the 134 court cases reviewed in the course of this research concerned disputes of this kind.[16] This mass of litigation in the nineteenth and twentieth centuries suggests, at the very least, a weakening at all levels of the link between investment in irrigation and its political rewards. The costs of irrigation maintenance had anyway probably increased. Chettiyar bankers were not warrior chiefs with power to mobilize scarce local labour (although their local Maravar contractors may have been).

The British legal system was no better able to force the zamindar representatives of the state to fulfil their obligations to invest in irrigation, than it was to compel 'community obligation' (*kutimaramat*) in *ryotwari* areas (Mosse 1999). British property law provided no substitute for local authority. In fact, Madras Presidency lacked any comprehensive irrigation law which defined clearly the rights of government, zamindars and others to irrigation water. The matter was left to English easement law and an incomprehensible batch of case law (Baker 1984: 473). The problem was only compounded by the sheer complexity of land tenure produced by a history of royal 'gifting', and which meant that hydrologically inter-linked villages and tanks were held on different joint or multiple tenures and share-holdings.

In the absence of defined rights, litigants and their advocates invariably had recourse to the principle of 'custom'. Indeed, in passing judgement on the many disputes over water flows[17] and repairs in these inter-linked networks of tanks and channels, the courts drew on an existing discourse to confirm *rights* on the basis of 'natural' water flow, 'customary' use and entitlement by royal grant, or *obligations* on the basis of receipt of customary *kulavettu* (tank cutting) shares.[18]

Unlike their representation by engineers, however, tanks and their catchments were (and are) not static physical or social systems. Water courses in this ecology do not follow unchanging channels. Flood flows breach or extend channels, cause diversions, establish new courses or obliterate old ones. Such changes have for long provided focused opportunities for disputants to reconstruct past landscapes and to redefine antecedent natural or 'customary' water flows to their advantage. The construction of new dams, repair of channels, diversion of seasonal water, extensions of tank bunds and so forth, in order to renew or increase water supplies to tanks, could be authoritative when represented as the recovery of an 'original' landscape. Nineteenth- and twentieth-century court-case 'exhibits' are full of competing 'natural histories' of rivers, channels and other water courses. They show that the meaning and purpose of any tank structure was not fixed, but defined by conflicting representations of landscape. As endless appeals and reversals of judgement show, in arbitrating between competing definitions and in passing judgement on the customary or *mamul* water flow, the courts of the colonial judiciary struggled hopelessly to lock an endlessly changing hydrology into an enduring set of 'customary' rights and obligations.[19] But Anglo-Indian law not only reified and fixed irrigation arrangements in terms of ideas of customary right, but ultimately also eroded the very institutions it evoked by introducing its own system of generalized rules, codes and precedents which was, in principle, independent of political power and the state (Dirks 1986: 321–2; Price 1996: 45).[20]

In sum, while patronage and segmentary authority created the semblance of continuity with an old state order, the dispersal of resources and authority, and the contestation of rights and responsibilities, in fact worked against the reinvestment of resources into irrigation at every level. Political incentives to invest were not what they were, tenures were insecure and economic returns were extremely uncertain. Government was unable to force the zamindars to fulfil their obligations. Expenditure on irrigation works, which was erratic, usually ad hoc and responsive to petitioning by village leaders, often amounted to no more than one per cent of the revenue demand.[21] Even the comparatively greater spending on tanks by the Court of Wards between 1921 and 1926 resulted in no expansion of cultivation or revenue.

Revenue and redistribution

Revenue collection itself was another arena which brought two 'modes of state'—kingly and colonial—into contradiction. This contributed to major and irreversible shifts in the political relationships linking zamindari 'states' with their villagers, and ultimately to their collapse within the colonial state. Zamindars employed the pre-colonial 'share' system to collect rent much as they had collected dues in the eighteenth century, as a means to build up their political following by redistributing state resources (Baker 1975: 20). Towards the end of the nineteenth and during the twentieth century, however, a delicate system of royal overlordship and a hierarchy of devolved power were breaking down. Zamindars were losing their capacity to direct resources in their estates: first wet-land paddy (on which revenue depended) was displaced from its centrality in the estate economy; second, the redistributive element in revenue administration was being undermined; and third, there was widespread failure of tank irrigation systems. Each of these changes occurred as zamindari rule became increasingly subject to the influence and control of the centralized colonial state with its more extractive tax regime, and significantly changed the relationship between state and society.

Wet-land paddy cultivation declined, partly because profitable cash-cropping of chillies, cotton, tobacco, plantain and other spices, oilseeds or vegetables at lower cash rents (*tirvai*) expanded in the zamindaris steadily after 1850,[22] especially in black cotton soil areas of Ramnad, where the 'productivity of dry lands increased in relation to wet lands' (Ludden 1985: 154). British policies, which opened up new markets for dry-land cash crops, encouraged the cultivation of previously unproductive dry land. Wet-land paddy cultivation and irrigation structures were reported as abandoned,[23] as *ryots* 'throw all their energy and money into their dry lands which bear a fixed cash rent and bring greater out-turn and larger profit'.[24]

The diversion of land and effort away from 'share' (*varam*) paddy was resisted. In the 1870s and 1880s, notifications prohibiting cash crop cultivation on these paddy lands were being made by collectors, cowle-holding overlords and other 'melvaramdars' (those with rights to the 'upper share' of grain). The obligation to grow paddy on wet land under tanks was being inserted as a clause in the land titles (*pattas*) issued, and *ryots* were made to give written undertakings not to cultivate cash crops in place of paddy. If they did so, they were challenged through law suits[25] and faced fines and punitive taxes, although the zamindari estates' attempt to impose additional taxes on dry-land cash crops was successfully challenged in the Madras High Court, especially where land was cultivated using wells dug by farmers themselves.[26]

What was at issue in the shift to dry-land cash-cropping, particularly in black cotton soil villages, was not just a loss of revenue, but a more fundamental disruption of the distinctive relationship between community and state which authorized the Maravar caste's political dominance. This had both local and regional implications. In the black soil village of Alapuram, for example, the authority of the old order— based on Maravar political office, and the control of wet-land production, revenue and redistribution as linked to the state—was challenged during the nineteenth century by the rising economic power of Utaiyar-caste cultivators, who were late eighteenth-century migrants granted title to dry land by the Ramnad raja). [27] Utaiyar landlords clearly gained from secure property rights and new economic opportunities from cash-cropping dry land (as well as entrepreneurial rice cultivation in Burma), all encouraged by British government policy. By the 1930s they had purchased much Maravar and Vellalar wet land, dug private wells, constructed new sluices, substituted private servants for village officers (e.g., hereditary Pallar 'water turners'), and in other ways eroded the social systems of irrigation which linked village production to the state through Maravar political office. Significantly, this new social challenge was articulated through the institutions of the old regime (Dirks 1987), that is in disputes over festival honours at regional temples, including *natu* temples, where Utaiyars acquired new rights and 'shares' in worship (Mosse 1997c).

At the estate level, zamindar influence dwindled. Firstly, the growth of cash cropping shifted the economic focus of the village away from the estate office and towards the railway connected market towns, many of which were beyond the borders of the two zamindaris so that the rajas began to lose what grip they had on the economics of their estates. Secondly, the colonial government's own direct involvement in the estates undermined the position and political role of the rajas. Moreover, the position of the zamindars was weakened by the growing use of various legislative and other government institutions by the villagers (Baker 1984: 433ff). But most significantly, the government (through the Court of

Wards) began to interfere with the primary institution linking village and state, the revenue system itself.

British officers not surprisingly were just as quick to condemn the 'redistributive' share revenue system as they were the 'land alienations' of royal gifting. But perhaps most disruptive of the older articulation of village and state was the shift, in Sivagangai estate, away from the share system altogether to a fixed land tax in cash. In the 1920s, believing that the share system was a serious disincentive to paddy cultivation, which reduced as much as half of the zamindari to uncultivated waste and caused a dramatic fall in revenue, the British government (through the Court of Wards) began to switch to fixed cash rents.[28] It intended that this would reduce the cost of revenue administration, reward ryots' investment in land by *ryots* and result in 'an expansion of cultivation and an increase in revenue'.[29] By 1931, nearly 80 per cent of Sivagangai wet land had been 'commuted' to cash rent. However the shift to fixed cash rents proved to be extremely ill-timed. Fixed rents, which were based on the high prices of the 1920s, became increasingly resented in the depression years of the 1930s when grain prices reached their lowest in twenty years.[30] The ability to pay rent through loans and remittances was further reduced as world depression affected Chettiyar businesses overseas, and hence access to credit and migrants' earnings. Rent arrears escalated as the relationship between the estate and the *ryots* deteriorated.[31] The misjudgement was political as much as economic. The rationalities of fixed cash rents failed to acknowledge the status and power of influential *ryots,* who had previously controlled the 'share' system and 'redistributed' estate revenue, and now faced a sharp increase in rent demand (cf. Baker 1984: 441). No longer incorporated into the 'moral economy' of the zamindari 'state', officials, revenue staff, Maravar headmen and village officers refused to act for it. The estate collector in Sivagangai complained repeatedly of disloyal estate staff who 'slyly connived with the *ryots* in making any coercive steps and proceedings in the court infructuous by tampering with evidence at the very source'. But equally, without their co-operation, the estate was powerless to collect rents.

In the 1930s there was a spate of reports, legal suits and convictions relating to embezzlement by revenue staff and village headmen.[32] But the Court of Wards was up against more than petty resistance by revenue officials. The resistance to the estate and its revenue collection became more organized. An estate *ryots* association, the Pattidars Sangam, began agitation against fixed cash rents in 1928–9. The Sangam was organized by ex-estate employees (notably the former personal assistant to the estate collector). Support for the Sangam declined after its tactics of withholding of rent and facing legal suits failed, however, and by 1931 it was considered discredited and defunct.[33] But organized resistance had more local roots. In many villages *ryots* joined village-level 'oppandams' (*oppantam*: 'agreement, contract' [Fabricius 1972: 160]) undertaking to resist rent payment and to exclude estate officials from villages, and they enforced their decisions by penalties and social boycotts (cf. Baker 1984: 441–2).

Significantly, the organized resistance to rent brought into focus precisely those elements of society which had formerly articulated warrior polity. That is to say, resistance focused on Maravar (and Kallar) caste centres (e.g., Maravarmangalam) and drew on strong caste organization and martial culture. In October 1931 (while Sivagangai was under the Court of Wards), a large deputation of Maravars from Tiruvegampat demanded from the collector 'a wholesale reduction of rent and a reversion to waram or in the alternative the rendition of the estate to the raja'.[34] Kallars of Paganeri organized by the Ramnad District Kallar Mahajana Sangam met at Paganeri (an old *natu* centre) and passed resolutions including a demand for a 50 per cent remission in cash rent.[35]

Despite the use of coercive measures, rent collection in these areas was all but impossible[36] and criminal charges relating to resistance simply accumulated.[37] When the Sivagangai Zamindar was reinstated in 1934, he virtually abandoned the idea of maintaining rent collections (Baker 1984: 442) and in Ramnad during the 1930s the zamindar made little attempt to impose revenue demand. When in 1935 the Ramnad zamindari was assumed by the Court of Wards at the zamindar's request 'for the discharge of debts', it was described as 'in a condition of complete wreckage'.[38] Villages were massively in arrears on rent, but there were no records to indicate by how much. The virtual collapse of the revenue system, together with extensive leases and debts, brought the estate into bankruptcy by the end of the 1930s (Ibid.: 442–3). In Ramnad (as in Sivagangai) the lack of investment in the irrigation systems lay at the root of peasant resistance to the zamindar 'state', and the failure of the zamindars to protect irrigation provided the strongest grounds for Maravar leaders disaffected with the estate to organize resistance to rent payment and to exclude estate officials from their villages.[39] Indeed, resentment ran so high that 'in two estates the ryots reacted to the zamindars' refusal to maintain irrigation works by running riot and shooting dead some estate employees' (Baker 1984: 436).

Just as zamindari rule had sought to maintain itself through largess and redistribution, so its collapse was reflected in the failure to protect and invest in public assets, especially tanks, but also forests and temples. In Sivagangai zamindari, several large devastanam (temple) establishments (e.g., Kalaiyarkovil in Sivagangai) were working in deficit while smaller temples were 'denied even a piper set'.[40] By neglecting the maintenance of irrigation tanks and demanding the wet-land 'upper share' from land which could no longer be cultivated as wet land for want of water, the zamindar abused his royal obligations, while in neglecting the temples he had 'forgone his moral right to the income' (Ibid.: 436, 442–3; Price 1979: 24–5).[41]

If nothing else, the history of irrigation in colonial Ramnad and Sivagangai demonstrates that, contrary to currently popular arguments (e.g., Agarwal and Narain 1997), small-scale irrigation systems suffered under colonial rule. This was not because centralized and bureaucratic state control eroded local village systems, but because of the internal contradictions arising from the persistence of kingly rule based on gift, 'redistribution' and decentralized authority within a colonial state based on centralized administration of property, law and revenue.[42] It is by appreciating the continuing *political* nature of local irrigation systems that sense can be made of their operation or decline. Indeed, the record of Ramnad and Sivagangai shows how comprehensively the permanent settlement had failed to separate resources management from political leadership, and how the fate of irrigation systems was inexorably tied to that of kingly rule. Land and water continued to be ruled rather than managed, and the collapse of irrigation systems in these estates was both caused by, and resulted in, the loss of legitimate *political* authority to rule in this way.

The development state and community

The erosion of older forms of political integration was coincident with the growth of a culture of 'stateness' which took its fullest form only after Independence (Ludden 1992). But to suggest that British rule disrupted a 'segmentary' political system is not to suggest that it replaced it with centralized control. The colonial state, 'despite its spectacular theatre of self-representation ... remained a rather thin stratum of institutions' mostly concerned with revenue and order (Kaviraj 1997: 232); or as Washbrook puts it, 'the British were much less present in the society which they governed than had been their warrior predecessors: in many ways they were "absent rulers"' (Washbrook 1976: 332). The post-colonial state project of national development, by contrast, justified a massive expansion of state bureaucracy and its extension into everyday society. In this conclusion, I want to suggest two things: firstly, that a stronger idea of the state has evoked stronger ideas of 'the community'; and secondly, that the state-community polarity has served to hide from view the continuing importance of some 'segmentary' relationships which remain part of the practices of the state today.

The Indian 'development state' defined a role for itself which made intermediary roles of community benefaction entirely redundant. At Independence, zamindars were viewed (as indeed they had long been) as anachronistic anomalies which separated the people from the government, their benefactor (Government of Tamil Nadu 1977: 197). Their removal (in 1949) was seen as an early welfare and land-reform measure. Indeed, the elimination of intermediaries between 'people' and 'state' was just as crucial a legislative and ideological imperative for Independent India's 'development regime' as it was for Thomas Munro, the architect of *ryotwari* tenure over a century earlier (Ludden 1992: 256). With the abolition of zamindaris, rights in all irrigation structures (tanks, foreshores, channels, etc.) became vested in the state.[43] Along with rights over irrigation, the state devolved to itself the responsibility for maintenance and repair, and for a short period a special technical cell was established to deal with 'ex-zamin' tanks with funds from the wartime Grow More Food programme. But the state extended its involvement in agricultural production far beyond this. Through controls on input and output prices and subsidized productivity investments, 'the state is deeply entrenched in the culture of farming, and farmers rest their livelihood on the work of the state as much as on the rain' (Ibid.: 275). And, of course, indirect and mediated or brokered access to state inputs and subsidies serve to underline and reproduce caste-based inequalities (cf. Jeffrey and Lerche, Dimensions of Dominance; Class and State in Uttar Pradesh, in this volume).

Most commentators would agree that the extension of state control has done little to improve the condition of Tamil tank-irrigation systems. On the contrary, the increased involvement of the post-Independence state is blamed for their continuing decline. There are two types of argument here. The first, echoing the sentiments of the earlier regime, complains that: 'The more the State has risen to a sense of its obligation, the more the people have become unmindful of their own'.[44] The second (alluded to earlier) blames the modernizing development strategies of the centralized state for eroding community rights in irrigation and destroying the wisdom of indigenous systems (e.g., Agarwal and Narain 1997).

Both commentaries on the state and irrigation endorse a similar set of policy prescriptions, namely that the state should divest itself of rights and responsibilities and transfer the management of irrigation to communities of users. Strongly shaped by an international discourse of 'participatory development', national strategies of 'irrigation management transfer' (IMT) now involve the establishment of village-level farmers' or water users' associations constituted as self-managed village institutions, promoted by, but crucially independent of, the state. Elsewhere I have argued that there is a strong parallel between this policy and that around *kutimaramat* in the nineteenth century (Mosse 1999). The contemporary over-extended state irrigation bureaucracy, weakened by performance deficiencies and fiscal crisis, requires village-level solutions to irrigation maintenance which are socially and financially self-supporting, in the same way as the newly-extended Public Works Department (PWD)in the mid-nineteenth century needed village traditions of irrigation maintenance (ibid: 320).

In both the colonial and contemporary cases, 'community develop-ment' institutions provide a means to delimit state obligations while re-taining (or extending) state control. Alternatively put, colonial 'oriental-ist' constructions of enduringly autonomous village communities have gained a new lease of life within irrigation as in other areas of rural development in India. Through the ideological elimination of illegiti-mate intermediaries (contractors, middlemen, absentee landlords, po-litical bosses) the 'village' and 'state' are constantly recreated as essential and separate categories. They then require the mediation of new devel-opment 'extensionists', 'community organizers' or non-governmental organizations (NGOs), and new instruments—meetings, village com-mittees or participatory planning exercises (such as 'participatory rural appraisal')—to articulate village society with the benefactor state.

The polarized simplifications of 'state' and 'community' conceal the continuing dispersal of state resources which tank irrigation and the culture of public works involves. In presenting irrigation tanks as village resources to be efficiently managed by autonomous water users' associations, the new development planning model ignores the continuing *political* significance of irrigation as 'part of a nexus of community and land which [links] local society to the state' (Gilmartin 1994). Although in post-zamindari Ramnad and Sivagangai tanks are now the property of the state (PWD or Panchayat Unions), they remain part of a village 'public domain' (*urpotu*). In pre-colonial and zamindari times, this domain—the tank, temple or threshing floor—was the point at which local authority, unequal access to resources and social hierarchy were validated by their connection with the state, expressed in the form of material or symbolic shares. Today, in many villages in Sivagangai and Ramnad, tank institutions continue to express hierarchical social relations through caste-specific roles (e.g., low-caste Pallar water turners, Paraiyar channel watchers, Maravar headmen), and rights, obligations and 'honours' expressed in terms of privileged shares of water, fish or other usufructs. While at one level the tank is an irrigation structure, at another its institutions still provide idioms of political relations and social standing. The symbolic importance of shares in tank resources gives them a significance far beyond their material value, and makes these the focus of social dispute, particularly where the authoritative structures which tank systems express are challenged by low-caste protest or withdrawal from public-service roles (Mosse 1997; 1997b). Conversely, tanks continue to provide the means to legitimize local power, and to acquire wealth and convert it into status. Common property continues to be 'ruled' rather than managed. Thus while contests of power and local water resources do not appear directly connected to the state, they do revolve around tanks as state property, providing opportunities for men of influence to access, control and redistribute state resources. Today, this is largely through systems of contracting for the public works of, for example, tank deepening, sluice or weir construction, tree harvesting or charcoal burning.

Although the dismantling of the share revenue system weakened the political position of Maravar headmen, many retain privileged access to public works contracts, as well as holding key positions in village administration. What is of interest here is not the acquisition of contracts *per se*, but the village-state links and the 'redistribution' of state resources which the system entails. Firstly, the acquisition of major public works contracts often involves political intermediaries. Indeed, the links between party affiliation, 'incentive' payments and the awarding of public works contracts in India are too well-known to need restatement here. These links are widely believed to have been especially elaborate in Tamil Nadu under Ms Jayalalitha's AIADMK administration between 1991 and 1996. Secondly, and equally important, is the maintenance of relationships with the state bureaucracy – especially middle-level revenue and public works officers. In common parlance, tank works involve 'three shares' (*muppanku*): one for the PWD or revenue officer (*atikarar*), one for the contractor (*kantrakkarar*) and one for labour (*vettukarar*).[45] But these 'shares' cannot be viewed as personal entitlements, since further distributions from junior to senior officers are often expected in order to maintain the wider sets of relations with the state. For example in Kiliyur (pseudonym), the contractor and the village administrative officer agreed to spend half the income from harvested trees in the tank bed on arrangements for the district collector's visit to the village, and this also involved an expectation that a number of middle-level officers (*tahsildar*, revenue inspector, etc.) would receive 'gifts'.

The private gains from public works do not only have to be shared 'upwards' with government officers and politicians. If they are to acquire legitimacy, they also have to be 'redistributed' locally in culturally acceptable forms of public expenditure, usually religious. For example, income from tank-fish and trees in Ramnad and Sivagangai generate significant village funds—especially in recent years, as government forestry plantations started on tank foreshores in the 1980s are harvested. Conspicuously, the village funds generated from these resources, and controlled by village contractor-leaders, are mostly accounted for by spending on temples—for their construction, repair or inauguration, or the celebration of their festivals—and hardly ever on tank repair or other public goods.[46] Tank resources are not used in ways which maximise economic utility, but rather in ways which minimize social conflict and enhance the prestige and credibility of contractor-leaders. As noted elsewhere, temples demand generosity not accountability; although the self-serving nature of contracting is common knowledge and many suspect that contractors have 'eaten public funds', financial transactions rarely get questioned (Mosse 1997).[47] Through temple works, contractor-leaders not only diffuse dispute over public money, but they also represent personally profitable contracts in the idiom of morally valued acts of public giving; they interpose themselves as religious donors in ways which win public esteem and honour, and underline the legitimacy of local authority and contracting (Sivakumar and Sivakumar 1996). This, of course, is only the local working of a much wider system of 'redistributive' resource flows which extends from village leaders to the Minister of Public Works, who (in the mid-1990s) was able to insert himself in the place of former kings and chiefs as a patron of public works and, through gifts for temple building and repair, as a generous religious donor in his native Sivagangai district.

Through such manoeuvres local power can legitimize its claim on state resources and transform state public works into personal patronage. Indeed, particular tank works (weirs, sluices, bund repairs, etc.) often retain the name of the contractor involved in their construction. Not only do village leaders incorporate public works into their strategies of reputation building, but the state itself is also incorporated into the ritual systems which express this honour. Junior revenue officials and police officers participate *ex officio* in village and regional temple festivals, and receive honours at their conclusion. Many festival cycles conclude with a public distribution of honours manifesting the rank and status of caste-based donors. Such systems conventionally begin with honours for the temple (*kovil*), the government (*carkkar*), the region (*natu*) and the village (*kiramam*). In this way upward linkages are expressed, legitimizing local power in a way which resembles an older state order.

Such ritual expressions of hierarchical caste order linked to the state strikingly contrast with developmental models of state and community mediated by professional extensionists or democratic committees. Although Maravar headmen and other leaders continue to play a role in mediating the state's development resources, their roles are officially viewed as illegitimate, because groups and institutions, not individuals, are the authorized points of contact with the state. Indeed one of the most striking features of recent years is the massive increase in the number of 'groups' or 'associations' or 'societies' in Sivagangai and Ramnad villages. Villagers participate in a plethora of local organizations and committees. Each government (or NGO) agency or programme promotes its own local institution. A village may have a watershed committee, a health committee, an education committee, several self-help savings groups, a women's income-generation group, a youth group, a women's health group, literacy groups, as well as the older co-operative and panchayat institutions. A lack of co-ordination between departments and programmes furthers this multiplicity.

In contemporary state irrigation development too, it is the 'tank users' associations' which, in theory, have the central role and the authority to contract with the state for tank repairs, manage tank usufructs and arrange water allocation. 'Local institutions' like the tank users' associations are, however, rarely the democratic or utilitarian instruments of village self-help that they appear to be in policy documents. Rather they become arenas for conflict or vehicles for political ambition, precisely because they mediate new linkages to external authority and access to material and political resources (Mosse 1997b). Individual big-men have not been displaced or lost their capacity to control and redirect state resources, but have instead begun to pursue these aims through the control of new local institutions.

What is also significant, however, is that new officially-backed institutions provide platforms for protest or the forging of alternative routes to the bureaucracy, for challenging existing access to public works contracts, or for demanding a new level of accountability from state officials and local contractors alike. When (in 1995) a Dalit-led women's group in Alapuram village petitioned the district collector and forced an upper-caste contractor from the village to do inadequate tank repair and deepening work again, it was clear that the tank as a public resource was articulating a set of society-state relationships which challenged the longstanding socio-politics of public works.

This essay set out to challenge the polar opposition between 'state' and 'community' by investigating the institutions, transactions and resource flows involved in small-scale irrigation under colonial rule. These reveal 'the state' as fragmented into several different forms of local overlordship. The principles of rule, discovered in pre-colonial political relations, continued in these colonial fragments, and in the local operation of the postcolonial 'development state'. Throughout this long period, the state has constituted its authority through gift transactions and the 'redistribution' of its resources in favour of the local power to which the state has had to be permeable. But in the twentieth century, the hierarchical moral order—the dharma—has repeatedly been challenged, both by the bureaucratic norms of a colonial state, and later by the principles of local autonomy and community development. The institutions and resource systems founded upon earlier segmentary political relations, such as the tank systems of Ramnad and Sivagangai have began to fall apart, but the hegemony of developmental ideas of the state and community can now offer other emancipatory opportunities.

Notes

1. Ramanathapuram and Sivagangai districts together formed the Ramnad kingdom until 1730 when Sivagangai was separated as an independent realm. From 1803 these kingdoms became zamindari estates under the British permanent settlement.
2. As domains of political authority, these *natus* undoubtedly had fluctuating territorial boundaries (cf. Kaviraj 1997: 229). The contemporary significance of *natus* is almost exclusively ritual and ceremonial. But to the extent that the powers and institutions of the past leave traces which 'have become compacted in the meaning systems of actors in the present' (Appadurai 1981: 5), ritual becomes a source for the ethnohistory of the political relationships of the *natu*.
3. For example, ninth-century inscriptions (AD 815–899) record several granite and brick works of tank construction, desilting, and repair of bunds and sluices by one Etticattan leader in the Irunjai Natu in modern-day Sattur and Mudukkulatur *taluks* in Ramnad. In recognition of such works the title '*kilavan*' was bestowed on Etticattan by the Pandiyan king Srimara Srivallabha (Gurukkal 1986:158).
4. Stephen Lushington's Report on the Province of Ramnad for Fasli 1208, Lushington to Petrie, 29 Dec. 1800, Attachment no.6, 'Sodundrums', Madurai District Records, vol. 1109, Tamil Nadu State Archives p.396;From J.B.Blackburn, Collector of Madurai to the President and Member of the Board of Revenue, 5 June 1835. Madurai District Records, vol. 1109, Tamil Nadu State Archives.
5. Raju 1941: 124, citing evidence presented to the 1869 Kudimaramat Committee.

6. Data compiled by the author from records of the Samasthanam (kingdom/estate) office, at the palace in Sivagangai. In Ramnad and Sivagangai, royal gifting was characterized by the granting of *entire* villages under charitable and other forms of patronage. The beneficiaries of granted villages paid only a small fixed tax (*poruppu*) per unit of wet land (*nanjai*) to the raja.

7. Collector of Madurai, R.Peter to Board of revenue 19 Aug 1816 (Madurai District Records No. 1164, p. 17–8).

8. Report of the Settlement of Ramnad Fasli 1227, Madurai District Records 9034, p. 53. Tamil Nadu State Archives.

9. Diary of the Superintendent of Tank Repairs and Watercourses for the month of January 1801 (B/R (XIV) Misc. vol 216, Tamil Nadu State Archives.)

10. Regulation XXV of 1802, quoted in Government of Tamil Nadu 1977: 51.

11. Letter from Mr Parishes 12 March 1803, quoted in Rajaram Row 1891: 254.

12. Quoted from one of many copper plates in which the king's gift is prefaced by a laudatory text particularly identifying the king as a warrior and donor.

13. Today in conversation, these leases are referred to as *kuttakai*, a fixed tenancy. Leases were of different kinds: most were for fixed-term periods of between five and forty years, but a number of villages were given on permanent lease or assigned as gift. In 1870 there were seventy-nine permanently leased villages in Ramnad zamindari, forty-two given to Chettiyar bankers, twenty-nine held by royal family members, seven for charity and one for irrigation repair (Price 1979b: 227). Cowles could produce profits (over the fixed payment to the zamindar) of between 25 and over 659 per cent, and the more profitable cowles feature prominently in those given away as forms of largess by estate managers (Price 1979a: 227). It was not always easy to recover leased villages (e.g., 'suit for recovery of Kiranur village', Court of Wards 1906, 15 August 2081M).

14. The extent of 'land alienations', and the massive erosion of the revenue base of the zamindari which they represented, was of growing concern to the British, who went to great lengths to challenge and reverse them through the courts. In 1873 the Ramnad Collector issued a notice—subsequently contested—to all cowledars informing them that their leases were to be cancelled and the villages resumed to the zamindar (Dirks 1986: 327). But even though 104 'alienated' villages in Ramnad were recovered by government under the management of the Court of Wards between 1873 and 1882, in 1886, 323 of the estate's 2,168 villages remained 'alienated' as zamindars continued to gift, grant or lease villages (Ibid.: 328–9; Rajaram Row 1891).

15. For example, N.Minchin report on the tanks of Sholapuram, Sivagangai Zamindari November 1889.

16. This set of cases concerning tanks (civil suits, criminal cases and appeals) and covering the period between 1880 and 1945 is almost certainly a small fraction of the total number of tank cases. Moreover, only a small proportion of irrigation disputes resulted in litigation. The cases represent those for which

papers could be found in the Sivagangai Samastanam Record Office; they particularly involve the Samastanam as plaintiff or defendant, and are thus village conflicts in which 'the state' has interests *vis-à-vis* other 'proprietors' or lease-holders such as temple trustees, *inamdars* or Chettiyar banker lessees.

17. Any change in water supply arrangements, command or storage capacity in one tank would change the hydrology of the wider system. Conflicts over water were therefore endemic to the system. In the nineteenth century, courts came to replace the personalized networks of chiefly authority as sources of arbitration in disputes over water rights. There was considerable litigation relating to water conflicts and rights over water flow. Out of the 134 Sivagangai cases 60 per cent concerned matters of inter-tank water allocation, mostly the interception or diversion of tank supplies.

18. Before 1850 inamdars or cowledars drawing water from Samastanam (estate) tanks were held to be under obligation to pass this grain share on to the estate, and having received *kulavettu* payments, the zamindar was bound to maintain the tank, or to compensate the cowledar if he undertook the repair. e.g., Sivagangai rane cowle dated 27 October 1874, CoW March 27 No. 426, 1900. After 1852 there was no longer a demand for *kulavettu* but for a proportion of the cost of work.

19. Fluidity in drainage is indicated by the fact that the name of a river is often applied inconsistently to different water courses.

20. In practice, the law was far from autonomous from the colonial state, which was characterized by the 'selective application of law, constant manufacture of acts and regulations to direct and constrain the free play of legal norms and procedures' (Dirks 1986: 322).

21. Court of Wards 70M 26 Feb 1901; CoW 292 Mis 28 Feb 1913. Villages differed widely in their capacity to mobilize estate resources for tank repairs. Villagers well-connected to the palace recall repairs every five years; less well-linked villagers hardly saw any repairs.

22. Judgements on small case suits nos 692, 695, 773, 778 of 1893 in the Subordinate Court of Madura, East (Sivagangai Samastanam Record Office, Sivagangai). These cases brought together a mass of evidence on expanding cash cropping in the century.

23. A report of 1889 on Sholapur Taluk of Sivagangai Zamindari, J.Minchin, 25 May 1889.

24. Letter from Estate Collector Uttumalai to Secretary Court of Wards, Madras 14 Dec 1910, Court of Wards Proceedings No. 1194, Mis 15 Sept 1911. Today black cotton soil dry lands—*karisalkadu*—are synomous with poorly maintained tank systems—see Mosse 1997a, 1997b.

25. MELAC Part II p113. Cf. Baker 1984:436; Sivagangai Samastanam Record Office, Sivagangai

26. MELAC Oral Evidence IV p. 306–7.

27. Alapuram (a pseudonym) is the village in which I undertook fieldwork in 1982–4 and intermittently in 1993–6.

28. Report (draft) by the Commissioner of Land Revenue, M.E.Couchman. 3 July 1920, Court of Wards (confidential) No. 1990/20, 'Waste lands (Sivagangai—Introduction of cash rent.' Madras, Sivagangai Samastanam Record Office, Sivagangai. MELAC pt II p. 144, Oral evidence Pt II p. 155, 316.

29. Statement of principles and procedures adopted by the Estate in arriving at the commuted rents. Cited in Court of the Special Deputy Collector, Manamadurai. S.S. No. 6311 of 28, Arunachalam Pillai vs The Estate Collector, Sivagangai.

30. Sivagangai—Administrative Report 1931 (F1340)—(Court of Wards 1931 9 December 31P)

31. Court of Wards 1932 15 December No.31P, Administrative Report Fasli 1341; Court of Wards 1931, 9 December No.31P , Administrative Report Fasli 1341.

32. For Sivagangai: Court of Wards 1931 31 Oct 482 M, e.g. Tiruvegampet Headman Pakkiyan Udayar, Court of Wards Aug 12 1931 349. For Ramnad: 1938 Court of Wards Proceedings 11 separate cases: 8 headmen, 1 Rev. Inspect, 1 karnam, I Servai [Court of Wards Index 1938].

33. In 1931–2, 4,389 suits were decided in favour of the estate, and only 157 against.

34. Sivagangai Administrative report 1931 (Fasli 1340). Court of Wards 9 December 1931 31P.

35. Sivagangai Samastanam Record Office, Sivagangai.

36. In one village alone (Radanoor) there were arrears of over Rs 37,000, 238 distraints, thirty-eight land attachments and ten criminal complaints filed, and in the following year thirty-three criminal complaints were filed. Sivagangai Administrative report 1931 (Fasli 1340). Court of Wards 9 December 1931 31P.

37. In the 5 years 1928–32 17,196 criminal complaints were filed under section 212 of the Estates Land Act.

38. MELAC (Madras Estates Land Act Committee) Part II p. 111, Court of Wards 858 Ramnad Administrative Report 12 Dec 1936.

39. Court of Wards 858 Ramnad Administrative Report 12 Dec 1936; Court of Wards 1174M,15 Dec 1937; Court of Wards 33 6 Dec 1935. Witnesses to the Madras Estates Land Act Committee (1937), set up to report on conditions prevailing in the zamindaris and chaired by Congress Revenue Minister Prakasam, were very clear that in respect of tank maintenance 'because they [zamindars] fail to do their duty, the tenants also did not pay *varam*'. MELAC Oral Evidence p. 311.

40. Report on the accounts of the temples under the management of the Sivagangai Samastanam for Faslis 1343 to 1346 (1937). Sivagangai Samastanam Record Office, Sivagangai.

41. Older villagers in Alapuram remember regular conflicts when estate officers attempted to collect the 'upper share' without repairing the tank. The officers would be accused, 'without cutting the tank you came to take *melvaram*?' (*kammay vettamal melvaram vanka vantingala?*). To pre-empt

conflict, the estate would rapidly organize superficial tank 'repair' work, derisorily referred to by villagers as 'sweeping' the tank.

42. Tank irrigation did not decline everywhere. In another paper I have contrasted the erosion of a social system of tank use in cash-cropping black soil villages inhabited by Utaiyar cultivators, with its persistence in Maravar-dominated red soil areas (Mosse 1997).

43. However, the surveys and settlements which sought to establish a firm demarcation between government land and private property had a difficult task and provoked widespread disputes and litigation (e.g., in relation to private titles claimed for land falling in tanks and channels).

44. 1901–2 Irrigation Commission . Part II Provincial, p. 113.

45. The extension of state control and *de jure* elimination of a range of 'customary' rights in tanks, trees, fisheries, communal lands, residual tank water, etc., has strengthened the hand of junior revenue officials since *de facto* continuance of these rights usually involves payments to them.

46. Details of the rapid survey covering eighty-five interconnected tanks in Ramnad and Sivagangai on which this conclusion is based are reported elsewhere (Mosse 1997; n.d.).

47. There are of course limits to the effectiveness of this strategy and a marked increase in the past decade in the demand for accountability for public works, so much so, in fact, that as one Maravar leader explained, between the demands of state officials and those of villagers there is no longer a livelihood from contracting.

References

Agarwal, A., and S. Narain.1997. *Dying wisdom* (Fourth citizens' report on the environment). New Delhi: Centre for Science and Environment.

Appadurai, A. 1981. *Worship and conflict under colonial rule.* Cambridge: Cambridge University Press.

Baker, C. J. 1975. Tamilnad estates in the twentieth century. *Indian Economic and Social History Review* 13: 1–44.

———. 1984. *An Indian rural economy 1880–1955: the Tamilnad countryside.* Oxford: Clarendon Press.

Chatterjee, P. 1995. *The nation and its fragments: colonial and postcolonial histories.* Delhi: Oxford University Press.

Dirks, N. B. 1986. From little king to landlord: property, law and gift under the Madras permanent settlement. *Comparative Studies in Society and History* 28, 2: 307–33.

———. 1987. *The hollow crown: ethnohistory of a south Indian little kingdom.* Cambridge: Cambridge University Press

Escobar, A. 1995. *Encouraging development: the making and unmaking of the third world.* Princeton: Princeton University Press.

Fabricius, J. P. 1972 [1779]. *Tamil and English dictionary* (4th ed.). Tranquebar: Evangelical Lutheran Mission.

Ferguson, J. 1994. *The anti-politics machine: 'development', depoliticization and bureaucratic power in Lesotho.* Minneapolis: University of Minnesota Press.
Gadgil, M., and R. Guha. 1992. *This fissured land: an ecological history of India.* Delhi: Oxford University Press.
Gilmartin, D. 1994. Scientific empire and imperial science: colonialism and irrigation technology in the Indus basin. *Journal of Asian Studies* 53: 1127–49.
Government of Tamil Nadu 1977. *History of land revenue settlement and abolition of intermediary tenures in Tamil Nadu.* Madras: Goverment of Tamil Nadu.
Granda, P.A. 1984. *Property rights and land control in Tamil Nadu: 1350–1600.* Ph.D. Dissertation, University of Michigan.
Gurukkal, R. 1986. Aspects of the reservoir system of irrigation in the early Pandya state. *Studies in History* 2, 2: 155–64.
Heitzman. J. 1997. *Gifts of power: lordship in an early Indian state.* Delhi: Oxford University Press.
Kaviraj, S. 1997. The modern state in India. *In* M. Doornbos and S. Kaviraj, eds, *Dynamics of state formation: Europe and India compared.* New Delhi: Sage.
Kadhirvel, S. 1977. *A history of the Maravars, 1700–1802.* Madras: Madras Publishing House.
Lansing, S. 1991. *Priests and programmers: technologies of power in the engineered landscape of Bali.* Princeton: Princeton University Press
Lardinois, R. 1989. Deserted villages and depopulation in rural Tamil Nadu c. 1780–c. 1830. *In* T. Dyson, ed., *India's historical demography.* London: Curzon Press.
Ludden, D. 1979. Patronage and irrigation in Tamil Nadu: a long-term view. *Indian Economic and Social History Review* 16, 3: 347–65.
———. 1985. *Peasant history in south India.* Princeton: Princeton University Press.
———. 1992. India's development regime. *In* N. B. Dirks, ed., *Colonialism and culture,* pp. 247–87. Ann Arbor: University of Michigan Press
———.1993. 'Orientalist empiricism: transformations of colonial knowledge'. *In* C. A. Breckenridge and P. van der Veer, eds, *Orientalism and the postcolonial predicament: perspectives on South Asia,* pp. 250–78. Philadelphia: University of Pennsylvania Press.
MIDS (Madras Institute of Development Studies). 1986. *Tank irrigation in Tamil Nadu: some macro and micro perspectives.* Madras: Madras Institute of Development Studies.
Mosse, D. 1997. Ecological zones and the culture of collective action: the history and social organisation of a tank irrigation system in Tamil Nadu. *South Indian Studies* 3: 1–88
———. 1997a. The ideology and politics of community participation: tank irrigation development in colonial and contemporary Tamil Nadu. *In* R.L. Stirrat and R. Grillo, eds, *Discourse of development: anthropological perspectives,* pp. 255–91. Oxford: Berg.
———. 1997b.The symbolic making of a common property resource: history, ecology and locality in a tank-irrigated landscape in south India. *Development and Change* 28, 3: 467–504.

——. 1997c. Honour, caste and conflict: the ethnohistory of a Catholic festival in rural Tamil Nadu (1730–1990). In J.Assayag and G. Tarabout, eds, *Alterité et identité: Islam et Christianisme en Inde. Purusartha* 19: 71–120.

——. 1999. Colonial and contemporary ideologies of community management: the case of tank irrigation development in south India. *Modern Asian Studies* 33, 2: 303–38.

——. n.d. *The rule of water: irrigation and society in south India* (provisional title).

Nelson, J. H. 1989 [1868] *The Madura country: a manual.* New Delhi: Asian Educational Services.

O'Leary, B. 1989. *The Asiatic mode of production: oriental despotism, historical materialism and Indian history.* Oxford: Basil Blackwell.

Price, P. G. 1979a. Resources and rule in zamindari south India, 1802–1903: Sivagangai and Ramnad as kingdoms under the Raj. Ph.D. Dissertation, University of Wisconsin-Madison.

——. 1979b.Rajadharma in Ramnad: land litigation and largess. *Contributions to Indian Sociology* (n.s.) 13,2: 207–39.

——. 1996. *Kingship and political practice in colonial India.* Cambridge: Cambridge University Press.

Rajaram Row, T. 1891. *Manual of the Ramnad Samastanam.* Madurai: Cleghorn Press.

Raju, S. 1941. *Economic conditions in Madras Presidency 1800–1850.* Madras: University of Madras.

Rudner, D. W. 1989. Banker's trust and the culture of banking among the Nattukottai Chettiars of colonial south India. *Modern Asian Studies* 23, 3: 417–58.

——. 1994. *Caste and capitalism in colonial India: the Nattukottai Chettiars.* Berkeley: University of California Press.

Sengupta, N. 1985. Field systems, property reform and indigenous irrigation. *MIDS Offprint 3*, Madras Institute of Development Studies.

——. 1993. *User-friendly irrigation designs.* New Delhi: Sage.

Scott, J. 1998. *Seeing like a state: how certain schemes to improve the human condition have failed.* New Haven: Yale University Press.

Shankari, U. 1991. Major problems in minor irrigation: social change and tank irrigation in Chittor district of Andhra Pradesh. *Contributions to Indian Sociology* (n.s.) 25, 1: 85–111.

——, and E. Shah. 1993. *Water management traditions in India.* Madras: PPST Foundation.

Sivakumar, S.S., and C. Sivakumar. 1996. Organisation of agriculture, society and ideology: an essay on the meaning of social order in the Tamil Country. In P. Robb, ed., *The meanings of agriculture: essays in South Asian history and economics.* Delhi: Oxford University Press.

Stein, B. 1980. *Peasant state and society in medieval south India.* Delhi: Oxford University Press.

——. 1985. State formation and economy reconsidered. *Modern Asian Studies* 19: 387–413.

Subbarayalu, Y. 1973. *The political geography of the Chola country from AD 800 to 1300 as gleaned from epigraphy and literature.* Madras: Madras University Press.

Vaidyanathan, A. 1992. *Strategy for development of tank irrigation.* Madras: Madras Institute of Development Studies.

Washbrook, D. 1976. *The emergence of provincial politics in the Madras Presidency 1870–1920.* Cambridge: Cambridge University Press.

—— 1988. Progress and problems: South Asian economic and social history c. 1720–1860. *Modern Asian Studies* 22: 57–96.

Wittfogel, K. A. 1957. *Oriental despotism: a comparative study of total power.* New Haven: Yale University Press.

Teaching nationalism in Maharashtra schools

Véronique Bénéï

... even the commanders of great armies prided themselves
more upon their being Patils and Deshmukhs in their old
villages in Maharashtra than on their extensive Jahagirs in
distant lands. This feeling of patriotism illustrates most
forcibly the characteristic result of the formation of a
Nation in the best sense of the word .... [T]he history of the
Marathas is the history of the formation of a true Indian
Nationality.

(M.G. Ranade, *Rise of the Maratha Power*, 1900, p. 4).

Kolhapur, southern Maharashtra, January 1999. It is already 12 noon
and the school day is just about to begin at Vidhyapeeth Marathi Shakha,
one of the oldest Marathi primary schools set in the heart of the bustling
city. The horns of rickshaws and two-wheelers can be heard from a
distance at times superseded by the shouting of hawkers or vegetable-
sellers going about their business. Just like on any other day, the pupils
have been assembled in the playground under the already scorching sun.
They are standing there in columns corresponding to their form divisions.
One of the teachers now signals to the peon, who starts playing a large
drum (*dhol*). From then on, the children are silenced by the teachers,

This essay is based on field research carried out from December 1998 to March 1999,
in Kolhapur, Maharashtra, which was made possible through a generous grant from
the Economic and Social Research Council. I have benefited from numerous
comments and help from people at the workshop, as well as before and after it;
amongst them are Jackie Assayag, Mukulika Banerjee, Arjun Dev, Henrike Donner,
Chris Fuller, Thomas Blom Hansen, John Harriss, Sudipta Kaviraj, Sunil Khilnani,
Caroline and Filippo Osella, Johnny Parry and Bharti Patil.

made to stand absolutely still, and the latecomers are hurried into their respective columns. After raising their right hands to the forehead in a military salute, they all begin to rock to the martial Hindi sound of '*ek-do ek-do ek, ek-do ek-do ek*', etc. ('one-two one-two one', etc.) shouted out by the primary teacher in charge and echoed by the children. The shrill yet powerful and energetic voice of the teacher is relayed by a microphone. The children then stand still again, their arms stretching downwards, whilst the sound of a harmonium is added to that of the drum. The teacher in charge bellows at them in Hindi, and they start singing the Indian national anthem (*rashtragit*), in Bengali, celebrating the various features (landscape, regions, etc.) of India:

Janaganamana- adhinayak jay he
Bharat-bhagyavidhata.
Panjab Sindhu Gujarat Maratha
Dravida Utkal Bang
Vindhya Himachal Yamuna Ganga
Ucchal jalidh tarang
Tav shubh name jage, tav shubh ashis mage
Gahe tav jay gatha.
Janagana mangaldayak jay he Bharat-Bhagyavidhata.

The other teachers stand nearby, with the same seriousness as the rest, singing the nation-state into existence. For this is *mulyashikshan* time, the time to pay tribute to the nation, the time to show it one's love and (re)create it through this act, the time to build future generations of loving and caring Indian citizens, in the state of Maharashtra.

Education is one of the crucial topics which an anthropological study of the Indian state should address. Such a study may obviously focus on the relationship between the centre and the regional states: how central and regional state educational policies sometimes contradict one another, or overlap, is no doubt a matter of importance. But leaving aside the tensions between these policies and their ideological implications, and the relative power of the central and state governments in the educational domain, what calls for more attention is the kind of 'imagined' nation (Anderson 1991) and region that is being reproduced through schooling, curricula and syllabuses. How such a construction is being relayed to the targeted population and what resonances it may or may not have for local social actors, whether in the form of symbolic or practical reappropriation, are also issues fundamental to anthropologists. Addressing these issues, by moving away from abstract political-science explanations or dichotomous interpretations in terms of irrational versus rational behaviour, can contribute to an understanding of people's political choices and attachments seen from the grassroots level.[1]

My intention in this essay is to shed light on some of the relationships between the nation and the region as seen from the vantage-point of institutionalized knowledge transmission in Maharashtra. As is well-known, it is through regional movements—drawing on what C.A. Bayly (1998) defines as 'regional old patriotisms' which were themselves instrumental in shaping the regions—that the idea of an Indian independent nation was born at the time of the British Raj and was eventually realized.[2] My argument is that, at the regional state level where such movements took place in the late nineteenth and early twentieth centuries, the nation is, *even today*, mostly conceived of and constructed through the prism of the region.[3] This is particularly—but not exclusively—so in the almost archetypal cases of Bengal, Maharashtra and Tamilnadu, where clear cases of 'old patriotism' elaborated over the last few centuries were tapped into in the process, not only by intellectuals and those often deemed to be 'instrumentalist' politicians, but also and more fundamentally, by the ordinary people. In this essay, how a regional construction of the nation is presently effected in the Maharashtrian case will be shown by studying the 'nationalist liturgy'—taking into account how children themselves speak about the nation—in Marathi primary schools in the southernmost city of western Maharashtra, Kolhapur.

Education and the relationship between the centre and the states

Dual authority

In India, education is a matter of both central and state policy. This generates certain tensions, particularly with reference to the political orientation of respective states and their governments. General guidelines produced by the National Centre for Education, Research and Training (NCERT) in New Delhi pertain to the aims and objectives of education and to the curricula to be evolved for different stages of schooling. So far, since Independence, NCERT recommendations have been based on two reports on education. The first report is that of 1964–6, more famously known as the Kothari Commission report (after the name of its president), and the second is that of 1986–8. The National Policy of 1968, based on the Kothari report, was the first to be designed properly after Independence and it is generally considered to have marked a significant step in the history of education in post-Independence India. The 1988 report was mostly a follow-up to the 1966 one, with greater emphasis laid on scientific and vocational education, in addition to a concern for universal literacy. The last guidelines evolved by NCERT came out in 1992, and are still based on the 1988 report.

The national goals of education which the respective states are expected to promote have been subjected to a noticeable change in their formulation.[4] Whereas the National Policy of 1968 was first and foremost aimed at promoting 'national progress, a sense of common citizenship and culture, and [at] strengthen[ing] national integration', the one of 1988 stressed how education should 'contribute to national cohesion, a scientific temper and independence of mind and spirit—thus further[ing] the goals of socialism, secularism and democracy enshrined in our Constitution'. The last three goals mentioned refer to political modes of governance which have increasingly come under attack since the 1980s, as the Congress government and party started losing ground to Hindu nationalist movements. Officials drawing up national recommendations may therefore have felt it necessary at the time to restate those previously taken-for-granted goals. Subsequent events have proved them right.

Since the pro-Hindutva Bharatiya Janata Party (BJP) came to power in Delhi in 1997, the central government has repeatedly been subject to pressures from the Rashtriya Swayamsevak Sangh (RSS) to give its policies an explicitly Hindu slant. In April 1998, RSS officials demanded that the central government put into force the application of a composite scheme of yoga, Sanskrit, and 'ethical education' (*naitik shiksha*) throughout India (Kesari 1998). Such a scheme was allegedly motivated by the will to build a 'strong nation', which would be proud of its rich Hindu heritage and ready to defend it by physical force.[5] The RSS also wanted the central government to issue guidelines to all academic institutions making it mandatory to display photographs of 'national heroes' who had contributed to the 'building of the Indian nation', specifically Hindutva ideologues such as V.D. Savarkar. Pressures in the educational field had proven mostly unsuccessful until recently, partly owing to the renewed opposition of so-called secular parties.[6]

The Hindu political party, however, has—together with the 'saffron family'—made further inroads into higher educational bodies and institutions at the Centre.[7] In December 1998, when I visited the NCERT in Delhi and met with the president of the history committee there (he had been in the job for over thirty years), his colleagues were busy preparing a report of *all* NCERT-designed textbooks as per the government's orders to assess the amount of ethical education already provided. Although the president of the history section seemed quite confident at the time that the Hindu right coalition would not stay in power long enough to impose any significant changes, subsequent events appear to have proved him wrong. Yet more recently, after infiltrating the NCERT, the present central government started putting its plan of revising the whole national curriculum framework for school education in action (Rajalakshmi 2000). In a document, it proposed substantive alterations to the existing system, over-emphasizing religious (Hindu) education 'as opposed to education about religions', together with an 'overplay of the importance of indigenous education without giving a coherent critique of the perceived dangers of globalization, an overdose of national identity bordering on jingoism, and an attempt to highlight the need to redefine the existing understanding of secularism'.

The NCERT has branches—known as SCERT, 'S' for state—in each state throughout the country. In spite of this states do enjoy a right of autonomy in educational matters and are free to decide whether or not to follow the national recommendations. This explains why particular kinds of politically or religiously influenced curricula have long existed in some states, such as in the northern Hindi belt over which the RSS has had a very strong influence for decades (Kumar 1992; Menon and Rajalakshmi 1998). The continual tension existing between centre and state policies also reflects the difficulty that a federal state like India has to face with respect to the simultaneous construction of a nation and strong regional states. Arguably, what kind of nation is desired determines what kind of education is imparted by the state, not only at the national level but even more so at the 'regional' level, although this does not necessarily mean that an emphasis on the nation-state implies opposition to regionalism. In this connection, I shall be looking at how these national goals are relayed to and implemented by the Maharashtra state.

Maharashtra state and recent educational 'achievements'

The state of Maharashtra, during fieldwork and until October 1999, was governed by a saffron-coloured BJP-Shiv Sena combine, whose famous 'remote-control' leader was ex-cartoonist and founder of the Shiv Sena, Bal Thackeray.[8] After this coalition came to power in March 1995, various schemes were carried out in different fields. Particularly prominent were social schemes (such as slum rehabilitation projects and the *jhunkar-bhakri* scheme, whereby people were provided with a basic meal for a rupee), and economic schemes (such as help given for setting up small business units). These were accompanied by a hardened 'sons of the soil' drive, at times nearly assuming the form of ethnic cleansing primarily targeted at Muslims (see Hansen, Governance and myths of state in Mumbai, in this volume), but also at Indians hailing from other regions. Most of the official schemes proved to be failures, which further strengthened the xenophobic attitude of the saffron coalition and its supporters.

In the educational field however, evaluating the state government policy is more difficult. In view of the pro-Hindutva orientation of the BJP-Shiv Sena coalition, it should be stressed that the government's power regarding educational matters is circumscribed by that of separate bodies such as the Maharashtra State Centre for Educational Research and Training (MSCERT) and the Maharashtra State Bureau of Textbooks, otherwise known in Marathi as Patthya Pustak Mandal or Bal Bharati, after the name of the building which houses it in Pune. The Bureau's creation dates back to 1967, following the Kothari report of 1966. Aimed at homogenizing primary and lower- secondary education throughout the state, this autonomous body is in charge of preparing textbooks for first to eighth standards in all subjects. It receives its directives from the MSCERT, whose autonomous status frees it from any possible pressure from the state government, unlike educational administrations in some other states, such as Uttar Pradesh, Madhya Pradesh or Bihar. Government control over these two bodies would therefore be a rather unlikely prerequisite for significant transformation of the school curriculum in Maharashtra.

Yet, what has happened seems both subtle and straightforward. It is subtle because the BJP-Shiv Sena government was also implementing measures voted in by the previous Congress government, although there is reason to believe that the SMART PT (Statewide Massive and Rigorous Training for Primary Teachers) programme allegedly conducted according to the last NCERT recommendations (1988) was also given a definite RSS twist. This programme came into existence in May 1997, and its main objective is officially to promote a new child-centred approach. This involved preparing new textbooks as well as training all primary teachers throughout the state of Maharashtra. The new textbooks include pedagogical information and teaching objectives. Their contents have also been modified and Marathi lessons have been given a much more nationalist and xenophobic bias. As for training, *all* primary teachers were called to their taluka headquarters for a two-week training session.[9] In the course of those sessions, special training was also imparted in yoga, as part of the morning 'value education' (*mulyashikshan*) to begin the day in school. Implementation of yoga classes had been carried out over the last three years throughout the state and seems relatively effective, although less so in the majority of private non-grant-aided schools. This yoga scheme, as noted above, is part and parcel of the RSS's nationwide educational policy. Some of these developments are however also quite straightforward. Thus the creation of special cadet corps courses in the primary section—formerly limited to eighth standard up to college level—was enforced in 1997, and seems to be implemented effectively in both state-run and grant-aided schools. Similarly, the creation of military schools for girls—one of the first measures taken within the first six months of the BJP-Shiv Sena government—has been implemented and there now exist several such schools all over Maharashtra, which have managed to attract a sizeable number of pupils of all ages. These schools provide military training, yoga and Sanskrit classes in addition to following the state syllabus.

That the pro-Hindutva state of Maharashtra was the first in promoting the dissemination of yoga classes is significant in the light of the pro-Hindutva educational attempts which have recently taken place at the centre. No less significant, bearing in mind the crucial place ascribed by RSS ideologues to (pseudo-)military training, was the decision taken by the government of Maharashtra to carry their own military schooling project one step further. The project was started in 1996 and had cost Rs 840 million by March 1999. In the last days of March 1999, official posters entitled 'A Military School in Every District' (*Pratyek jilhyat sainiki shala*) were sent to each and every school throughout Maharashtra. They displayed photographs taken in already existing military schools. The posters also provided information on the project and its very formulation exemplifies the use made of regional traditions, such as the martial Maratha one, for nationalist purposes:

From the riverside of the Bhima the Marathas extended their empire up to Atka [north India]; in order to protect this fiercely glowing heritage and to 'sacrifice one's life for swadesh', in order to protect this fiery and impetuous race, one military school [will be set up] in every district.

The poster further boasted of the committed participation of 900 students in the twelve districts of the state where such military schools had already been started.[10] It also mentioned the opening of a naval school in June in Raigad, 'where Kanoji Angre, naval chief under Shivaji, had served'. The poster ended with these words: 'With our Shivshahi [government] alliance, Maharashtra will rise to new heights'.

Whether the plan for these military school's could have been successful matters less than the plan's embodiment of the BJP-Shiv Sena government's ideological pretensions and motivations, and how the latter may echo or resonate with the sensitivities and sensibilities of the

Maharashtrian population at large. In this respect, it is important to note the continuities existing between different discourses of the nation prevailing in Maharashtra, from that of the non-Brahman movement to the Congress and the Shiv Sena.[11] Indeed, it may be worth noting that since the return to power of the Congress in October 1999, the scheme has not been stalled; on the contrary, it has been further implemented.[12] All these discourses in varying ways play upon an 'old patriotism' which bound Maharashtrians in the immediate pre-colonial period to their regional homelands, and which the Indian national movement later drew upon. Arguably, this type of patriotism or 'sense of loyalty to place and institutions' (Bayly 1998: vii, 1) remains in Maharashtra even today in the form of particular identifications. Describing aspects of present-day *ordinary* schooling in a Maharashtrian city will help to disclose these.

Kolhapur, January 1999

A Maharashtrian city with a reformist past

Kolhapur is the southernmost city of western Maharashtra and has a population of over 400,000.[13] Now a developing industrial town, it was once the capital of the princely state of Kolhapur, which was later merged as a district into the present-day Maharashtra state. Under the leadership of Maharaj Chhatrapati Shahu at the turn of the century, Kolhapur initiated social reform movements which took their inspiration from the nineteenth-century non-Brahman leader Mahatma Jyotiba Phule (Bénéï 1999). At the core of these non-Brahman movements lay the goal of elementary education. In 1919, the king made elementary education free and compulsory for all his subjects by means of an edict, and he also founded boarding schools, hostels and colleges in the princely city. From the 1950s onwards, other educational movements based on the same reformist principles saw the light of day in the whole of southern Maharashtra. All these movements established themselves as institutions, which ran several educational centres, and to this day they remain instrumental in providing access to education in even remote places in the countryside.[14] In Kolhapur, many of these institutions created a veritable network of primary and secondary schools and colleges as early as the 1920s, a large number of which have come to supersede the government-run ones in terms of public recognition. This historical configuration accounts for both today's literacy rate (about 75 per cent) and the educational structure in Kolhapur. The total number of primary schoolchildren in Kolhapur was 61,000 in 152 primary schools in 1998, out of which eighteen were English-medium, six Urdu-medium, one

Gujarati-medium, while the remaining 127 schools (84 per cent) were Marathi-medium.[15] Primary schools are of three types: those run by the Municipal Corporation, government-aided ones run by private educational institutions, and private ones which are government-recognized but receive no grant.[16] It is only partially true to say that an overwhelming majority of children enrolled in Corporation schools come from the lower classes, whereas children in the second type of schools are predominantly from the middle classes, and those in the third type are from middle- or upper-class backgrounds. Preliminary observations made in slum areas suggest somewhat more nuanced and interesting data about parents and processes of school selection.

There is of course no one school that is representative of all others in Kolhapur, even within any one category.[17] Each school has its own history and ways of doing things; in some cases, these may owe much to the personality of, say, the head of the school or a particularly influential teacher. Yet regardless of institutional idiosyncrasies, every school day must start with *mulyashikshan*, 'value education', formerly known as *paripath*. Only after this is done can the children go to their respective classrooms and start their lessons. All *mulyashikshan* sessions follow the same routine to a certain extent. In some schools, as we shall see, children may even continue the *mulyashikshan* after entering the classroom. The school day is also ended according to a set pattern, although it may include songs which vary from one school to another. Let us now return to Vidhyapeeth Marathi Shakha, where this essay began.

Nationalist liturgy and amor patriae at Vidhyapeeth Marathi Shakha

Located in the heart of the ever-bustling city, just a stone's throw away from the Mahalakshmi temple, the Vidhyapeeth Marathi Shakha school boasts a long-standing educational tradition rooted in local history. The land for the school premises was given by Chhatrapati Shahu Maharaj himself in 1917.[18] At that time, it was a high school only and no educational institution was in charge of it. It was only in 1933 that an educational society, the Vidhyapeeth Shikshan Sanstha (VSS), was founded together with a primary school. Since then the VSS has been running both schools and has set up branches all over the city, ten in all, each one of which is endowed with kindergarten, primary, secondary and junior college sections. Recently, the VSS has even started an English-medium kindergarten and primary school in the premises of the branch situated on the outskirts of the city, in the university area. The Shakha caters for kindergarten, and standards one to four. Its roll for the school year 1998–9 was a total of 1,280 pupils, both boys and girls, and it had twenty teachers, male and female. With five divisions for each standard, the school boasts twenty divisions of approximately sixty-five students each.

The *mulyashikshan* started with the singing of the *rashtragit* (national anthem). This was initiated by the teacher in charge who militarily summoned the children in Hindi: 'Attention! Ready to start the *rashtragit*: start!' After the *rashtragit*, the singing and chanting which followed took place exclusively in Marathi, although some of the orders were still being given in Hindi. The children were told, again in Hindi, to stretch out their arms so that they would be standing in evenly spaced rows, and they were similarly summoned to start reciting the pledge of India, which they did in Marathi, holding the right arm horizontal as if taking a pledge in court. A literal translation of it is given in English-medium textbooks as follows:

India is my country. All Indians are my brothers and sisters. I love my country, and I am proud of its rich and varied heritage. I shall always strive to be worthy of it. I shall give my parents, teachers and all elders respect, and treat everyone with courtesy. To my country and my people, I pledge my devotion. In their well-being and prosperity alone lies my happiness.

The pledge was followed by the school prayer, a *shloka* from the great Marathi work *Dnyaneshwari*, written by Saint Dnyaneshwar in the thirteenth century and then by 'Tara's song' (*taragit*), which is a recent addition of the SMART PT training for girls' schooling.[19] All these items were interspersed with simple calisthenics, which involved arm-raising, repeatedly putting the legs apart and together, sideways movements with the arms, and so on. All the while, the second-standard teacher was orchestrating the session, at times gesturing towards the drummer who played continuously, thus contributing to the martial tone of the whole event, and leading the children in gymnastic movements whilst singing along with them. Most of the other teachers stood by their divisions and joined in the singing. Then the 'thought for the day' (*suvichar*) followed, together with 'moral stories' (*boddh katha*),[20] and 'news' (*batmya*) in which both children and teachers participated in turn. After slightly more than twenty minutes, the teacher in charge raised her fist in a military gesture, shouting *Vande*, inviting an energetic response of *Mataram* from the pupils as they too raised their fists in response. This was done twice after which the 'value education' session ended.

Ideally, of course, the performance described above should be followed daily by each and every primary school in the state. Nevertheless, although at the beginning of my research, the heads and teachers used to go through the whole session at great length and without omitting the slightest detail. As soon as the personnel in these schools were sufficiently reassured that I was not an envoy from the state government checking out the implementation of official orders, they shortened the daily nationalist 'fuss', probably reverting to their usual practice. This happens to be rather ironically confirmed by the use of the Marathi word *paripath*, which is preferred today to that of *mulyashikshan*. *Paripath* actually means 'habitual action; custom, prevalence; routine' (Deshpande 1990: 298). The use of such a word in the present context is therefore indicative of the strong resilience to an externally-imposed state policy found in the daily routine of specific schools. What all schools invariably perform are the school prayer, the national anthem and the pledge of India, followed by either 'good thought for the day' (*suvichar*) or 'moral stories'. The Vidhyapeeth Marathi Shakha is no exception in this respect, either in content or duration of *mulyashikshan*.

The collective shaping of the nation at the most basic, 'grassroots' level of a primary school in southern Maharashtra is, then, re-enacted daily. What takes place is not only the shaping of the nation, but also the eliciting of an emotional attachment to it. This is by no means specific to Indian schools; mass education plays a similarly prominent role in building such national love the world over. In European schools, for instance, it is also through the idea of the nation that children are taught about legitimate feelings of love whilst learning paeans and poems celebrating the nation's grandeur and beauty (Thiesse 1999: 238). In the Indian case, however, there is ambiguity about the object of national love. Indeed, it is debatable whether it is love for the 'nation' or for the 'country' that is being nurtured through this nationalist teaching. For instance, what was translated in the pledge as 'country' is the word *desh*, whereas *rashtra* (the closest equivalent to 'nation') is seldom mentioned in this context. This has further implications to which we need to come back later. For the moment, I shall use the phrase 'nation' without specifying further.

The length of schooling, in Maharashtra as elsewhere in India, is about ten years (that is, if the child completes its secondary education). At the rate of twenty minutes every school day during these ten years, so crucial to identity formation, it is indeed a singularly insular love for the motherland which the system attempts to ingrain in each schoolchild. Further efficacy is arguably sought in collective ingraining. Whether this attempt is actually successful is difficult to assess. Yet in this process, it is not only a sense of 'collective identity' that is being tentatively constructed, but also a social body of future generations of Indian citizens: a social body which, ideally, should be unconditionally devoted to the nation's love and service. These last two aims (unity of the nation together with love for the nation), as we saw, are made explicit in the pledge of India. The pledge, it should be stressed, is in Maharashtra printed on the first page of *every* school book from second standard onwards, for *all* subjects and in *all* languages used as a medium of instruction. Even kindergarten and first-standard schoolchildren learn it from older children at the time of *mulyashikshan*, mumbling it as well as they can.

Incorporating the nation

To be sure, daily rituals publicly worshipping the nation are in no way specific to Maharashtra or India. In England, too, daily assemblies are still carried out in some schools and religion is taught as part of the curriculum, and there have been flag-raising rituals in schools in the United States since the 1880s wherein the nation celebrates itself routinely (Billig 1995: 50). What may be more specific to Maharashtra, even as compared with other parts of India[21] is how, in a secular educational system, religious ideas are presently taught together with nationalist ideas in schools, and how physical exercise and language play a prominent part in the process.

Of bodies and tongues

One of the most striking aspects of the educational process in schools in Maharashtra is how the body is used as a pedagogical tool. By the same token, nationalism is taught by physical means. Even in cases where, as I was later to find out after repeatedly observing these rituals in different schools, the *paripath* would take no more than ten minutes on a regular basis, the body would however always be made the fundamental vehicle for transmitting the national message, with different drills being practised at each stage. In the process, the idea of the body of the nation (Assayag 1997) was physically integrated by the pupils, congruently with the idea about the bodily aspect of nationhood which was advanced by Ernest Renan (1882: 40) over a century ago. This integration is made very explicit in some of the supplementary books which are actually used for physical education, and prepared for each standard by private educational publishers (I know nothing of their respective political orientations), as well as in the official textbooks produced by the Maharashtra State Bureau.

Thus the Vikas 'vocal and physical education' (*sangeet ani sharirik shikshan*) meant for fourth standard starts with the *pratidnya* ('pledge of India', in Marathi) and the *rashtragit*, in Bengali. It also includes a song entitled *Jay Bharta*, inspired by the national anthem, which additionally glorifies the gods, and all the various revolutionaries and makers of modern and independent India. This song was written by the famous Marathi poet Kusumagraj. Interestingly, it is also to be found in the official third-standard Marathi language book, together with explicit instructions about how it should be practised and repeated individually and collectively, accompanied by or interspersed with calisthenics.

The same third-standard Marathi book contains another example of the incorporation of the nation in the form of its first story, which emphasizes the bodily and moral rectitude to be observed whilst the *rashtragit* is being sung. It is a masterpiece of the nationalist pedagogical genre. The story is narrated by a schoolteacher and is about untrained schoolchildren on their first day in school. It very adroitly weaves another story into the plot, about a retired *subhedar* (army officer) who, on passing by the school and hearing the *savdhan* (the loud call to attention that marks the beginning of military as well as nationalist school drills), 'instinctively' straightens himself up, dropping his water jug to the ground. The last words of the story are worth quoting at length, for they provide an excellent illustration of the intricate relationship between the teaching of nationalistic values and the disciplining of bodies:

Like [that of] the *subhedhar,* the body of each schoolchild should become proper, fit .... Whilst singing the *rashtragit,* correctness should be displayed. Whenever and wherever our country's *rashtragit* is played we must stop and stand in the *savdhan* position; we must show respect to our *rashtragit!* (p.11, English translation mine).

It should be emphasized that such an intricate relationship is also found in RSS ideology and activity, as demonstrated by Joseph Alter (1994) in his comparative study of somatic nationalism in Indian wrestling and militant Hinduism. The physical training exercises carried out by RSS volunteers are strikingly similar to what takes place in schools in Maharashtra.[22] Moreover, the professed aim of some of the RSS ideologues, such as Mohan Lal, is to ingrain 'discipline and obedience' with the aim of building up 'collective strength' which is at the core of military power. Similarly, the primary purpose of the RSS programme is to organize, bring together and 'build strength through unity' in Maharashtrian schools. Worth noting in this respect is that whereas such RSS-style bodily discipline has permeated the educational sphere, nothing of the Indian wrestling tradition seems to have been put into use in schools, despite the tradition's power throughout northern India, with Kolhapur being one of its key centres in southwestern Maharashtra. This is consistent with the idea of a *collective* forging of the national character in young minds. Alter (Ibid.: 566) points out that individuality is denied to RSS trainees, whereas a gradual building up of a sense of *individuality* is stressed among wrestlers. Things are obviously much more complicated, however, as further inquiry into the parallels between school physical training and Indian somatology reveals. For example, the two specificities of a wrestler's training are periods of physical exercise, called *vyayam*, and actual practice of wrestling (*jor*). The Sanskrit word *vyayam* may be used by teachers in Kolhapur to refer to physical education, but all of them prefer *kavait*, which ironically comes from Arabic and means 'military manoeuvres, parade' (Deshpande 1990: 89). This confirms that some of these more popular notions and values (about 'traditional' wrestling in the present case) which permeate the school environment are also Muslim ones, and not exclusively Hindu. It also suggests that schools are a privileged site to observe the meeting or even imbrication of this set of values with RSS and Hindutva ones, which place emphasis on the physical strength that RSS members and 'True Hindus' are expected to build so that they can defend the 'Hindu nation' by force.

It is noteworthy that the BJP-Shiv Sena government was only in power in Maharashtra for a few years, because a lot of the actual physical training going on in schools is definitely not the outcome of a short-term plan. As many teachers confirmed, there has been physical education, just as there has been 'value education', in schools ever since the creation of the Maharashtrian state. This is where the specificity of the Maharashtrian case is important, as compared with other parts of India. Indeed, the educational tradition there reaches out to the longstanding martial tradition embodied by Marathas and 'allied castes', and in particular by the prominent seventeenth-century historical figure, Shivaji, regarded since the late nineteenth century as the 'founder of the Maratha nation'. Such a resonance with earlier sensibilities existing in Maharashtra is important; it also ties in with a 'humoural notion' encompassing physical well-being and social and ecological harmony, together with an ethical mode of governance which is characteristic of 'old patriotisms' in India (Bayly 1998: 17, and 1–35, 63–97). It is significant that on these older notions, RSS ideologues have successfully drawn in part; let us not forget that the RSS was a Maharashtrian creation.[23]

The idea of India, together with love for the country, is not only taught physically; it is also crucially transmitted through language. In Kolhapur schools, orders pertaining to national songs and the pledge are given in Hindi, even though the performance is for the most part carried out in

Marathi. Both languages serve as powerful vectors of nationalist ideology and knowledge. As Anderson remarks, language alone suggests—mostly in the form of poetry and songs—'a kind of contemporaneous community' (1991: 145). The crucial role played by language in the transmission of a regional and national sense of belonging deserves particular attention. To use Hobsbawm's apposite formulation, a 'mystical identification of nationality with a sort of platonic idea of the language ... is much more characteristic of the ideological construction of nationalist intellectuals ... than of the actual grassroot users of the idiom' (1997: 57). As Renan said much earlier: 'La langue invite à se réunir ; elle n'y force pas' (1991: 38).[24] In other words, there is no necessary equation between language and nation. Moreover, the very notion of 'mother tongue', which is often associated with a national language, is itself a historical construct that took shape in Europe at the time of written vernacularization, and in India in the latter half of the nineteenth century (Ramaswamy 1997: 15–17). Yet, its constructed nature does not preclude the concept of 'mother tongue' from being a powerful vector of regional and national identity today, in Europe or elsewhere, particularly if the state assumes its promotion. In India, for instance, in regions such as Tamilnadu, the mother tongue is seen as both bonding its speakers in a 'net of unity' 'as firmly and surely as the love of their mother(s)', and potentially transforming its speakers into 'patriots and citizens' (Ibid.: 53, 57, 140).

The concept of 'mother tongue' holds a powerful influence over the nationalist liturgy in Maharashtra as well, judging by the large number of prayers and poems addressed to both the mother and the motherland learnt throughout the primary years of schooling. This is already apparent in songs and poems like *Ai majhya guru* (Mother, my guru). It becomes particularly obvious when looking at the actual contents of the Marathi language textbooks, from first to fourth or fifth standards, wherein the 'idea of India' is celebrated at length. All primary Marathi language manuals are replete with poems, stories and songs glorifying 'India'. Thus, the third-standard Marathi textbook, in addition to the poem *Jay Bharta* and the story about the moral and physical rectitude to be observed at the time of singing the *rashtragit*, includes other stories set at the time of Independence, or ones about nationalist fighters, such as Mahatma Gandhi. Even the first-standard Marathi textbook, in addition to reproducing the words of the national anthem on the last page of the book under the title 'Our national song' (*Aple rashtragit*), also has a twelve-line poem entitled *Ha majha Bharat desh*, 'This is my country of India'. The poem's first and last lines read thus:

Ha majha Bharat desh.	This is my country of India.
Chhan chhan majha desh.	Superb, superb is my country.
...	...
Majha desh chan ahe.	My country is superb.
Bharat majha desh ahe.	India is my country.

Western parallels, 'integral' nationalism and 'banal' Hinduism

Although similarities have already been noted by scholars of South Asia between western nationalisms and Indian nationalism—more recently between totalitarian regimes and Hindutva ideology—no detailed comparative study has yet been carried out. I suggest that educational agendas and their realization might provide a valuable vantage-point for such a study. Indeed, the educational programme conducted in Maharashtra shares many common features with certain nineteenth-century European nationalist programmes, particularly German ones. For instance, in Maharashtra, singing and songs play a central part in developing and spreading national and regional culture and language amongst the children and, indirectly, within the larger population.[25] Similarly, in the very first years of the nineteenth century, Ludwig J. Arnim dreamt of creating singing schools in order to spread German language and culture deeply within the population; Arnim's collection of 'folklore', *Des Knaben Wunderhorn* (*The Child's Wonderhorn*), gathered with Clemens Brentano and published in Heidelberg, was considered to define *deutsches Liedgut* ('German singing stock') as part of a tradition salvaged for the purpose of creating German national unity (Thiesse 1999: 63).[26] In addition, as early as 1808 and at the very time when Johann G. Fichte published his *Reden an die deutsche Nation* (*Addresses to the German nation*), wherein he advocated an educational system suitable for 'regenerating' the German nation, Friedrich L. Jahn attempted to promote German patriotic education by founding physical education societies designed to build young people's character as well as their corporeal resistance (Ibid.: 60). In the meetings held under the aegis of such societies, the young minds would be read the *Nibelungenlied*.[27] This practice may be compared with reading extracts from the great Hindu epics, the *Ramayana* and *Mahabharata*, to children in RSS units where, in addition, they are taught very biased Indian history (Sarkar 1995; Setalvad 1995). Moreover, these German nationalist programmes also emphasized bodily discipline in the same way as the RSS does today.

210 of The Everyday State and Society in Modern India

It should be emphasized, that in the present case, such features are not restricted to RSS schools, but have permeated the official educational domain as a whole by becoming a part of physical education in Marathi schools more generally. In other words, these features have been fully integrated into the daily school life in Maharashtra, to the extent of becoming almost 'banal'.

This 'banal' character of nationalism—the extent to which it is so ingrained in people's everyday lives that it goes unnoticed most of the time—is another point which has not received much attention in studies of nationalism. According to Michael Billig (1995), many students of western nationalism have tended to restrict the word 'nationalism' to the description of 'irrational' events generated by it, such as outbursts of violence, riots and civil wars. By doing so, these scholars have arguably denied the concept of 'nationalism' any other reality, so that other non-violent and non-conflictual forms of nationalism—that is, 'our own'—are not acknowledged as falling into the category of nationalism. Instead, the term 'patriotism' is preferred and, of course, positively valued, so that 'our good patriotism' stands in opposition to 'their evil nationalism'. The dichotomy introduced by Billig is certainly debatable, since the concept of patriotism seems, on the contrary, to have been discarded over the last hundred years or so (Bayly 1998). Nevertheless, Billig is right to point out that: 'Daily the nation is indicated, or "flagged", in the lives of the citizenry. Nationalism, far from being an intermittent mood in established nations, is the endemic condition' (1995: 6, and ch. 3).

It will be noted that Billig's comment applies to 'established nations', by which he means western ones. In this respect, the criticisms addressed by Billig to students of western nationalism might be turned against him for failing to see the applicability of his argument to non-western nationalisms, thereby denying them the very qualification of 'nationalisms'. This 'banal nationalism', meant to 'cover the ideological habits which enable the established nations of the west to be reproduced' and which 'are not removed from everyday life' but very much ingrained in them, may arguably be used to describe nationalism in non-western countries as well, particularly India. Schools are obviously one of the privileged sites where such habits are ingrained. The value of *amor patriae* is nurtured together with the love for parents, the family, elderly people, and so on, and is even made part of basic knowledge, as physical-cum-value education and Marathi lessons show. Let me take you to one of the classrooms in the same Vidhyapeeth Marathi Shakha school to illustrate this point further.

When, at the end of the twenty-minute 'value education' session, the pupils went to their respective classrooms, I followed the second-standard teacher—the one in charge of the *mulyashikshan*. The classroom had bare floors covered with rugs, with no benches or tables, unlike some other classrooms in the same school, and its walls were decorated with posters illustrating various topics, among them Hindu religion and nationalist leaders. After the children had greeted us on entering the classroom, the teacher invited me to carry out Saraswati Puja in front of a poster on one of the walls. She first lit an oil lamp and made me light incense sticks from that lamp to do the goddess's *arti* (worship with offering of incense and flowers). Some children had brought flowers and these were added on to the tray which was presented to the deity. Then the lesson started or, rather, the *mulyashikshan* continued, but was again referred to as *paripath*: the singing of a Ganapati *stotra* (a hymn for elephant-headed Ganesh) was followed by that of a Maruti *stotra* (for the monkey-god Hanuman). Without observing a pause, the pupils then struck up a song devoted to the love of and for mothers (*Ai majhya guru*), followed by the 'five *namaskars*' (the first three of them addressing the country, the parents and the teachers). They then recited the Marathi and the English months followed by the days of the week, the *tithis* of the Hindu lunar month, the seasons (in both Marathi and English), the *nakshatras* (lunar asterisms), and the numbers (multiplication tables). This was then followed by all the songs and poems so far learnt from the second-standard Marathi language textbook (sung one after the other, with the students hardly pausing for words or breath), and lastly, the currency charts (how many *paise* in a *rupee*, how many *annas* in a *rupee*, etc.).

All this was done in a matter of ten minutes, in a very mechanical way, with the pupils rocking their bodies imperceptibly for most of the time while enumerating those strings of lists in repetitive tones, except for the poems and songs, which they also enacted by miming. For the pupils, body language and tone of voice were mnemonic devices. It was also as if the daily liturgy carried out in the playground through singing and gesticulating with drills was being continued in the classroom. Moreover, according to the well-known practice of rote-learning in Indian schools, the material from the language textbook had been committed to memory, and its daily repetition was meant to ensure effective rooting in the young minds.

One should also note how the *paripath* ends with the currency charts. Flags are indeed not the only conspicuous emblems of nationhood, coins and notes are too. (Billig 1995: 41). Currency is taught and learnt daily in primary schools in Maharashtra, and, more often than not, it is also displayed on the classroom walls, together with maps depicting the 'body of India'. Usually, these maps have been drawn or brought by the pupils themselves. There are also many more occasions at school when children are invited to connect themselves to the nation; creative activities (*karyanubhav*) are some of them, when celebration of the nation is effected principally by means of drawings. Thus, it is not isolated 'nationalist propaganda' which is transmitted at school, but a nationalism that is totally integrated into school life and knowledge. What we are observing here is indeed an example of plain daily nationalism, or, as in Billig's phrase, 'banal nationalism'.

Yet this 'banal nationalism' is also peculiarly tainted with religion. Indeed, it is significant in the present case that there are many references to Hindu culture and religion; not only is a (Hindu) *puja* effected at the beginning, but religious hymns (*stotra*) are also incorporated into the litany, together with elements of the Hindu calendar and astronomy. In other words, it is as much 'banal Hinduism' which is being inculcated as 'banal nationalism'.[28] I should mention that Hindu rites or *puja* are not necessarily conducted in all schools, or even in all the classrooms in this particular school. Yet, when I discussed this aspect with other schoolteachers and the headmistress at the next break, many teachers—even those who did *not* carry out any such *puja*—pointed out that there was nothing special about it, since 'this is our Hindu culture; Saraswati is the goddess of learning, this is why [it is done]' (*amci Hindu sanskruti ahe, ti; Saraswati shikshanaci devi 'he, mhanun*). These teachers were not particularly sympathetic to Hindu militant nationalism, or even to RSS ideals, as conversations with them later revealed. Yet, since it was such a part of their own lives, they did not seem to see anything wrong with Hinduism being taught at school as part of 'Hindu culture', the overwhelmingly predominant culture in India if judged only by the number of adherents to the Hindu faith. This is one of the most serious difficulties in studying religious nationalism at the grassroots level in India; many people—even those *not* belonging to the Hindu fold—conceive of Indian culture and the Indian nation as essentially Hindu, without this conception *necessarily* being accompanied by any communalist claim or politically militant Hindu identity. Such is the ambiguity of Hinduism as both culture *and* religion. It is on this very ambiguity that militant religious nationalists play, often appealing to the local or regional components of Hinduism as culture. In the present case, these are regionally dominant traits that include long-existing ethical and political modes of governance, characteristic of an 'old Maharashtrian patriotism' which is more generally drawn upon in constructing the idea of India as a whole.

Marathi-speaking nation, Hindi-speaking nation

How, precisely, is the idea of India perceived by Marathi schoolchildren? What does India signify for them, apart from a parroted 'my country' to which they pledge allegiance? My contention is that, at least for children up to 9 or 10 years, and most probably also for adults, as shown by interviews with teachers, the idea of the nation is mostly mediated through that of the region, in this case, Maharashtra. The interviews and conversations carried out in classrooms of various standards in different schools will not be discussed in detail here. Suffice it to say that when I asked fourth-standard children about all those songs which they sing daily, their answers pointed towards an idiomatic congruence of the Indian nation with Marathi. The different languages in which national and other songs and poems are performed by the schoolchildren have been noted above. Perhaps I should emphasize again that in no school was the national anthem ever sung in any other language but Bengali, the one in which it was originally written by Rabindranath Tagore, though pronounced as in Hindi. Yet, whenever I asked the pupils—at the Vidhyapeeth Marathi Shakha or elsewhere—in which language the national anthem was written, 'Bengali' was never the answer. 'Marathi' was the first answer of the overwhelming majority. In some instances, but no more accurately, clarification or denial would come at a second stage: 'Well, actually, it is in Sanskrit, but we sing it in Marathi'. Tagore's poem may have been chosen as the national anthem at the time of Indian independence precisely because its highly Sanskritized form keeps intact the names of the various regions mentioned so that the inhabitants of each of them can recognize theirs in the 'echoed physical realization of the imagined community' (Anderson 1991: 145). But this does not undermine my argument; on the contrary, it reinforces it by showing the quintessential place of regions in the very imagining of the Indian nation. As sharply observed by Bayly (1998: 98): 'Even the Indian national anthem ... conjures up a virtuous set of patrias linked into a wider national community'.

In this respect, it is noteworthy that 'Hindi' would come as only a second-best answer to the same question, in spite of most of the orders at the time of *mulyashikshan* being given in Hindi, which has a wide currency in Maharashtra. As the official idiom of the 'wider national community', Hindi is commonly taught in Maharashtra as a second language and it certainly possesses an ambivalent value for Maharashtrians.[29] Children studying in any medium start learning Hindi from fifth standard onwards. The official language is moreover commonly spoken—in urban settings and, to a lesser extent, in rural ones as well— and it does not generally elicit the kind of antagonism expected in the southern states. In the first half of this century, even the founding fathers of the RSS, after thoroughly reflecting on the issue, decided that their movement's language would be Hindi rather than Marathi for national purposes (McKean 1996). The almost intimate relationship that Marathi native speakers entertain with the Hindi language is such that, in some instances, it would sound somewhat strange to them—as many primary school teachers and one university student told me—to utter some slogans in Marathi. This is even true for such typically Maharashtrian slogans as *Shivaji Maharaj ki jai*, in praise of the regional as well as the national hero already referred to.

Speaking in Hindi, therefore, is not a controversial issue for Marathi people, particularly in relation to the idea of nation. Yet, Marathi as the tongue of the 'Maratha nation' (McDonald 1968) remains a powerful idiom and it is arguably through this idiom only that Maharashtrians are willing and able to relate to the nation and appropriate it for themselves. This is also illustrated by available translations into Marathi (although I did not see them used in schools) of national songs such as *Vande Mataram* (*Rashtriya Geete* 1998), and even by national songs written in Marathi by well-known Marathi poets who were writers and freedom fighters, such as Kusumagraj. Perhaps the very best exemplification of this is the nationalist Marathi song by N.V. Tilak which, playing on popular reminiscences of other songs celebrating Hindustan, is entitled 'Beloved Hindistan' (*Priyakar Hindistan*, emphasis mine).

Conclusion: 'nation', 'state' or 'country'?

Despite the existing variety of educational institutions in Kolhapur which are a product of local history, the schooling pattern is relatively homogenized not only in terms of general education, but also when it comes to teaching the idea of nation. The body of the nation is metaphorically constructed and reconstructed each day by the social body of primary schoolchildren and teachers, which, in the process, is also (re-)constructing itself. Such national construction is mediated through the bodies of the children themselves by means of collective singing and physical exercise. It might be asked whether there is an 'experiential specificity of effect' (Csordas 1994) of this nationalist liturgy upon the schoolchildren themselves. Do the children also get transformed in the process and to what extent? It is through this public worship of the nation that the children are also physically creating themselves. Just as they are metaphorically embodying the nation into existence, the very idea of the nation also becomes embodied in their physical selves. Children are phenomenologically taught to 'feel' the nation, within their own bodies.

What we have been looking at, finally, is how the incorporation of a 'spontaneous' national sentiment is effected (Thiesse 1999: 14). Hindi and Marathi are part and parcel of such patriotic ingraining, as illustrated by the intricate emotional and political relationship existing between the two languages. All these, in short, illustrate the workings, at the grassroots level, of a regional Indian state's nationalist purpose through mass education. These workings have to be understood as both official implementation processes *and* social actors' agency. In both these processes, the regional 'bodies' (i.e. states) also play a predominant part.

Indeed, such national sentiment cannot be imposed from above, whether by an army of politicians or by other means. Hobsbawm argues that 'a proto-national base' may be desirable or perhaps 'even essential for the formation of serious state-aspiring national movements', but he claims that it is *not* essential for 'the formation of national patriotism and loyalty ... once a state has been founded' (1997: 78). This claim is arguably wrong. Indeed, such a proto-national base, or 'old patriotic' base, as Bayly (1998) would call it, is necessary for the national sentiment to feed on at a local level, regardless of the state's designs. In other words, the regional 'bodies' (states) are themselves necessary for constituting the national body of India. It is through regional movements that the idea of an independent Indian nation came into existence, and the nation is being constructed by means of regional inputs today as well, such as Maharashtrian patriotism in the present case. The effectiveness of old patriotisms up to the 1930s noted by Bayly may arguably be extended to the present day. These old patriotisms have of course been significantly transformed over time. Nevertheless, their history is still one of the most powerful resources for building (regional and) national consciousness, as shown by the way in which the martial Maratha tradition is summoned in the process of constructing the nation in Maharashtra today. Such a Maratha tradition has been strongly sustained by and embodied in the recurrent narration of Shivaji's life since the nineteenth century, and this has been further continued—for example, in school textbooks—since the inception of the Maharashtra state in 1960. All this is consistent with the pattern, highlighted by Anderson (1991: 201), in which state historiographical campaigns are pursued through school systems.

The retention of these powerfully significant old patriotisms today might in turn account for a sense of belonging to the nation being more effectively created through the idiom of the region, despite the 'official' language (i.e. Hindi) also being used to inculcate the idea of the nation. It also helps to explain the currency enjoyed by RSS ideology in Maharashtra, whose promoters have successfully tapped into this 'old patriotic' reserve. This is also why such a convergence is found between RSS militant religious nationalism and the Maharashtrian sensibilities alluded to above, which, in turn, makes it difficult to draw a clear-cut line between extreme Hindutva forms of militant religious nationalism and mere resonances of or sympathies for it.

The object of nurturing this national love still remains in question: is it the state, the nation, or the nation-state that is actually being sung and cherished into existence? None of these, it seems. Rather, at least as I was able to observe it in this part of Maharashtra, it is the 'country' (*desh*). Only in such composed words as *rashtriya-git* is the word commonly translated as 'nation' (Deshpande 1990: 471) actually used. This use occurs for instance in the last pages of the civics part of the fourth-standard textbook. Moreover, in the register of *rashtragit*, no distinction whatsoever is actually made between India and Maharashtra: both are called *rashtra*. Likewise, both are also, and more frequently, referred to as *desh*. There is obviously an ambiguity here, which partly lies in the variety of meanings—and their evolution over time—of the words *desh* and *rashtra* (see Deshpande 1990; Molesworth 1975), and which may not be easily resolved.[30] Yet, *most* of the expressions, phrases, songs and discourses about India are about *desh*, i.e., 'country'. Patriotism and nationalism are being transmitted through the idiom of *desh*, and not that of *rashtra* or *rajya*. This is consistent with the Marathi as well as Hindi words expressing love for one's country, *swadeshabhiman* and *swadeshhitkari*. These two words were deliberately coined from the earlier cognate words *desh* and *deshmukh* within Indian intellectual circles, by students and teachers at the Poona College among others, in the late nineteenth century (Bayly 1998: 90), in parallel with a phenomenon which has so far been amply documented only in studies of western nationalism (Hobsbawm 1997; Thiesse 1999). It does not mean, however, that this lexical invention is totally artificial. On the contrary, it is congruent with old patriotic bonds, which may account for the root *desh* being chosen in the first place.

Consequently, the idea of the nation-state is downplayed to the benefit of the more powerfully emotional one of 'country'. To be sure, it is through the state's apparatus that the ideology of *desh* is transmitted, and one might see in this process a manifestation of the state's very power in masking its reality as 'nation' and *desh*. On the other hand, we should not attribute too much power to the state. Indeed, the converse argument might be put forward, that the only way for the state to be effective is to appeal to sentiments of *desh*. As pointed out by Bayly, 'old patriotisms may provide a way of linking political sentiment and political service in a variable geometry of politics which eliminates many of the tensions of the modern Indian state' (1998: 127). Perhaps it is high time that more studies of nationalism and the nation-state—whether in political science, history or anthropology—reintroduced the patriotic idiom in which people affectively and emotionally relate to the state.

Notes

1. The dangers of over-interpreting people's behaviour noted by Hobsbawm obviously still apply. As his apt formulation summarizes (1997: 79): 'We are constantly running the risk of giving the people marks in terms of a syllabus they have not studied and an examination they are not taking'.
2. See also the seminal work of Cohn, particularly (1988).
3. There is obviously a difficulty with the word 'region' and it is not my intention here to dwell on the possible meanings of the word (see Cohn, 'Regions Subjective and Objective: Their Relation to the Study of Modern Indian History and Society' in Cohn 1988: ch. 6). I am aware that using this term with respect to Maharashtra may create some confusion, since the state which bears this name is itself made up of what might be called 'regions'.
4. In addition to the national goals, the same general schooling pattern was recommended for adoption throughout India. Familiarly known as '10+2+3', it dates from the 1968 National Policy and is in force in most states today: children are expected to enter school at the age of 6, and after ten years of schooling (five in the primary section and five in the lower secondary), they may take their Secondary School Certificate (SSC), followed by two years of Junior College leading to a Higher Secondary Certificate (HSC), and they then aim for a BA or BSc, to be completed in three more years.
5. This is made very explicit in the presentation by the RSS on its internet website; see http://www.rss.org.com.
6. On subsequent unsuccessful attempts, see Baweja (1998), Muralidharan and Pande (1998), and Krishnakumar *et al.* (1998). It should nevertheless be noted that the BJP coalition government has managed to infiltrate higher education advisory boards.
7. One such institutional body is the Indian Council for Historical Research which has in the course of the last two years been 'restructured' with right-wing Hindu sympathizers replacing all the former members. The objective is obviously to rewrite Indian national history in a particular way, that is, with a Hindu bias (Muralidharan and Pande 2000).
8. Although Bal Thackeray was not himself a member of the government, he nevertheless was most instrumental in appointing ministers to office, as was demonstrated again in February 1999, when the then Chief Minister

Manohar Joshi was asked to resign. Hence the epithet usually attributed to him of 'remote-control' leader.

9. A first session was held in May 1997 for first- and second-standard teachers, a second one took place in May 1998 for third- and fourth-standard teachers, and a last session was held in May 1999 for fifth-standard teachers.

10. Certainly one of the most striking sections of the poster is the one devoted to military schools for girls: 'In order to protect the responsibility of sati, the heritage of Rani of Jhansi, the military Rani Lakshmibai school for girls [was set up] in Pune'. Such rhetoric is fully congruent with the ideological stand of Hindutva parties on the paradoxical role that women are expected to play, i.e. submissive housewives embodying the pillars of 'tradition' *and* fierce goddess-like fighters for the latter's preservation (Jeffery and Basu 1998; MacKean 1996; Sarkar and Butalia 1995). Women's sacrificial bodies represent here the body of Mother India incarnate.

11. This was rightly pointed out to me by Thomas Blom Hansen.

12. As pointed out by a student of political science in Kolhapur, it is doubtful that the new government should want to stall the scheme, for they are in deep ideological resonance with it.

13. Figures given by the Population Institute (Sankhyeci Sanstha) of Kolhapur and based on the 1991 Census of India, Kolhapur series.

14. Wherever the state failed to provide a *gram panchayat* school, these educational institutions set one up, which was later recognized and at a subsequent stage, granted and/or taken over by the state government. Amongst the most famous ones are the Annasaheb Latthe Education Society in Sangli, the Rayat Shikshan Sanstha in Satara, and the Swami Vivekananda Shikshan Sanstha in Kolhapur.

15. All these figures were provided by corporation officials of the Primary School Bureau (Prarthamik Shikshan Mandal) in August 1998 and February 1999. The following figures are based on those given by the corporation officials in February 1999 for classes one to seven as of 1997.

16. The first type accounts for 47.4 per cent of the total number of schools and caters for only 40.6 per cent of the total pupil population, whilst the second and third type account for 45.4 per cent and 7.2 per cent of the schools and cater for 50 per cent and 9.4 per cent of the student population respectively. Out of the thirty or so schools observed, fifteen of them were of the first type, ten were of the second and five of the third type respectively.

17. Only the first four standards of the primary section were taken into consideration for observation and interaction with the pupils and the teachers. Despite the fifth standard being officially included in the lower primary section since 1988, the fifth standard remains in the upper primary section in many schools; this made it less convenient to observe.

18. This is far from being the only educational institution or school whose premises were given by the local benefactor. Many such establishments are found throughout Kolhapur city even today.

19. Drawing on its social reformist heritage (that of Mahatma Jyotiba Phule in particular, who started the first schools for girls in the 1870s in Pune), the state of Maharashtra started a policy in favour of girls' education in the 1970s, which was further reinforced in the early 1990s; this song should be seen in this context.

20. A more accurate term would perhaps be 'instructive' or 'educative' (Deshpande 1990: 379) which lays greater stress on conveying knowledge, as well as awakening, than the English word 'moral' does. Nevertheless, the latter word was the one most often used by teachers—Marathi and English—for translating *boddh katha*.

21. Nita Kumar did not note anything comparable in Benares schools (personal communication, London, May 2000).

22. 'P.T. exercises are common in many Indian schools and are done as much with an eye toward promoting disciplined behavior as individual fitness. In the RSS program, as in schools, the boys are made to line up, stand at attention and then space themselves one arm's length apart. ... P.T. exercises are done in unison, under the command of a drill teacher who barks out orders. The exercises are primarily aerobic calisthenics .... The idea is to get everyone to do each exercise in exactly the same way, at the same time: to make the whole rectangular grid act as one body' (Alter 1994: 565).

23. Although the physical education carried out by the RSS trainees owes much more to western military ideology and gymnastics (Alter 1994).

24. 'Language provides a means for people to unite; it does not force them to do so.'

25. As Hobsbawm points out (1997: 115), the primary school is one of the two 'great institutions'—the army being the other—contributing to the penetration of the official language into people's homes.

26. I thank Henrike Donner for clarifying this point for me (personal communication).

27. These songs refer to the Germanic saga of Siegfried, whose plot is also found in the Icelandic *Edda* and the Scandinavian *Völsunga saga*. Although the saga was written in the early thirteenth century in Austria, it was Johann J. Bodmer who popularised it anew by publishing parts of it in 1757. Richard Wagner partially drew upon it for his well-known *Tetralogie* ('Tetralogy').

28. As suggested to me by Chris Fuller.

29. Note that at the time of writing the Constitution, after lengthy debates over the issue of a national language, it was finally decided that Hindi would be called an 'official' and not a 'national' language, lest the southern states disputed it.

30. Interestingly, no reference to government, nation or state is made by Kincaid and Parasnis (1968) in any occurrence of their translation of 'rashtra' as in 'Maharashtra', but only to 'country'. In this sense, 'rashtra' was by the beginning of the twentieth century a close equivalent to today's 'desh', as in 'Madhya Pradesh' or 'Uttar Pradesh' (i.e. the medium country', 'the northern country').

References

Alter, J.S. 1994. Somatic nationalism: Indian wrestling and militant Hinduism. *Modern Asian Studies* 28, 3: 557–88.

Anderson, B. 1991[1983]. *Imagined communities: reflections on the origin and spread of nationalism.* London: Verso (revised edition).

Assayag, J. 1997. Le corps de l'Inde: la carte, la vache, la nation. *Gradhiva* 22: 15–29.

Baweja, H. 1998. Failing the test. *India Today,* 2 November: 16–17.

Bayly, C.A. 1998. *Origins of nationality in south Asia: patriotism and ethical government in the making of modern India.* Delhi: Oxford University Press.

Bénéï, V. 1999. Reappropriating colonial documents in Kolhapur (Maharashtra): variations on a nationalist theme. *Modern Asian Studies* 33, 4: 913–50.

Billig, M. 1995. *Banal nationalism.* London: Sage.

Census of India 1991. Maharashtra. Series 14. Part XII, A and B. District census handbook. Kolhapur. Village and town directory. Village and townwise primary census abstract. Bombay: Maharashtra Government.

Cohn, B.S. 1988. *An anthropologist among the historians and other essays.* Delhi: Oxford University Press.

Csordas, T.J. 1994. *The sacred self: a cultural phenomenology of charismatic healing.* Berkeley: University of California Press.

Deshpande, M.K. 1990 [1967]. *Marathi-English dictionary.* Nagpur: Suvichar Prakashan Mandal.

Education and national development. 1966. Report of the Education Commission 1964–6. New Delhi: NCERT.

Hobsbawm, E.J. 1997[1990]. *Nations and nationalisms since 1780: programme, myth, reality.* Cambridge: Cambridge University Press.

Jeffery, P., and A. Basu, eds. 1998. *Appropriating gender: women's activism and politicized religion in south Asia.* New York: Routledge.

Kaviraj, S. 1992. Writing, speaking, being: language and the historical formation of identities in India. *In* D. Hellman, Rajanayagam and D. Rothermund, eds, *Nationalstaat und Sprachkonflikte in Süd- und Südostasien,* pp. 28–65. Stuttgart: Franz Steiner Verlag.

Kesari, V. 1998. RSS wants Sanskrit, yoga in all schools. *The Asian Age,* 28 April : Mumbai.

Khilnani, S. 1998. *The idea of India.* New Delhi: Penguin Books.

Krishnakumar et al.. 1998. A spreading network. *Frontline,* 20 November: 11–13.

Kumar, K. 1992. Hindu revivalism and education in north-central India. *In* M. Marty and S. Appleby, eds., *Fundamentalisms and society,* pp. 536–57. Chicago: University of Chicago Press.

Kumar, K. 1994. *Learning from conflict.* Delhi: Orient Longman.

McDonald, E. E. 1968. The growth of regional consciousness in Maharashtra. *Indian Economic and Socialy History Review* 5, 3: 223–43.

McKean, L. 1996. *Divine enterprise: gurus and the Hindu nationalist movement.* Chicago: University of Chicago Press.